Birder's
GUIDE TO
PENNSYLVANIA

Gulf Publishing Company

PENNSYLVANIA

Paula Ford

Illustrations by Stan Kotala
Maps by Mark Hood

Gulf Publishing Company
Book Division
P.O. Box 2608, Houston, Texas 77252-2608

10 9 8 7 6 5 4 3 2 1

Library of Congress Cataloging-in-Publication Data
Ford, Paula.
   Birder's guide to Pennsylvania/Paula Ford; illustrations by Stan Kotala; maps by Mark Hood.
      p. cm.
   Includes bibliographical references (p.252) and indexes.
   ISBN 0-88415-073-9
   1. Bird watching—Pennsylvania—Guidebooks. 2. Pennsylvania—Guidebooks. I. Title.
QL684.P4F67 1995
598′.07′234748—dc20   94-34830
                                                              CIP

To my wonderful family—
My husband, Craig J. Cameron,
for his love and support
in this project and in everything.
My daughter, Jessica Ford Cameron,
for all the love and laughter
she has brought into my life.

Contents

Acknowledgments ix

About the Author xi

Introduction 1

1. Lake Erie Coastal Plain 11

Erie. Presque Isle State Park. Roderick Reserve.

2. Glaciated Northwest 21

Edinboro. Meadville. Pymatuning Area. Maurice K.
Goddard State Park. Sharon. Erie National Wildlife
Refuge. New Castle. Slippery Rock. Oil City.

3. Allegheny Plateau 45

Laurel Highlands. Johnstown. Blue Knob State
Park. Prince Gallitzin State Park. Clarion. Warren.
Bendigo State Park. Elk State Park. Moshannon
State Forest. "God's Country." Grand Canyon of
Pennsylvania. Tioga/Hammond Lakes.
Susquehannock State Forest. Northeast Northern
Tier. The Poconos (Eastern Glaciated Plateau).

4. Pittsburgh Plateau 96

Pittsburgh. Uniontown. Kittanning. Indiana.

5. Ridge and Valley Province 117

Bedford. Altoona. Huntingdon. State College. Williamsport. Wilkes-Barre/Scranton. Hawk Mountain Sanctuary. Tuscarora State Forest. Little Buffalo State Park. Buchanan State Forest. Delaware Water Gap National Recreation Area. South Mountain.

6. Piedmont 169

Harrisburg. Susquehanna River. Shippensburg. York. Lancaster. Reading. Allentown/Bethlehem/Easton. Doylestown. Norristown. West Chester.

7. Atlantic Coastal Plain 215

Philadelphia. John Heinz National Wildlife Refuge at Tinicum. Neshaminy State Park.

Appendixes 228

A Checklist of Pennsylvania Birds. Pennsylvania Bird Organizations. Scientific Bird Collections in Pennsylvania. Selected References.

Indexes to Birds and Locations 255

Acknowledgments

A book like this would be impossible to write without the help of many people, and I have many to thank for helping me with this one. State parks staff in nearly every park, forest district managers from nearly every state forest, refuge managers, historic site managers, Army Corps of Engineers staff, and several managers of county parks filled out questionnaires and provided maps, brochures, management plans, bird checklists, and other useful information. Mary Herrold, who helped me contact state park managers early in the project, also provided much useful information about sites in north-central Pennsylvania. Paul Zeph and Keith Taylor of the Bureau of State Parks, Walt Pomeroy of National Audubon Society, and John Jakoby of Greater Wyoming Valley Audubon Society provided information and contacts.

For early help, including publication of my questionnaire in their wonderful journal, *Pennsylvania Birds,* I thank Frank and Barbara Haas. I could not have written this book without the excellent county reports published each quarter in *Pennsylvania Birds.*

For permission to use the Pennsylvania Ornithological Records Committee bird list, I thank Ed Kwater and Steve Santner.

The following birders and naturalists provided information about specific sites: Derry Bird, Charlie Brightbill, Margaret Buckwalter, Morris Cox, Jerry Dyer, Wes Egli, Robert Funiga, Alan Gregory, Greg Grove, Don Henise, Margaret Higbee, Barb Jacoby, Nancy Karp, Bill King, Marylea Klauder, Robert Knepshield, Stan Kotala, Sherri La Bar, Cheryl Leahy, Robert Leberman, Karen Lippy, Jocelyn Little, Tony Marich, Chris McCabe, Pam Meade, Charlie Miller, Grace Randolph, Tom Reeves, Robert Ross, Steve Santner, Cal Schildknecht, Martin Selzer, Dan Sinal, Jerry Skinner, Voni Strasser, Stephanie

Streeter, Jean Stull, Fran and Jack Williams, Robert Williams, Judy Wink, and Peter Wulfhorst. I thank them all.

Many thanks are due to the fine people at Gulf Publishing Company. My former editor, Julia Starr, is a stellar person; I thank her for her enthusiasm and patience in the early stages of this project. Claire Blondeau joined Gulf just in time to edit the manuscript and usher it through the publishing process. She has been a delight to work with, and I appreciate her excellent counsel.

I thank Stan Kotala, M.D., for his drawings and Mark Hood for the maps for this book.

My parents, Paul and Kate Ford, made sure that I was raised in Pennsylvania and close to nature. Who could ask for more? I thank them for this and a million other reasons.

I've been birding with my husband, Craig Cameron, for more than 20 years, and with my daughter, Jessica Ford Cameron, since her first birding trip to Canoe Creek State Park at age one week. She enjoyed it so much we took her to Hawk Mountain when she was seven weeks old. A family like mine is an advantage to someone who wants to write a book such as this. Craig and Jes tolerated many days when I was "checking a site for the book" and many, many hours when I put everything on hold while I wrote, and wrote. They never complained. In fact, both accompanied me on many of my field trips and made the project very pleasant. I appreciate their support (and Jessica's neck rubs!) much more than they know.

I believe that those of us who love birds should do all we can to protect them and their habitats; therefore, I will donate a portion of my royalties for this book to the Pennsylvania Society for Ornithology, the Audubon Council of Pennsylvania, and the Western Pennsylvania Conservancy.

For some parks, bird data are almost nonexistent or are not up to date. If you bird a park regularly, please share your information with the park manager. The more managers know about the birds in their parks, the better job they can do protecting the habitats birds depend on. While you are sharing, if you will send updated lists to me, I will include the information in future editions of this book. You have my thanks in advance!

About the Author

Paula Ford is an environmental writer and consultant. She has published training manuals, technical reports, proposals, and articles in magazines ranging from *Country Journal* to *Bluegrass Unlimited*.

In recent years, Paula has traveled north of the Arctic Circle in Norway, to the Sonora Desert in Arizona, to the bayous of Louisiana, to Florida's Everglades, to Acadia National Park in Maine, to Rocky Mountain National Park in Colorado, and, many times, to the halls of Congress in Washington, D.C. Her consulting work has taken her to Utah, New Mexico, Kansas, Tennessee, Oklahoma, and New York.

She is an active member of the National Audubon Society and has presented talks at its past three national conventions, in Arizona, Colorado, and Washington. Paula has served as president of the Audubon Council of Pennsylvania and previously edited its newsletter, *The Drummer*. She currently serves on the steering committee of the National Citizens' Network on Oil and Gas Hazardous Wastes.

She has a master's degree in technical writing and a bachelor's degree in English literature, both from Penn State. She lives in Hollidaysburg, Pennsylvania, with her husband, daughter, two cats and one dog. Until recently, she always had a pet mouse or two—or seven!—but her husband has finally convinced her that the short lifespans of mice lead only to heartbreak.

Birder's
GUIDE TO
PENNSYLVANIA

Introduction

This book is intended to provide birders, especially newcomers and visitors to Pennsylvania, an inventory of places to visit. It is not intended to be a comprehensive list of every possible location in which one might see every bird ever recorded in Pennsylvania. This book is intended to be portable. This book attempts to answer those frequent birding questions: We are visiting my in-laws in Williamsport; are there any places to go birding nearby? I have a business trip to Philadelphia; should I take my binoculars?

Pennsylvania has only four Rare Bird Alerts, but they cover fairly wide territories. Use them to check for local rarities, and don't forget to report your best finds.

Table 1
Rare Bird Alerts

Region	Telephone
Western Pennsylvania	(412) 963-6104
(Audubon Society of Western Pennsylvania)	
Eastern Pennsylvania	(215) 567-2473
(Academy of Natural Science)	
To report sightings, call	(215) 299-1181
Wilkes-Barre/Scranton	(717) 825-2473
(Wyoming Valley Audubon Society)	
Lehigh Valley	(215) 759-5754
(Lehigh Valley Audubon Society)	

A very valuable tool for birders is a personal computer. Using databases and E-mail, birders can find out about rarities in an area or ask questions of birders who are knowledgeable about a particular site. I believe this tool will become increasingly popular as more birders discover its usefulness.

BIRDLINE provides the same information as the Eastern Pennsylvania bird alert. If you have a modem, you can read BIRDLINE by connecting to PENpages, a computerized information service provided by Penn State's Cooperative Extension Service. In addition to the weekly BIRDLINE update, PENpages also provides information about wildlife, forestry, land management, wetlands, and many other topics of interest to birders. In Pennsylvania contact your county extension agent, who will provide an instruction booklet, phone number, and "username" for the county. Birders outside Pennsylvania may write to PENpages, Cooperative Extension Service, University Park, PA 16802. PENpages is also available through the Internet; the node is PSUPEN.PSU.EDU.

I assume that readers know how to identify birds in the field. Most birders rely on one of three field guides that cover the eastern United States, including Pennsylvania: *A Field Guide to the Birds* (Eastern edition) by Roger Tory Peterson, *Birds of North America: A Guide to Field Identification,* by Chandler Robbins et al., or the National Geographic Society's *Field Guide to the Birds of North America.* Two additional books recently published that will provide much information and many delightful hours of study are *Atlas of Breeding Birds in Pennsylvania* edited by Daniel Brauning, the non-game ornithologist for the Pennsylvania Game Commission, and *Annotated List of the Birds of Pennsylvania* by Steven Santner, Daniel Brauning, Glenna Schwalbe, and Paul Schwalbe of the Pennsylvania Ornithological Technical Committee.

PENNSYLVANIA'S HABITATS

Every person who has been educated in a Pennsylvania school has read the famous letter William Penn wrote in 1683 to prospective settlers in England: "Here . . . the air is sweet and clear, the heavens serene, like the south parts of France. The waters are generally good, there are diverse plants. And the woods are adorned with lovely flowers for color and variety. I have seen the gardens of London best stored with that sort of beauty, but think they may be improved by our woods." Our founder also praised the birds of his new home: "Of fowl of the land, there is the turkey (40- and 50-pound weight), which is very great, pheasants, heath-birds, pigeons, and partridges in abundance. Of the water, the swan, goose, white and gray, brants, ducks, teal, also the snipe and curlew, and that in great numbers; but the duck and the teal excel . . ."

Roger Tory Peterson has called Philadelphia the cradle of American ornithology because both Alexander Wilson and John James Audubon lived near the city, but Pennsylvania is an important state for bird watchers not only because of its birders (add to the list William Bartram, Spencer Fullerton Baird, W. C. Clyde Todd, George Miksch Sutton, Witmer Stone, and Earle Poole) but also because of the rich diversity of its bird life.

Appendix 1 lists 418 birds on the official state list (as of May 1993). An additional 40 hypothetical species, two extirpated, and two extinct are also included in this list. Why so many birds in a state that is not very large? A glance at the list may prompt another question: Why such a rich diversity of bird life? One answer to these questions lies in the fact that Pennsylvania is at the northern range limit for southern birds such as Yellow-crowned Night Heron, Black Vulture, and Swainson's Warbler and at the southern limit for northern birds such as Sora, Swainson's Thrush, and Canada Warbler.

Pennsylvania, the Keystone State, covers 45,308 square miles and ranks 33rd in size of the 50 states. The state is a rectangle that extends about 280 miles east to west and 160 miles north to south. Within that rectangle are found two coastal plains (Lake Erie and the Atlantic), a band of mountains (the Appalachians), a deeply cut plateau (the Allegheny), and a band of rolling hills (the Piedmont).

If this physical variety weren't enough to guarantee a rich diversity of wildlife, including birds, Pennsylvania is also blessed with a wealth of habitats: three major river systems (the Allegheny-Monongahela-Ohio, the Susquehanna, and the Delaware), swamps, glacial lakes, bogs, marshes, freshwater intertidal marshes, and of course, Penn's Woods. The commonwealth also has farms with croplands and pastures, reservoirs, urban areas, reclaimed strip mines, and hundreds of parks.

The climate is varied as well. The northwestern region receives lake-effect snow from Lake Erie and is the coolest, snowiest region of the commonwealth during the winter; however, its summers are the sunniest in Pennsylvania. At the opposite corner of Pennsylvania, in the Philadelphia region, the summers are significantly longer than in the north. The average dates of the frost-free season are from April 30 to October 31 in the southeast. In the north-central region of the commonwealth, these dates are from May 20 to September 30. Rainfall is fairly consistent across Pennsylvania with an average range of 38 to 42 inches. Snowfall ranges from less than 30 inches per year in the Southeast to nearly 100 inches per year in McKean County.

An additional guarantee of exciting birding is Pennsylvania's location on the Atlantic Flyway. To many birders, Pennsylvania means outstanding waves of warblers in the spring and birds of prey in the fall. Rarities are occasionally blown into Pennsylvania by hurricanes.

Pennsylvania is divided into seven ornithological regions that correspond to the commonwealth's physiographic provinces: the Lake Erie Coastal Plain; the Northwest Glaciated Region; the Allegheny Plateau, including the Poconos and the Laurel Highlands; the Southwest Plateau; the Ridge and Valley Province; the Piedmont; and the Atlantic Coastal Plain. In most cases, the divisions between the regions are recognizable. For example, the Allegheny Front defines the boundary of the Ridge and Valley Province and the Allegheny Plateau.

I have visited most of the locations listed in this book; however, one or even several visits by one person would not do justice to them. I have been helped in this effort by dozens of people who shared their extensive knowledge of birding locations in Pennsylvania (see Acknowledgments). I have also relied on regional checklists, Audubon chapter newsletters, replies to questionnaires, and other sources of information. Especially useful has been *Pennsylvania Birds,* a quarterly journal edited by Frank and Barbara Haas.

NOMENCLATURE

Bird names used in this guide follow the American Ornithologists' Union *Check-list of North American Birds,* Sixth Edition, 1983, as amended through the 38th Supplement, 1991.

ABUNDANCE

Just as birds are diverse, bird checklists differ in the use of the terms "abundant," "common," "uncommon," "rare," and "accidental."

In some cases, I have had to "translate" terminology from checklists. In doing so, I have tried to be consistent with the usage of the Pennsylvania Ornithological Technical Committee. The Committee uses the following terms to rate the probability of finding a species:

Table 2
Abundance Terms

Term	Probability
Excellent	found on more than 99% of trips
Good	found on 50–99% of trips
Fair	found on 10–50% of trips
Poor	found on 1–10% of trips
Casual	found on fewer than 1% of trips; more than 10 records in Pennsylvania
Accidental	Fewer than 10 records in the state

I find these terms very useful in a checklist, but in describing bird species, I hesitate to use words such as "good" or "poor," so I will use the following terms:

Table 3
Abundance Terms Used in This Book

Term	Probability
Abundant	Excellent probability of being found
Common	Good probability of being found
Uncommon	Fair probability of being found
Rare	Poor probability of being found

Abundant birds, sure to be seen almost anywhere in Pennsylvania, include the following year-round residents: Mallard, Downy Woodpecker, American Crow, European Starling, and House Sparrow. In winter the Brown-headed Cowbird is easily found.

The following birds nest in all seven regions of Pennsylvania: Killdeer, Chimney Swift, Northern Flicker, Tree Swallow, House Wren, American Robin, Gray Catbird, Yellow Warbler, Common Yellowthroat, Indigo Bunting, Chipping Sparrow, Red-winged Blackbird, and Common Grackle. These 13 species are so easily found they will not be highlighted in the location accounts. In this book, breeding birds are those categorized as "probable" or "confirmed" during the Atlas project (1983–1989).

Abundant spring migrants in all regions are Ruby-crowned Kinglet, Yellow-rumped Warbler, and White-throated Sparrow. Abundant fall migrants in all regions are Ruby-crowned Kinglet, Yellow-rumped Warbler, White-throated Sparrow, and Brown-headed Cowbird.

According to the National Audubon Society Christmas Bird Counts for 1993, a total of 160 species winter in Pennsylvania. Thirteen species were seen in all 63 of Pennsylvania's count circles. Twenty species were seen in only one count circle. Forty species were seen in 53 or more counts, and may thus be considered widespread (at least as of 1993).

Table 4
1993 Christmas Bird Count

Number of Counts	Bird
63	Red-tailed Hawk, Mourning Dove, Downy Woodpecker, Hairy Woodpecker, Blue Jay, American Crow, Black-capped Chickadee, White-breasted Nuthatch, European Starling, Northern Cardinal, Dark-eyed Junco, House Finch, House Sparrow
62	Rock Dove, Tufted Titmouse, American Tree Sparrow, Song Sparrow, American Goldfinch
61	Brown Creeper
60	Cooper's Hawk, Carolina Wren, Golden-crowned Kinglet, American Robin
59	Mallard, American Kestrel, Red-bellied Woodpecker, Red-breasted Nuthatch, White-throated Sparrow
58	Northern Flicker
57	Sharp-shinned Hawk, Great Horned Owl, Belted Kingfisher
56	Cedar Waxwing
55	Canada Goose, Pileated Woodpecker
54	Great Blue Heron, Eastern Bluebird, Northern Mockingbird
53	Eastern Screech-Owl, American Black Duck

For some sites in this book, no abundance data are available. Projects like the Special Areas Project (SAP) coordinated by the Pennsylvania Society for Ornithology will help develop checklists with abundance data. Why not volunteer to help with a SAP for your favorite park or get to know a "new" park better by doing a SAP? As Doug Gross, "the Father of SAPs," says, "If you bird one spot consistently and methodically, you will see rarities." And even if you don't discover a new species, I guarantee you will have fun doing a SAP.

Another way to help get better checklists and abundance data for state parks is to ask for them. If park managers know what the park users want, they usually try to provide it. Birders should participate in developing management plans for parks.

BIRDING SAFELY

Birders care about their own safety and the safety of the birds they watch. Some of the sites discussed in this book are State Game Lands. These properties, administered by the Pennsylvania Game Commission, are heavily used during hunting season, especially during buck season (the last Monday in November to the second Friday in December). Some areas of many state parks also are open to hunters. Check at park offices for details. Hunting is not allowed on Sundays (except for fox, crow, and coyote), so wise birders will plan trips to hunting areas then. If you cannot adjust your schedule, practice the same safety measures the Game Commission suggests for hunters:

- Wear 250 square inches of daylight fluorescent orange on the head, chest, and back combined. This is required of hunters in the fall season. In the spring, they must wear 100 square inches visible in a 360-degree arc while moving through the woods. The Game Commission suggests that hunters mark their calling locations by wrapping an orange band around a tree. Watch for them.
- Eliminate red, white, and blue from your clothing during spring turkey season (usually the month of May, from a half hour before sunrise to noon). These colors are found on the head and neck of mature Wild Turkey. Birders should be very careful during turkey season. In 1991, two hunters were killed, and 51 others were wounded during turkey season.

- Shout "STOP" to alert a hunter who is approaching you. Do not move or wave.

For more information about hunting in Pennsylvania, contact the Pennsylvania Game Commission, 2001 Elmerton Avenue, Harrisburg, PA 17110-9797, (717) 787-4259. For more information about hunting regulations in state parks, contact the specific park you are planning to visit or call the Bureau of State Parks, 1-800-63-PARKS.

Another safety issue for birders is Lyme disease. When you go afield, wear protective clothing and/or insect repellent. If you notice an unusual rash, see your physician. Early detection is important if treatment is to be successful.

For the safety of the birds you are observing, practice the following habits:

- Do not destroy habitats.
- Do not disturb the birds, especially during nesting season.
- Minimize the use of recorded calls.
- Never handle eggs or young.
- Do not tap den trees to see if they contain nests.
- Remove litter, especially fishing line and plastic six-pack holders, you find while birding.

ADDITIONAL NOTES

I have used a variety of criteria in selecting sites for this book. I have tried to include accessible samples of all habitats and have included familiar locations such as Hawk Mountain and Presque Isle State Park as well as hidden treasure sites usually known to local birders. These are not necessarily the best places to find the most birds. Nor are these the only places worth birding. We've all had the happy accident of stumbling across a wonderful bird in a totally unexpected place. A book that could identify every location where one might see every bird possible would be impossible to write. If such a book were possible, it would make birding in Pennsylvania seem like a trip to a zoo. Much of the magic of discovery would be lost.

I have emphasized sites open to the public. Luckily, Pennsylvania has plenty of these. The Bureau of State Parks alone manages 104 state parks, four environmental education centers, and six undeveloped parks for a total of 114 sites that include 277,164 acres of a variety of habitats. The Bureau of Forestry manages nearly two million acres of land, and the Pennsylvania Game Commission owns more than a million acres. Federal lands include more than 500,000 acres in the Allegheny National Forest and two national wildlife refuges. Many counties and towns also own parks.

Especially in the northwestern region of Pennsylvania, landowners tend to frown upon trespassers. If you see a "No Trespassing" sign anywhere, do not enter the property.

In several cases I have not included sites because my questionnaires were not returned, and I did not have time to visit the sites. Perhaps those birders given questionnaires are jealously guarding secret treasures. Or maybe they feel their birds are not worth mentioning. More likely, the staff was busy. In any case, I hope readers will give me feedback and suggest additional or alternative sites for a possible second edition of this book.

The directions and conditions in this book are as accurate as possible at the time I gathered the information. Birders may know of shortcuts to favorite sites, but my goal has been to keep the directions simple, so I have tried to use main highways and obvious landmarks. (Directions such as "a half mile before the road turns to dirt" are useful only to people who already know the area well.)

The maps in this book are intended to give a general overview of the areas being discussed. For a free current road map of Pennsylvania, stop at any state park or roadside information center or call the Bureau of State Parks at (800) 63-PARKS.

New highways will play havoc with this edition, as will construction of new housing developments, malls, and industrial parks. If we birders lose a little convenience because of changes in landscapes, we will do well to remind ourselves that the birds are losing their homes.

Finally, a comprehensive bird checklist for each of the sites would be far beyond the scope of this book. I have tried to select samples, both common and rare, of what might be found at a particular location. I hope this book helps you decide which locations to visit, and I hope you find many more birds than I have listed. Happy birding!

Paula Ford

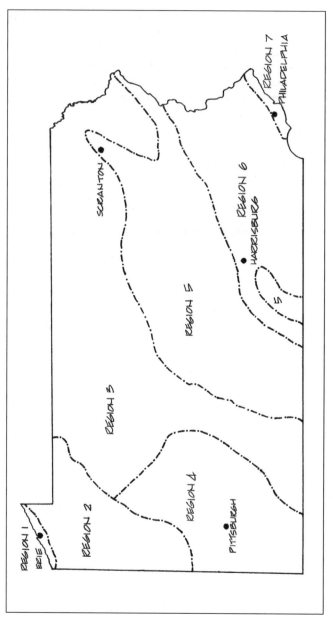

Regions of Pennsylvania

Chapter 1
Lake Erie Coastal Plain

 The Lake Erie Coastal Plain is a very narrow strip of land along the northwest boundary of Pennsylvania. This region covers less than 1% of Pennsylvania. The plain extends about 45 miles diagonally from the Ohio border to New York along the shore of Lake Erie and gradually rises toward the southeast where its boundary is defined by a cliff known as the Erie scarp, which is parallel to Interstate 90. The elevation ranges from 571 feet at the shore of Lake Erie to about 800 feet at I-90.

Habitats include urban communities, parks, wetlands, forests, glacial lakes, beaches, orchards, vineyards, and Lake Erie and Erie Bay. At Lake Erie's shore, the beach has little or no vegetation. As you move inland, you will find a zone of sand dunes with beach grasses followed by a flat area with plants such as goldenrod, silverweed, and bluejoint. A final zone is a forest with Virginia pine.

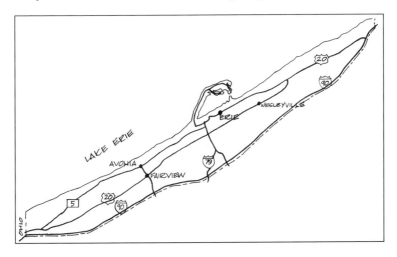

Lake Erie Coastal Plain

The climate of the Lake Erie Coastal Plain ranges from cold winters characterized by lake-effect snow (Erie averages more than 80 inches a year) to mild summers. Rain in the plain averages 38 to 44 inches per year.

Jean Stull, James A. Stull, and Gerald M. McWilliams have documented 327 bird species in their excellent guide to the region, *Birds of Erie County Pennsylvania Including Presque Isle* (Allegheny Press, 1985). The Presque Isle Audubon Society offers a checklist (1992) with bar graphs. Send $2 to PIAS at P.O. Box 1783, Erie, PA 16507.

According to the records of the Pennsylvania Ornithological Technical Committee (Santner, et al. 1992), the following birds are abundant year-round in this region: Canada Goose, American Kestrel, Ring-billed Gull, Rock Dove, Mourning Dove, Black-Capped Chickadee, Northern Cardinal, House Finch, and House Sparrow.

American Kestrel

Abundant winter residents include Canvasback, Redhead, Common Goldeneye, Bufflehead, Common Merganser, Herring Gull, Great Black-backed Gull, and Dark-eyed Junco. Abundant summer residents are the Bank Swallow and the Red-eyed Vireo.

Abundant spring migrants include Ring-necked Duck, Red-breasted Duck, Sharp-shinned Hawk, Red-shouldered Hawk, American Coot, and Purple Martin.

Abundant fall migrants are Common Loon, Ring-necked Duck, Red-breasted Merganser, American Coot, Dunlin, and Purple Martin.

Nesting birds include Least Bittern, Wood Duck, Virginia Rail, Common Moorhen, Spotted Sandpiper, American Woodcock, Black Tern (which nests only in this region and the adjacent Northwest Glaciated Region), Barred Owl, Northern Saw-whet Owl, Ruby-throated Hummingbird, Belted Kingfisher, six woodpecker species, seven flycatchers (including Willow and Least Flycatcher), Horned Lark, six swallows, five wrens (including Marsh Wren), Eastern Bluebird, four vireos (including Warbling Vireo), 13 warblers (including Blue-winged, Chestnut-sided, Black-throated Green, Cerulean, Black-and-white Warbler, American Redstart, Prothonotary Warbler, Louisiana Waterthrush, and Mourning, Hooded, and Canada Warblers), and eight sparrows (including "probable" Clay-colored, Vesper, and Henslow's Sparrows and "confirmed" Savannah and Swamp Sparrows).

In late summer, swallows gather in large flocks before migrating, and flights of shorebirds arrive—usually after a cold front has passed through the area. These flights begin in July, peak in August or early September, and continue until October. According to Stull, Stull, and McWilliams, rarities have included godwits, phalaropes, Whimbrel, Red Knot, Buff-breasted and White-rumped Sandpiper, and Willet. Thirty-seven shorebird species have been recorded, all at Presque Isle State Park.

Autumn migration includes vireos, thrushes, blackbirds, and warblers. Terns fly over the lake, and ducks swim in Presque Isle lagoons and on inland waters. Surface feeders arrive in September, while diving ducks begin arriving in October. Wintering birds include Common Loon, Horned Grebe, scoters, Oldsquaw, and very large flocks of Bonaparte's, Ring-billed, and Herring Gulls. Less common are Glaucous, Iceland, and Little Gulls.

Spring migration is the highlight of the birder's year in this region. When the wind is from the south, hundreds of birds of prey pass through the region, especially in April. Thirty-six species of warblers have been recorded in May. The birds are most concentrated at Presque Isle State Park.

ERIE

Erie is the county seat of Erie County and the third largest city in Pennsylvania. The population in the 1990 census was 108,718 in the city and 275,572 in Erie County. Industry, agriculture, and shipping are important to the region's economy, but tourism is well established. In fact, during spring migration, many motels and restaurants fly "Welcome Birders" banners. Although the city boasts more than 3,200 hotel and motel rooms, reservations are essential (and can be difficult to obtain) during mid-May when spring migration is at its peak. Plan trips in advance.

The foremost birding location in the Erie area is a hot spot of national significance: Presque Isle State Park. Other birding locations worth checking are the David M. Roderick Wildlife Reserve, Asbury Woods Nature Center, and Scott Park (Sixth Avenue and Sommerheim Drive). The city also has a zoo.

The public docks at the foot of State Street are locally famous for the hundreds of thousands of gulls that gather in winter to feed on dying Gizzard Shad. Most common are Bonaparte's Gull, Ring-billed Gull, Herring Gull, and Great Black-backed Gull. Check flocks carefully for Little Gull, Iceland Gull, and Glaucous Gull. These are not found in great numbers, but they have been recorded most years. Less common are Laughing Gull, Franklin's Gull, Thayer's Gull, Lesser Black-backed Gull, and Black-legged Kittiwake.

Asbury Woods Nature Center

Asbury Woods Nature Center, owned by the Millcreek Township School District, is approximately 50 acres of pine forest, oak forest, beech/maple forest, vernal ponds, wetlands, and old fields. The center is located in Millcreek Township, southwest of Erie near the Erie International Airport. From Exit 3 on I-90, drive north on I-79 to US

20. Just west of the airport, turn left onto Asbury Road and continue one-quarter mile past 38th Street. Turn left at the barn.

The center has 2 miles of trails and a quarter-mile boardwalk that is wheelchair-accessible. The trails may be used between dawn and dusk, 7 days a week. Food is not available at the center, and picnicking is not permitted.

A nature center with exhibits of small live animals and seasonal displays is open Monday to Saturday from 9 a.m. to 5 p.m. and Sunday from noon to 5 p.m., March to November. It closes at 4 p.m. during the winter months. Asbury Woods offers daylong school programs, scout programs, and monthly public programs. Members receive a quarterly newsletter, *Woods Talk,* and discounts for admission to programs and at the gift shop.

Nineteen warblers have been recorded at the center. Notable breeding birds include Green-backed Heron, Red-breasted Nuthatch, and Hooded Warbler. Rose-breasted Grosbeak, Hooded Warbler, and Blue-winged Warblers may nest at Asbury Woods. Check with the center's staff for the latest information.

Wintering species include Red-breasted Nuthatch, Golden-crowned Kinglet, American Tree Sparrow, and White-Throated Sparrow. Pine Siskin and Evening Grosbeak appear irregularly.

The address is Asbury Woods Nature Center, 4105 Asbury Road, Erie, PA 16506, (814) 835-5336.

Scott Park

Located on the bank overlooking Presque Isle Bay, Scott Park's habitats include mixed woodlands, ravines, open fields, and bluffs. The park is located on West Sixth Street and Sommerheim Drive, just east of Peninsula Drive.

Erie Zoo

The Erie Zoo, a 15-acre facility located at Exit 7 off I-90, displays 300 animals. There is a fee for admission. The address is Erie Zoo, 423 West 38th Street, Erie, PA 16508, (814) 864-4091.

PRESQUE ISLE STATE PARK

Presque Isle State Park, 3,200 acres, is located on a 7-mile-long peninsula adjacent to the city of Erie. To reach the park, drive north on I-79 to Exit 43 and turn left. Drive west on 26th Street for one mile to Peninsula Drive (SR 832). Turn right and drive downhill to the park entrance. Ferry service to the park is available from the Erie Public Dock. Stop at the park office, about a mile past the entrance, to pick up a free checklist, brochure that explains the park's geology, and map.

The park is located on a sand spit that was created when glacial ice melted and a moraine, now covered by Lake Erie, emerged. As the lake slowly rose, the shoreline migrated, and the combination of winds, currents, and waves acted on glacial deposits and created Presque Isle. Presque Isle has been designated a National Natural Landmark by the National Park Service because of diverse habitats: dune, sand plain, forest, pond, marsh, swamp, and lagoon. The park is a good place to observe the succession from lake to climax forest within two miles. The geologic complexity of the peninsula means that a variety of habitats is available for birds, and its position on Lake Erie makes it an important resting point for birds during both spring and fall migrations. Monarch butterflies also migrate through the park in large numbers in the fall. In addition, the park is a good place to observe unusual plant life. The Pennsylvania Natural Diversity Inventory lists 55 of Presque Isle's 500 wild plant species as "special concern." The park is included in the Erie Christmas Bird Count.

Presque Isle State Park is open daily from 5 a.m. to 9 p.m. The park does not have campgrounds or cabins, but these are available in the Erie area. Food concessions are operated during the summer months at Beach 6, Beach 11, Pettinato Beach, and Budny Beach. Picnicking is permitted, and pavilions are available for groups. Seasonal mooring leases are offered at a 473-slip marina, and canoes, rowboats, and motorboats may be rented at a watercraft concession on the bay side of the park. Approximately 7 miles of trails wind through a variety of habitats. A 5.8-mile multi-purpose trail from the park entrance to the Perry Monument on Misery Bay is accessible to wheelchairs.

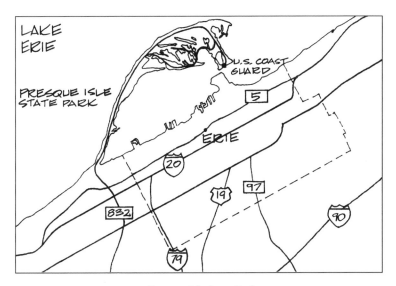

Presque Isle State Park

The park has a visitor center that provides environmental education and interpretive programs. A program brochure is published monthly and is available at the headquarters. One popular interpretive program offered from Memorial Day to Labor Day features a pontoon boat ride through the park's lagoons. Check at headquarters for a schedule.

A bird banding station is operated by the Stulls on weekends in May and September either behind the park administration building or near the Niagara boat launch area. Visitors are welcome to observe the banding, which provides a good opportunity for close-up study of migrants. Children especially appreciate seeing the birds at such close range.

During migration, any place in the park can be productive, but several spots are birders' favorites both during migration and year-round. The Old West Boat Livery with its lagoon and cattail and sedge marsh is home to Common Moorhen and Marsh Wren. The Lily Pond (near the park office) is especially good for migrants. The Stulls report that the most common are White-throated Sparrow, Golden-crowned and Ruby-crowned Kinglet, Magnolia and Yellow-rumped Warbler,

Swainson's Thrush, Yellow and Tennessee Warblers, Black-throated Blue Warbler, and Gray Catbird. The Sidewalk Trail (East Fisher Drive) goes through low bushes that teem with migrants in the spring. It's very pleasant to see all those warblers without abusing your neck. The east side of Misery Bay with its trees and undergrowth is attractive to Palm, Yellow, Blackburnian, Chestnut-sided, and Bay-breasted Warblers in May, August, and September. The Thompson Circle-Dead Pond Trail area is a good place to watch raptors migrate in the spring. Take the trails to Niagara Pond to search for Soras, Virginia Rails, and bitterns.

The Pines, an area planted in the 1930s near Budny Beach, is good for Great-horned, Long-eared, and Saw-whet Owls, and Eastern Screech-Owl, especially in winter and spring. Gull Point Sanctuary was designated a bird sanctuary in 1927. It is the best place in western Pennsylvania to see migrant shorebirds and water fowl. Piping Plovers and Common Terns historically nested at Gull Point, and the Pennsylvania Department of Environmental Resources is working with the Presque Isle Audubon Society to encourage the return of the birds as nesting species. (**Note:** A new management plan for the park is being developed. Entrance to portions of the Gull Point Sanctuary may be restricted during the breeding season. Check with the park staff for details.)

Black Terns have nested at Horseshoe Pond and Long Pond in recent years. The species is endangered in Pennsylvania, and birders should take special care not to disturb the birds if sighted.

Other nesting birds in the park include Least Bittern, Green-backed Heron, Virginia Rail, Common Moorhen, Spotted Sandpiper, American Woodcock, Willow Flycatcher, Great Crested Flycatcher, Marsh Wren, Blue-gray Gnatcatcher, Warbling Vireo, Black-throated Green Warbler, Prothonotary Warbler, Savannah Sparrow, and Swamp Sparrow. During August and early September, especially after a storm front has passed through, Gull Point is excellent for shorebirds. Winter visitors to Gull Point have included Snowy Owl and Northern Shrike. A sampling of rarities recorded at Presque Isle State Park includes Brown Pelican, Snowy Egret, Little Blue Heron, Yellow-crowned Night-Heron, Barrow's Goldeneye, Marbled Godwit, Swainson's Warbler, and Summer Tanager.

The park's address is P.O. Box 8510, Erie, PA 16505, (814) 871-4251.

RODERICK RESERVE (SGL 314)

The David M. Roderick Wildlife Reserve, also known as State Game Lands 314, is 3,131 acres of gently rolling uplands with wetlands, second-growth forests, streams, and steep shoreline bluffs composed of fine clays and silts deposited by the Wisconsin glacier. To reach the reserve, drive west on I-90 to Exit 1. Drive north about a mile on Route 6 to Route 20. Turn left onto Route 20, and drive just over a mile to the intersection with Route 5. You are on the right arm of this "Y" intersection and will make a right turn onto Rudd Road, just past where Route 5 joins Route 20. (This is a bit tricky.) Continue on Rudd Road to a "T" intersection and turn left onto Lake Shore Road (called "Lake Road" on some maps). Drive about 2 miles to the parking lot.

The reserve is open 7 days a week, 24 hours a day. Camping is not permitted. There are no picnic tables, but picnicking is allowed. A detailed map is available for $0.50 from the Pennsylvania Game Commission, 2001 Elmerton Ave., Harrisburg, PA 17110-9797. Ask for SGL #314.

It is possible to walk along the Lake Erie shore when the waves are calm and view the nesting sites of numerous Bank Swallows. This 1.5-mile expanse is the longest stretch of undeveloped shoreline between Buffalo and Toledo. It was originally purchased by Andrew Carnegie, and USX planned to build a steel mill on the site in the 1960s. When market conditions changed and the steel mill plans were scrapped, the land was sold to the Western Pennsylvania Conservancy, which then transferred it to the Pennsylvania Game Commission in 1989.

Young forests are a mixture of aspen, beech, swamp and white oak, and red and sugar maples. Fruit-bearing shrubs are abundant, and Bohemian Waxwings were found with Cedar Waxwings in the winter of 1992.

Spring hawk flights are good here when the wind is from the south or southwest. In spring 1991, a Mississippi Kite was recorded. Peregrine Falcons and Bald Eagles also migrate through the reserve.

A single count season for the Pennsylvania Breeding Bird Atlas project recorded more than 50 species of nesting birds. Because the reserve has not been in public ownership for very long, records are sparse. This may be a hot spot waiting to be discovered.

The reserve is managed by the Pennsylvania Game Commission office in Franklin. Its address is PGC Northwest Region Headquarters, P.O. Box 31, Franklin, PA 16323, (814) 432-3187.

Chapter 2
Glaciated Northwest

Both the Illinois and Wisconsin glaciations affected Pennsylvania's landscape in the northwestern corner of the commonwealth. As glaciers advanced into Pennsylvania, they carved the landscape and deposited till, or glacial debris, often in layers hundreds of feet deep. Before the glaciation, the rivers in this region drained northward. Dams of till blocked the ancient river channels and created lakes such as Conneaut Lake, the largest natural lake in Pennsylvania, as well as many smaller lakes. Some of the lakes eventually filled with sediment and became wetlands, including the vast Pymatuning Swamp, which was 10,400 acres before it was altered to create the Pymatuning Reservoir. Today, the Glaciated Northwest has approximately one-fifth of Pennsylvania's wetlands.

Examples of glacial features in the region include the West Liberty Esker (created when gravel filled a tunnel in the ice at the edge of the glacier) near Jennings Environmental Education Center and the Slippery Rock Gorge and Kildoo Falls in McConnell's Mill State Park.

The Glaciated Northwest extends from the Pennsylvania-Ohio border north of the Ohio River diagonally to the Pennsylvania-New York border just west of the Allegheny Reservoir. The northern boundary of the region is I-90; the southern boundary runs roughly parallel to the shore of Lake Erie. The region is a gently rolling terrain, with elevations ranging from 800 feet at I-90 to 1,400 feet at the southern boundary. Rivers and streams have carved paths through the plateau.

Glacial till is found on uplands, and alluvial soils are prevalent on flood plains. Average annual precipitation is 40 to 42 inches. The average annual temperature is between 46° and 50° Fahrenheit, with an average July extreme maximum temperature between 90 and 92, and an average January minimum of −4 to −8. Forests in the region are Northern Hardwood Forests with a mix of Sugar Maple, Yellow

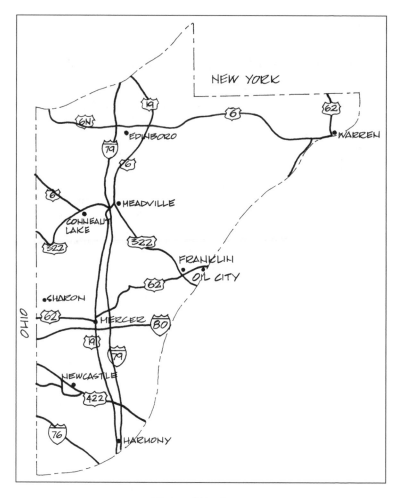

Glaciated Northwest

Birch, Beech, and Hemlock, or Beech/Maple Forest with Sugar Maple and Beech dominating.

This region was the birthplace of the world's oil industry, and oil and gas continue to be important in the local economy; however, oil production peaked in 1981. Other local economic activities include agriculture, manufacturing, and tourism.

Ovenbird

Abundant year-round residents in the Glaciated Northwest include Canada Goose, American Kestrel, Rock Dove, Mourning Dove, Black-Capped Chickadee, Tufted Titmouse, and Northern Cardinal. The Ring-billed Gull is an abundant winter resident. Abundant summer residents (all breed in the region) are Eastern Wood-Pewee, Barn Swallow, Blue Jay, Wood Thrush, Red-eyed Vireo, Ovenbird, and Field Sparrow.

Abundant spring migrants are Tundra Swan, Common Merganser, and American Coot. Although no fall migrants are abundant enough that birders would expect to see them on every field trip in the fall, many birds—including waterfowl, shorebirds, and songbirds—migrate through the region.

Siegel Marsh (SGL 218)

Siegel Marsh is located on State Game Lands 218, a tract of 1,343 acres of rolling open fields with several ponds and a 200-acre lake. To reach the marsh, depart I-90 at Exit 8 and travel south on Route 8 for approximately 5 miles. To reach the visitors' center, turn right at

Bogus Corners onto State Route 1005 and drive past the breast of the dam. The center is on the left.

The marsh itself is used by the game commission for Canada Goose propagation. This species is common all year. During migration, look for Snow and White-fronted Geese. Hooded Merganser and Wood Ducks both have bred here. In winter, look for Rough-legged Hawks. When water levels are low in late summer and early fall, check for migrating shorebirds.

For more information about SGL 218, contact the Northwest Division Headquarters, Pennsylvania Game Commission, P.O. Box 31, 1509 Pittsburgh Road, Franklin, PA 16323, (814) 423-3187.

EDINBORO

Edinboro, population 7,736, is the home of Edinboro State University. Edinboro Lake, northwest of the town, like other lakes in the area is good for migratory waterfowl in spring and fall. Black Tern, a species that is on the Pennsylvania endangered list, has been reported at the lake.

Union City Dam

Union City dam is a dry-bed reservoir on French Creek. It does not provide the usual menu of recreation facilities at typical Army Corps of Engineers' facilities, but because its water levels fluctuate depending on the rainfall in the area, it can be very good for birds. If extensive mudflats are exposed during migration, you'll want to check Union City Dam for migratory shorebirds. The following have been recorded: Greater and Lesser Yellowlegs, Short-billed Dowitcher, Least Sandpiper, Semipalmated Sandpiper, Pectoral Sandpiper, and Solitary Sandpiper. Rare species include Wilson's Phalarope, Red Knot, and Buff-breasted Sandpiper. Northern Shrike also has been seen in the area.

The address for Union City Dam is c/o Woodcock Creek Lake, P.O. Box 629, Saegertown, PA 16433, (814) 763-4422. For recorded recreation information call (814) 763-2008.

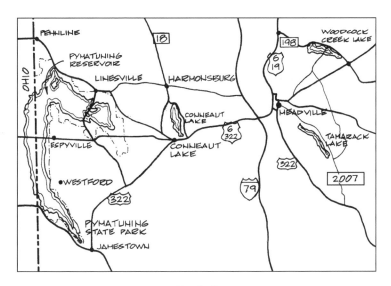

Meadville

MEADVILLE

Meadville, population 14,318, is the home of Allegheny College and birthplace of the modern zipper. In recent years there have been increased numbers of Red-bellied Woodpeckers in the area. In winter look for Rough-legged Hawks in open fields outside the city. Check Tamarack Lake, just south of Meadville off Route 2007 for migrating Horned Grebe in early April, as well as other waterfowl that migrate through the region.

Woodcock Creek Lake

Woodcock Creek Lake is a 1,732-acre lake and surrounding hardwood forest owned by the U.S. Army Corps of Engineers. To reach the Lake, drive north from Meadville on Route 86 for about 2 miles to Route 198, where you will turn right. The lake is just ahead on the right.

There are two observation blinds at the lake, both on the Bossard Nature Trail. Maps and brochures are available at the information center. Programs are offered on request. There are a fitness trail and hiking trail, and 1,000 feet of the Bossard Nature Trail is wheelchair-accessible.

The south shore of the lake is operated by Crawford County as Col. Crawford Park. A camping area has 111 sites. Food is available at the lake, and picnicking is permitted.

The lake is good for migratory waterfowl in the spring and fall. Look for Tundra Swan, Blue-winged Teal, Northern Shoveler, American Wigeon, Greater Scaup, Red-breasted Merganser, Hooded Merganser, and Ruddy Duck. During the drought of 1991, shorebirds such as Black-bellied Plover, Lesser Golden-Plover, Semipalmated Plover, Greater Yellowlegs, and Buff-breasted Sandpiper were recorded. This is a place worth checking when conditions are dry. An occasional Bald Eagle is seen in the area.

The address is Woodcock Creek Lake, P.O. Box 629, Saegertown, PA 16433-0629, (814) 763-4477. For recorded recreation information call (814) 763-2008. The address for Col. Crawford Park is RD 3, Meadville, PA 16335, (814) 724-6879.

PYMATUNING AREA

The area around Pymatuning Lake includes Pymatuning State Park, State Game Lands 214, and Pymatuning Wildlife Management Area. The latter two areas, about 11,000 acres, are managed by the Pennsylvania Game Commission. Ohio also has a state park on the western shore of the lake. The total area in Pennsylvania, including the state park, is 25,000 acres, of which 17,000 is water. The area is very popular for hunting, and the Game Commission chooses hunters who will be allowed use of a hunting blind by lottery. If possible, visit on Sundays during hunting season. "Pymatuning" is said to be a Native American term for "Crooked-Mouthed Man's Dwelling Place."

Pymatuning Wildlife Management Area & SGL 213

The lake and its adjacent facilities are located near Linesville, population 1,166. From Meadville take Route 6/322 southwest to Route 6. Just after you pass between Conneaut Lake on your right and the Conneaut Marsh (SGL 213) on your left, you will enter the town of Conneaut Lake and come to the intersection of Routes 6, 285, and

18/322. Turn right and drive north to Linesville on Route 6. At the stop light in Linesville, turn left onto State Route 3011 and drive 1.25 miles to Ford Island and the Game Commission's visitors' center.

The Pymatuning visitors' center is managed by the Pennsylvania Game Commission and is open from 8 a.m. to 4 p.m. during the week and 9 a.m. to 5 p.m. on weekends. There is no food concession at the center, but picnicking is allowed, and convenience stores are found in the area. As of early 1993, a wheelchair-accessible trail is under construction. The area is included in the Linesville Christmas Bird Count.

The area is popular with both hunters and tourists, as well as birders. The Pymatuning Waterfowl Expo is held every year on the third weekend in September. It features arts, crafts, a parade, an auction, exhibits, demonstrations, and the annual Pennsylvania Duck Stamp competition. Also popular with tourists is a concession at the Linesville spillway that sells bread to feed fish (carp) and waterfowl (Mallards and Canada Geese). So many converge that birds walk on the fishes' backs to get to the bread. Postcards showing this surreal scene are available.

The Game Commission properties do not have camping or picnicking, but both are permitted at the nearby state park. The visitors' center houses the Waterfowl Museum, which is open from 8 a.m to 4 p.m. weekdays and from 9 a.m. to 5 p.m. on weekends. The grounds are open 24 hours a day, except for restricted areas set aside for waterfowl propagation. **Do not under any circumstances enter the restricted areas; people have been fined for doing so.** This is why you stop at the visitors' center first. Pick up maps, brochures for a self-guided car tour, and a bird list—all are free. Restricted areas are shown on the maps and are posted.

The museum has exhibits of about 300 mounted birds and other animals. A very small bookstore sells Game Commission publications and items such as wildlife patches and Pennsylvania Duck stamps. Many birders buy the stamps to help support areas like Pymatuning.

The visitors' center staff will explain current regulations and restrictions and will point out notable birds. For example, when Bald Eagles are nesting directly across the water from Ford Island, the staff puts up spotting scopes so visitors can watch the birds from the center's patio. Wildlife programs are presented regularly. Topics may include beaver, bluebirds, a photo clinic, raptors, gypsy moth, wood carving, and endangered plants and animals. Special programs are arranged for groups. A nature trail begins at the visitors' center and ends at the parking lot. Brochures, available at the visitors' center, describe the 36 numbered trees and shrubs and the surrounding habitat. Pymatuning is popular with researchers. You will undoubtedly see birds with color-coded leg bands and neck collars.

A 25-mile driving tour that stops at six points of interest begins at the visitors' center parking lot. Maps are available at the center. Highlights of the driving tour include the Pymatuning Wildlife Management Area—forests, fields, crops, and water habitats. Goose nesting platforms and boxes for American Kestrel and Eastern Bluebird are provided here. Look for woodpeckers, plovers, yellowlegs, and Eastern Meadowlark. When you reach the paved road, Route 285, turn left. Drive 300 yards to a parking lot. Look for Bobolinks and Northern Harriers in the fields. In the late summer, shorebirds can be seen at the ponds. After leaving the parking lot, turn left and drive 2.2 miles, turn right onto Canal Road and drive another 1.5 miles, turn right and drive to the parking area. Walk across the small stream and turn right. This area was once a part of the Erie Canal system. Beaver have constructed a dam here. Look for songbirds, especially warblers in the spring and fall. From the parking area, turn right onto Canal Road and drive 1.4 miles to a stop sign. Turn right and drive 0.3 mile to Route 322. Make a sharp left onto Route 322 and drive 0.4 mile and turn right onto Pine Road. Drive 1.8 miles to the parking area for stop 4. At this impoundment, look for Grebe, Osprey, Kingfishers, and warblers.

Return to Route 322 and turn left toward Hartstown. Drive 1.4 miles and turn right at the railroad tracks, just before you would cross the bridge. While driving or walking down this dirt road, scan the marsh for eagles, ospreys, grebes, rails, snipes, bitterns, and egrets. Watch for Black Tern, which has been seen here.

Just north of the Game Commission visitors' center is a fish hatchery operated by the Pennsylvania Fish Commission. Cliff Swallows nest here. When the hatchery ponds are drained, the area is attractive to shorebirds. The hatchery parking lot offers a good view of Pymatuning Lake. Use a scope to look for Great Blue Heron, Great Egret, Bald Eagle, Osprey, Wood Duck, and other birds on the lake. If you do not have a scope, hatchery staff have them. A walking tour of the hatchery is available at the Fish Commission visitors' center.

Virginia Rail

The address is Pymatuning Wildlife Management Area, RD 1, Box 8, Hartstown, PA 16121, (800) 533-6764.

Pymatuning State Park

The entire Pymatuning Lake area is publicly owned, either as State Game Lands or as Pymatuning State Park. The state park office is located on Route 322 near the breast of the dam. Facilities at the state park include 807 campsites in four areas; both tent and trailer facilities are available. An organized-group camping area can accommodate 400 people. Modern cabins designed for families are available by advance reservation. There are four protected swimming beaches and numerous boat-launch areas. This is a busy park.

Fall migrants at the park include Green-winged Teal, American Black Duck, Northern Pintail, Northern Shoveler, Gadwall, American Wigeon, Canvasback, Redhead, and Ring-necked Duck.

The address is Pymatuning State Park, P.O. Box 425, Jamestown, PA 16134, (412) 932-3141.

MAURICE K. GODDARD STATE PARK

This park is named for one of Pennsylvania's outstanding environmentalists, Maurice K. Goddard, who is known to his thousands of friends as Doc Goddard. The park is the perfect tribute to this former Penn State forestry professor who became the first secretary of the Pennsylvania Department of Environmental Resources. Under the leadership of Doc Goddard, the Department accomplished the goal of Project 70: to establish a state park within 25 miles of every Pennsylvanian.

The park is located at Exit 34 of I-79. From I-79, drive west on Route 358 for about 0.4 mile and bear right at the "Y" intersection. Drive 1.1 miles to the intersection with Route 1009, Lake Wilhelm Road. Turn right, and drive north, about 2.3 miles to the park office. There are directional signs.

The park is 2,856 acres of old fields, hardwood forest, and the 1,860-acre Lake Wilhelm, a 6-mile-long, narrow, flood-control lake. Adjoining the park is State Game Lands 270, an additional 2,027 acres of open fields interspersed with woodlands. A portion of Lake Wilhelm in this area is used by the Pennsylvania Game Commission as a propagation area. Do **not** enter posted areas. The McKeever Environmental Learning Center is adjacent to the park (see next listing). The park does not have camping facilities, but it does have a food concession during the summer months.

The park has 21.5 miles of trails; some of the trails are designated for snowmobiles and cross-country skiing in winter. The Falling Run Nature Trail is a self-guided interpretive trail. A bird checklist of 219 species and 25 accidentals is available at the park office, which is open from 8 a.m. to 4 p.m.

A sampling of the birds recorded at the park includes the following: Pied-billed, Horned, Red-necked, and Eared Grebes; Greater and Lesser Scaups; Northern Harrier; Sharp-shinned and Cooper's Hawk; Northern Goshawk; Red-shouldered, Broad-winged, and Red-tailed Hawks; Marsh Wren; Louisiana and Northern Waterthrush; Grasshopper and Henslow's Sparrow; and Lapland Longspur.

The address for Maurice Goddard State Park is RD 3, Box 91, Sandy Lake, PA 16145, (412) 253-4833. For more information about SGL 270, contact Pennsylvania Game Commission, Northwest Division Headquarters, P.O. Box 31, Franklin, PA 16323, (814) 432-3187.

McKeever Environmental Learning Center

Located near M.K. Goddard State Park, the McKeever Center is a facility designed for groups of up to 120 people. The Goddard-McKeever Trail begins near the breast of the dam in Goddard State Park and connects the center to the park. The center has a discovery building, and there are trails nearby. For more information contact McKeever Environmental Learning Center, RD 3, Box 121, Sandy Lake, PA 16145, (412) 376-7585.

SHARON

Sharon, population 17,533, is located near the Ohio border on Route 62. Sharon is a steel town.

Shenango River Reservoir

Shenango River Reservoir, also known as Shenango Lake, is 3,560 acres of water and 15,071 acres of land in a federal flood-control project. The lake is located on the Shenango River near Hermitage. To reach the lake, take US 62 east from Sharon to Hermitage. Turn left onto SR 18 north from Hermitage, and continue about 6 miles to the lake. Recreation facilities are spread out but are well identified by signs.

The lake is open 7 days a week from sunrise to sunset. There are 330 campsites (including a limited number of tents for rent), picnic facilities, and the trailhead of the Shenango Trail. A visitors' center is open at the breast of the dam from May to September on weekends from noon to 4 p.m. Exhibits feature Corps of Engineers history, a district map, and local history. Campground programs are offered during the summer; most are nature-oriented.

Habitats at the lake include deciduous woods, wetlands, open fields, and water. Look for Great Blue Heron, Green-backed Heron, Double-crested Cormorant, and Osprey during the summer. There is a Cliff Swallow colony at the headquarters building.

When water levels have been low during late summer, the following shorebirds have been recorded: Black-bellied Plover, Lesser Golden-Plover, Semipalmated Plover, Killdeer, Greater Yellowlegs, Lesser Yellowlegs, Ruddy Turnstone, Sanderling, Semipalmated Sandpiper, Least Sandpiper, White-rumped Sandpiper, Baird's Sandpiper, Pectoral Sandpiper, Dunlin, Stilt Sandpiper, Buff-breasted Sandpiper, Ruff, and Short-billed Dowitcher.

In late September, the following migrants have been observed in the area: Blue-winged and Nashville Warblers; Yellow, Chestnut-sided, Magnolia, Black-throated Blue, Yellow-rumped, Black-throated Green, Blackburnian, Pine, Bay-breasted, and Black-and-white Warblers; American Redstart; Ovenbird; Kentucky Warbler; Common Yellowthroat; and Hooded and Wilson's Warblers.

The address is Shenango River Reservoir, 2442 Kelly Road, Hermitage, PA 16150. Phone for general information: (412) 962-7746; for lake information: (412) 962-4384; for campground registration: (412) 646-1115.

Brucker Great Blue Heron Sanctuary

The Brucker Great Blue Heron Sanctuary is a 45-acre sanctuary that protects the largest breeding colony of Great Blue Herons in Pennsylvania. More than 200 herons nest here.

Entry is prohibited during the active nesting season; however, an observation shelter allows birders to study the birds. Between September 1 and January 31, the entire sanctuary is open to the public, and hunting is permitted.

To reach the sanctuary, drive north from Sharon on Route 18, about 10 miles. A sign identifies the sanctuary, which is on the left.

For more information contact Brucker Great Blue Heron Sanctuary, P.O. Box 362, Greenville, PA 16125.

ERIE NATIONAL WILDLIFE REFUGE

The Erie National Wildlife Refuge is not located on Lake Erie but is named for the Erie Indians, a tribe that lived in the region. The refuge was established in 1959 with the primary objective of providing waterfowl with nesting, feeding, brooding, and resting marshes. More than 2,500 acres of the refuge's 8,750 acres are wetlands, including beaver ponds, marshes, swamps, impoundments, creeks,

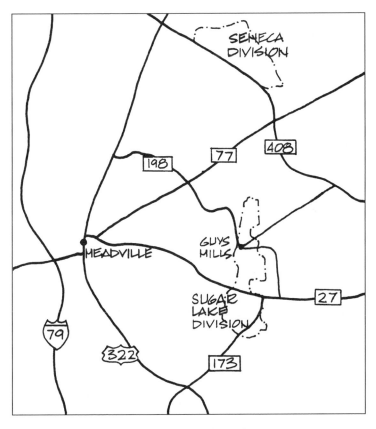

Erie National Wildlife Refuge

and wet meadows. The remainder of the refuge is open field, grass-lands, and timbered uplands. This wide variety of habitats has result-ed in a variety of species. A bird checklist (1986) lists 236 species, of which 112 are breeders, and an additional 15 accidentals that have been recorded at the refuge.

The refuge consists of two divisions. The Sugar Lake Division, 5,205 acres, is located 8.5 miles east of Meadville near the village of Guys Mills. The Seneca Division, 3,463 acres, is located 4 miles southeast of Cambridge Springs in a forested valley.

From Meadville take Route 27 and travel 7 miles east to State Route 2032, the left arm of a "Y" intersection (Route 27 bends to the right). Drive 3 miles on Route 2032 to a stop sign in Guys Mills. Con-tinue east on Route 2015 and drive 0.8 miles (past Union Cemetery) to the refuge headquarters on the right. The Seneca Division is 10 miles north of the Sugar Lake Division on Route 408.

Three trails, a wooded drive, an overlook, and an observation blind at Reitz's Pond offer options for viewing birds and other wildlife. The Tsuga Trail near the headquarters building follows either a 1.2-mile or 1.6-mile route through a variety of habitats. Stops at numbered sign posts are described in a brochure that explains management practices by both humans and beavers. A wheelchair-accessible trail is under construction as of this writing. The headquarters features wildlife exhibits.

Waterfowl migrations in March to early April and again in September to November are the main attraction at the refuge. Common migrants include Canada Goose (as many as 4,500 may be seen in a day), Wood Duck, Green-winged Teal, Mallard, Blue-winged Teal, American Wigeon, Ring-necked Duck, Bufflehead, and Hooded Merganser.

Twenty-four species of shorebirds have been recorded, most during migration. Check mudflats at the edges of impoundments for species such as Greater and Lesser Yellowlegs, Solitary Sandpiper, Spotted Sandpiper, and Dunlin. American Woodcock is common during migra-tion, less so in the summer months, but they do breed in the refuge.

Other breeding birds include Great Blue Heron, Green-backed Heron, Wood Duck (common), American Black Duck, Blue-winged Teal, Hooded Merganser, Bald Eagle (apparently expanding their range from Pymatuning), Red-shouldered Hawk, Broad-winged Hawk, Sora, American Coot, Spotted Sandpiper, Black-billed Cuckoo,

Hooded Merganser

Barred Owl, Red-headed Woodpecker, Yellow-bellied Sapsucker, Pileated Woodpecker, Acadian Flycatcher, Willow Flycatcher (common), Least Flycatcher, Great Crested Flycatcher (common), Bank Swallow (common), Eastern Bluebird, Veery, Wood Thrush, Brown Thrasher, Solitary Vireo, Yellow-throated Vireo, Warbling Vireo, Blue-winged Warbler (common), Chestnut-sided Warbler, Black-throated Green Warbler, Blackburnian Warbler, American Redstart, Northern and Louisiana Waterthrush, Hooded Warbler (common), Canada Warbler, Scarlet Tanager, Rose-breasted Grosbeak, Rufous-sided Towhee, Savannah Sparrow, Henslow's Sparrow (rare), Swamp Sparrow, Red-winged Blackbird, and Eastern Meadowlark.

Available at the refuge headquarters are the bird checklist, a guide to the Tsuga Nature Trail, a checklist of amphibians and reptiles, and brochures with maps showing locations where hunting and fishing are permitted. Programs are available for groups; arrangements should be made in advance. The refuge address is Refuge Manager, Erie National Wildlife Refuge, RD 1, Wood Duck Lane, Guys Mills, PA 16327, (814) 789-3585.

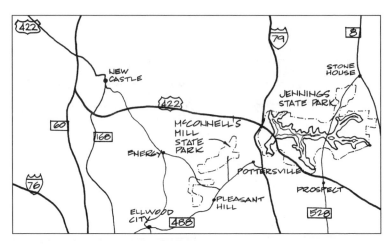

New Castle

NEW CASTLE

New Castle, population 28,334, is the county seat of Lawrence County. The city is located where the Shenango and Mahoning Rivers join to form the Beaver River. The location served as the regional capital of the Delaware tribe and was an important trading center. In the early days of European settlement, pig iron was manufactured from local iron ore; in recent years steel manufacturing has been an important local industry. Pottery is manufactured from deposits of clay in the area. Birders will want to visit nearby McConnell's Mill State Park, Moraine State Park, and Jennings Environmental Education Center.

Check reclaimed strip mines in the area for Short-eared Owl; they are not common, but have been recorded.

McConnell's Mill State Park

McConnell's Mill State Park is 2,512 acres in the Slippery Rock Creek Gorge, which was created when the Wisconsin Glacier dammed Muddy Creek and Slippery Rock Creek, creating a lake system. As the ice melted, the glacial Lake Arthur drained into the Slippery Rock Valley and cut the gorge to a depth of 400 feet. The water flow before the glaciation had been north to the St. Lawrence River but now drains to the Ohio River.

Warning: This park has a special hazard. The water in the creek is very swift in places, and there are deep pools. The rocks along the bank are smooth, and when wet, slippery. Be careful. Watch your children.

From New Castle, take Route 422 east, about 6 miles to the park entrance. Camping is not permitted in the park, but picnic facilities are available. Whitewater rafting is allowed, as are climbing (near Breakneck Bridge!) and rappeling. Guided nature walks are offered on Saturdays and Sundays during the summer. Check with the park office for a schedule. A 2-mile self-guided section of the Kildoo Nature Trail passes through a hemlock ravine. Pick up a trail brochure at the park office, located at the main entrance. Part of this trail is paved and wheelchair-accessible.

Of historical interest are McConnell's grist mill, built in 1868, and a covered bridge located nearby. Guided tours of the grist mill are available from Memorial Day to Labor Day.

Birds at McConnell's Mill State Park are similar to those found at Moraine State Park, which is 2 miles east on Route 422. Pick up a bird checklist at Moraine for your visit to McConnell's Mill. Of course, you will not see the waterfowl here that you saw at Moraine. You should see Pileated Woodpecker, Scarlet Tanager, and Rose-breasted Grosbeak. When Gypsy Moth populations are high, numerous Black-billed and Yellow-billed Cuckoos can be found.

The address of the park is RD 2, Box 16, Portersville, PA 16051, (412) 468-8091.

Moraine State Park

Lake Arthur lies at the site of a glacial lake that existed about 20,000 years ago during the Wisconsin glaciation. The present lake, 3,225 acres, was completed in 1969 after a decade of planning, clearing land, plugging more than 400 abandoned oil and gas wells, and restoring hundreds of acres of abandoned surface mines. To reach the park, leave I-79 at Exit 29. Take Route 422 east 2 miles to the park entrance. Stop at the park office to pick up a free map, Moraine State

Park "Facts" brochure, and a bird checklist of 239 species. Also of interest is a Pennsylvania Trail of Geology brochure that explains the glacial features of the park.

Day-use areas of the park open at 8 a.m and close at sunset seven days a week, year-round. A food concession is operated in the summer,

Sedge Wren

and picnics are allowed. Other facilities include swimming beaches, marinas, a restaurant, a 7.5-mile paved bicycle trail (wheelchair-accessible) and five hiking trails, a visitors' center, and 10 modern cabins. The Hilltop Trail is a self-guided interpretive trail near the boat concession. The propagation area managed by the Game Commission is closed to the public. The park has a bluebird trail with 37 boxes. Moraine is included in the Butler County Christmas Bird Count.

Environmental programs are presented by park staff on a regular basis. Check with the park office for a schedule. While at the park office, birders may want to look at the small wetlands exhibit.

Like other lakes in the Glaciated Northwest Region of Pennsylvania, Lake Arthur is very good for migratory waterfowl, especially in late March and early April. Twenty-nine species have been recorded. A sampling includes Tundra Swan, Snow Goose, Green-winged Teal, American Black Duck, Northern Pintail, Blue-winged Teal, Lesser Scaup, Common Goldeneye, Bufflehead, Common Merganser, Redbreasted Merganser, and Ruddy Duck.

A Cliff Swallow colony on the Route 528 bridge was discovered in 1990 with 5 nests. By 1992 it had more than 45 nests. Old farm fields that are in the shrubby stage of succession are good for Prairie Warbler, Yellow-breasted Chat, White-eyed Vireo, and Field Sparrow. Savannah and Grasshopper Sparrow can be found in open fields.

Sedge Wren has been a confirmed breeder in the park's propagation area. Fortunately for the birds, this area is strictly controlled and access is not permitted. Birders who are desperate to list a Sedge Wren should check moist upland sedge meadows in the park. Please report sightings to the park office.

The park's address is Moraine State Park, RD 1, Box 212, Portersville, PA 16051, (412) 368-8811.

Jennings Nature Reserve

The Jennings Environmental Education Center, 295 acres adjacent to Moraine State Park, is owned and managed by the Bureau of State Parks. The center was established to protect a unique ecosystem in Pennsylvania: a relict prairie and its stand of Blazing Star (*Liatris spicata*). The Blazing Star blooms in early August. Many other prairie plants also are found at Jennings. Another interesting species found at the center is the Massasauga Rattlesnake (*Sistrurus catenatus catenatus*). This snake, an endangered species, is very shy but is poisonous. Jennings staff reminds visitors to stay on the trails for their own safety as well as the safety of the snake.

To reach Jennings, exit I-79 at Route 422 (Exit 29) and drive east on 422 for 7 miles to Route 528. Take Route 528 north for 8 miles to the second entrance sign for Jennings.

The center is open from dawn to dusk, 7 days a week, and has approximately 8 miles of trails through the relict prairie, woodlands, and stream valleys. Wood Whisper Trail and portions of Massasauga Trail and Blazing Star Trail are wheelchair-accessible.

The education center offers programs on some weekends. (Call or write for a schedule). Examples from a previous fall/winter brochure include "Leave it to Beaver," "Pennsylvania's Bald Eagles," and "Winter Tracks and Traces." Programs for organizations, schools, or teachers are available but must be arranged in advance.

Jennings has a bluebird trail and conducts research on endangered plants and animals, prairie management, and wetlands treatment systems. A free bird checklist of 145 species is available at the nature center.

Nesting birds recorded at Jennings include Wood Duck; Sharp-shinned, Cooper's, Red-shouldered, Broad-winged, and Red-tailed Hawks; American Woodcock; Black-billed and Yellow-billed Cuckoos; Barred Owl (very near the nature center; young are easily viewed after fledgling); Pileated Woodpecker (common); Great Crested Flycatcher; Blue-winged Warbler (common); Chestnut-sided Warbler; Black-throated Green Warbler; Prairie Warbler; Black-and-White Warbler; American Redstart; Kentucky Warbler (common); Hooded Warbler (common); Rose-breasted Grosbeak (abundant); and Swamp Sparrow. Horned Lark have been observed here.

Migrants include 35 species of warblers recorded in the spring and 33 in the fall. Abundant spring and fall warblers are Tennessee, Nashville, Yellow, Chestnut-sided, Cape May, Yellow-rumped, Black-throated Green, Blackburnian, and Bay-breasted Warblers. An occasional Rusty Blackbird is seen during migration, as are Lincoln's and Swamp Sparrows.

A feeding station is operated during winter months, and binoculars are available for loan. Wintering species include Red-breasted

Nuthatch, Brown Creeper and, occasionally, Golden-crowned and Ruby-crowned Kinglets and Evening Grosbeak. Rare wintering birds include Yellow-bellied Sapsucker, Red Crossbill, White-winged Crossbill, and Common Redpoll.

The address is Jennings Environmental Education Center, RD 1, Box 281, Slippery Rock, PA 16057-8701, (412) 794-6011.

SLIPPERY ROCK

Slippery Rock, population 3,008, is the home of Slippery Rock University. The area around Slippery Rock has many fields and reclaimed strip mines. In summer, check these areas for sparrows, especially Vesper, Savannah, Grasshopper, and Henslow's. Large flocks of Bobolinks are sometimes seen. In winter, look for irregular visitors: Snow Bunting, Common Redpoll, and, less commonly, Lapland Longspur.

Wolf Creek Narrows

Wolf Creek Narrows is a 125-acre tract owned by the Western Pennsylvania Conservancy. To reach the area, take I-79 to Exit 30 (Slippery Rock). Drive east on SR 108 to Slippery Rock, and turn left onto SR 258 at the traffic light. Drive one block to Water Street and turn left. Stay on Water Street until it crosses Wolf Creek (about 2 miles). Cross the bridge and park in the small parking area, but be careful not to block the lane. The Narrows Trail begins at a sign on the opposite side of the bridge. This area is well-known for wildflowers in spring, including a spectacular tract of White Trillium in early May. As many as 30 species of warblers have been recorded when waves pass through the Wolf Creek Narrows area in mid-May. Both Orange-crowned and Yellow-throated Warblers have been observed here.

For more information, contact the Western Pennsylvania Conservancy, 316 4th Ave., Pittsburgh, PA 15222-9843, phone (412) 288-2777, fax (412) 281-1792.

OIL CITY

Oil City, population 11,949, has been the heart of Pennsylvania's oil industry since oil was first drilled at Titusville in 1859. Today oil remains an important part of the local economy because Pennsylvania's oil has a high paraffin content and is widely used as a lubricant. Refineries line both sides of Route 8 north of Oil City; thousands of active and abandoned wells dot the countryside. The Venango Museum of Art, Science, and Industry, 270 Seneca Street, has displays about the region. Admission is charged. Phone (814) 676-2007 for more information.

The area is important for recreation, especially fishing and hunting. The Allegheny River is popular with anglers seeking Small-mouthed Bass, Walleye, and Muskelunge.

Allegheny River Canoe Trips

Birding from a canoe can offer a relaxing, close look at river species such as Great Blue Heron and Green-backed Heron. The stretch of river between Franklin and Emlenton has Black-crowned Night-Heron in summer. For information about outfitters in the area, con-

Black-crowned Night Heron

tact the Venango County Area Tourist Promotion Agency, P.O. Box 147, Emlenton, PA 16373, (814) 867-2472 or (800) 867-2472.

Oil Creek State Park

Oil Creek State Park is 7,007 acres located in the Oil Creek valley between Titusville and Oil City. To reach the park, drive north of Oil City on Route 8 for 4 miles. Immediately after crossing the bridge over Oil Creek, turn right into the park. Take State Route 1007 to the park office, located near the second bridge.

The park is open daily, year-round from 8 a.m. to sunset. A free map and bird checklist are available at the park office located near the intersection of Routes 1007 and 1004 at Petroleum Centre. Nearby attractions include the Drake Well, drilled in 1859, and the Drake Well Museum. Also nearby is Pithole, a boom town where oil was discovered in January 1865. By September of that year, the town had 15,000 inhabitants, but the oil reserves were depleted and the town was deserted by 1867. Both the Drake Well and Pithole are administered by the Pennsylvania Historical and Museum Commission. The Oil Creek and Titusville Railroad runs excursions through the valley from May to October. Call (814) 676-1733 for more information.

Oil Creek State Park habitats include the stream valley, brushy and wooded wetlands, hemlock/maple woodlands in side valleys, and oak/hickory forests. The Oil Creek Hiking Trail is 36 miles long, a paved bike trail is 9.5 miles long and is wheelchair-accessible, and an interpretive trail is 5 miles long. An interpretive display in the park office and visitors' center features the oil history of the area. Programs are offered on historical topics, environmental education, and natural history. There are 12 Adirondack shelters available for backpackers. Food is available near the park, and picnicking is permitted.

The park has a bluebird trail and is part of the Pleasantville Christmas Bird Count. Notable birds include 34 species of migrant warblers in late April and May, breeding Blackburnian, Black-throated Green and Black-throated Blue Warblers; Dark-eyed Junco; and Whip-poor-will. Also breeding are Common Merganser, Eastern Bluebird, Rose-breasted Grosbeak, Wild Turkey, Cedar Waxwing, White-eyed Vireo, Wood Duck, Hooded Warbler, and Black-and-white Warbler.

Fall migrants include 33 species of warblers and Common Nighthawk. In winter look for Great Horned Owl, Barred Owl, and Eastern Screech-Owl. Pine Siskin, Evening Grosbeak, and Purple Finch also have been recorded in the winter. Osprey and Bald Eagle have been seen spring through fall.

Oil Creek State Park's address is RD 1, Box 207, Oil City, PA 16301, (814) 676-5915.

Chapter 3
Allegheny Plateau

The Allegheny Plateau is a "T"-shaped region that extends from the Mason-Dixon Line to the New York border. The western boundary of the region runs from Laurel Hill north to the boundary of the Northwest Glaciated region. The eastern boundary of the region is the Allegheny Front, a prominent scarp that marks the boundary of the Allegheny Plateau. The hook-shaped region on the right arm of the "T" is known as the Poconos or Pocono Mountains. This important recreational area in Pennsylvania was influenced by the Illinois and Wisconsin glacial advances. The Allegheny Plateau is characterized by rolling uplands deeply cut by rivers and streams, especially in the northern counties. The region makes up about 40% of Pennsylvania.

Average annual precipitation in this region is about 40 inches, slightly less in the eastern part of the region. Average snowfall ranges from 40 to 90 inches per year, with more snow in the north. The average annual temperature is between 48° and 50° Fahrenheit in the southern part of the region and between 44° and 48° in the north. The average July extreme maximum temperature is approximately 90° while the average January extreme minimum ranges from −2° in the south to −10° in the north.

Forests in the region are Northern Hardwood Forests (Sugar Maple, Yellow Birch, Beech, and Hemlock dominating) and Appalachian Oak Forests (White and Red Oak dominant). Soils are sedimentary in the south and west of the region and glacial till in the east. In most areas the soils are too rocky for growing crops, but livestock farming is possible.

The Allegheny Plateau is a region of extremes. In the some areas—especially Somerset and Clearfield counties—you will see the effects of strip mining for bituminous coal. Other areas—some parts of the

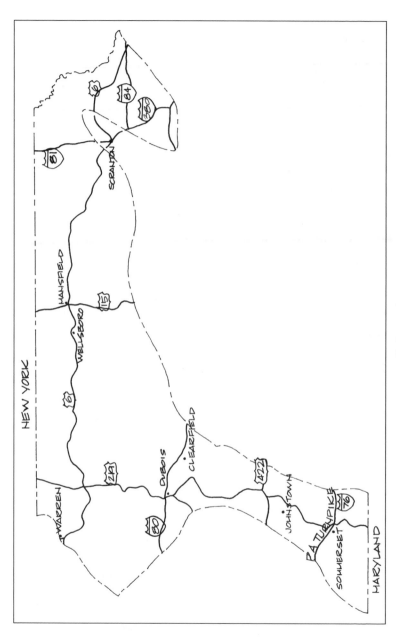

Allegheny Plateau

Allegheny National Forest and the "Northern Tier" of counties—are essentially wilderness. This is the most sparsely populated region of Pennsylvania. Local economic activities include manufacturing, forestry, coal mining, livestock farming, and tourism.

Abundant year-round residents of the Allegheny Plateau include Black-Capped Chickadee, Dark-eyed Junco, and House Sparrow. Abundant summer residents (all breed) include Eastern Wood-Pewee, Barn Swallow, Blue Jay, Wood Thrush, Red-eyed Vireo, Black-throated Green Warbler, Ovenbird, and Field Sparrow. The Common Merganser is certain to be seen during spring migration.

LAUREL HIGHLANDS

The Laurel Highlands section of the Allegheny Plateau is the "down line" of the "T"-shaped region. It extends from the Allegheny Front to the edge of the Pittsburgh Plateau. The highest point in Pennsylvania, Mount Davis (3,213 feet), is located here in southern Somerset County. Because of the high elevation of the plateau, birds such as Canada Warbler and Northern Junco are breeding species. In valleys cut by streams, more southerly species can be found. For example, Swainson's Warbler has been found in rhododendron thickets at Ohiopyle State Park and Bear Run Nature Reserve.

Youghiogheny River Lake

Youghiogheny River Lake is 3,915 acres of U.S. Army Corps of Engineers' flood-control project spanning the Mason-Dixon Line in southern Somerset County. The lake itself is 2,840 acres.

To reach the lake, take SR 281 south from Somerset to Confluence. The lake is just south of Confluence; there are several access points. Free maps are available at the visitors' center at Jockey Hollow. The lake is open from 7:30 a.m. to 10 p.m. in summer and from 7:30 a.m. to 4 p.m. the rest of the year. There are 206 campsites.

The lake has Wood Duck boxes, Osprey platforms, and bluebird boxes. Spring migrants include Common Loon, Horned Grebe, and Canada Goose. Summer species include Ruffed Grouse, Wild Turkey, Cooper's Hawk, Red-tailed Hawk, Eastern Screech-Owl, Great Horned Owl, and Wood Thrush.

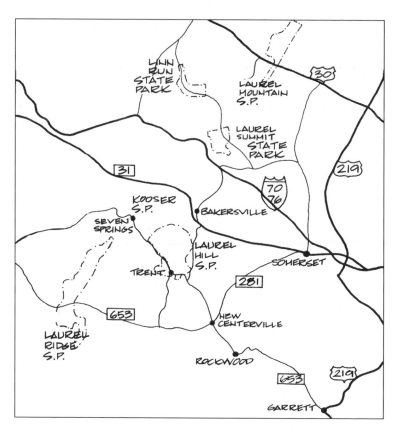

Laurel Highlands

Fall migrants include Common Loon, Bufflehead, Ruddy Duck, and Common Merganser. In winter, Bufflehead and Common Merganser have been recorded.

The address is Youghiogheny River Lake, RD 1, Box 17, Confluence, PA 15424-9103, (814) 395-3242.

Ohiopyle State Park

Ohiopyle State Park is 18,719 acres of fields; thickets; deciduous, coniferous, and mixed forest; and 14 miles of the Youghiogheny River.

To reach the park from the Pennsylvania Turnpike use the Donegal exit, Exit 9. Drive east on SR 31, 2 miles to Jones Mills, where you will turn right onto SR 381. Drive south about 17 miles to the park. The park office is south of the village of Ohiopyle, on LR 2012. Birders can pick up a free bird checklist and map of the park at the office.

The park is open every day from dawn to dusk. There are 223 campsites; reservations are advisable. Accommodations also are available at the Ohiopyle Youth Hostel. A food concession and gift shop are operated during the summer months near the waterfalls in the village of Ohiopyle. Park staff offers environmental and nature programs for the general public. During the summer, special children's programs are offered. Schools, scout groups, and other organizations may schedule free programs by contacting the park office.

The park has 42 miles of trails through a variety of habitats and is the southern terminus for the 70-mile Laurel Highlands Trail. The 126-page *A Hiker's Guide to the Laurel Highlands Trail* is available from the Pennsylvania Chapter of the Sierra Club, Allegheny Group, P.O Box 7404, Pittsburgh, PA 15213. The 28-mile Yough River Hike/Bike Trail is wheelchair-accessible.

A hike through the Ferncliff Natural Area gives a glimpse of plants such as Carolina Tassel-rue and Large-flowered Marshallia usually found in more southern areas.

Ohiopyle State Park is good for songbirds, especially during migrations. Olive-sided Flycatcher; Eastern Wood-Pewee; Yellow-bellied Flycatcher; Acadian, Alder, Willow, and Least Flycatcher; Eastern Phoebe; Great Crested Flycatcher; and Eastern Kingbird have been recorded in the park. Of these, Eastern Wood-Pewee, Acadian and Least Flycatchers, Eastern Phoebe, Great Crested Flycatcher, and Eastern Kingbird are breeding birds.

Vireos recorded in the park include these breeding species: White-eyed, Solitary, Yellow-throated, and Red-eyed Vireo. Warbling Vireo is found throughout the spring, summer, and fall. Philadelphia Vireo is an uncommon migrant in both spring and fall.

The park is also good for warblers. Thirty-six species have been recorded (*italics* indicate breeding species): Blue-winged, *Golden-winged,* Tennessee, Orange-crowned, and Nashville Warblers; *Northern Parula, Yellow, Chestnut-sided, Magnolia,* Cape May, *Black-throated Blue,* Yellow-rumped, *Black-throated Green, Blackburnian,*

Yellow-throated, Pine, *Prairie,* Palm, Bay-breasted, Blackpoll, *Cerulean,* and *Black-and-white Warblers; American Redstart; Worm-eating* and *Swainson's Warblers; Ovenbird;* Northern and Louisiana Waterthrushes; *Kentucky,* Connecticut, and Mourning Warblers; *Common Yellowthroat; Hooded, Wilson's,* and Canada Warblers; and *Yellow-breasted Chat.*

Black-throated Blue Warbler

Check the Cucumber Falls area, where numerous Rhododendron bushes grow, for Swainson's Warbler. This bird was recorded only in Ohiopyle State Park and nearby Bear Run Nature Reserve during the Atlas project. **Warning:** The Cucumber Falls Trail passes over some rocky, wet areas that are very slippery. Watch your step.

Sparrows recorded at the park include (*breeding*): American Tree, *Chipping, Field*, Vesper, *Savannah*, Grasshopper, Henslow's, Fox, Song, Lincoln's, White-throated, and White-crowned Sparrows.

"Fallingwater," designed by Frank Lloyd Wright, is 3 miles north of the park on SR 381. Many birders enjoy a visit to this architectural masterpiece as a side trip to Ohiopyle.

The park's address is Ohiopyle State Park, P.O. Box 105, Ohiopyle, PA 15470, (412) 329-8591. For information about the Youth Hostel, contact American Youth Hostels, Pittsburgh Council, 6300 Fifth Avenue, Pittsburgh, PA 15232.

Laurel Ridge State Park

Laurel Ridge State Park is 15,000 acres of mature northern hardwoods, mixed oak forests, and old fields that traverse Fayette, Somerset, Westmoreland, and Cambria counties. The park features the 70-mile Laurel Highlands Trail, a backpacking trail from Ohiopyle to the Conemaugh Gorge near Johnstown. The trail itself passes through or near several other state parks: It begins in Ohiopyle State Park and runs through Laurel Ridge (headquarters), Laurel Hill, Kooser, Laurel Summit, Linn Run, and Laurel Mountain state parks. The trail traverses several state game lands, sections of the Forbes State Forest, and other public and private lands. It ends at the Charles F. Lewis Natural Area in the Gallitzin State Forest.

To reach the park office, where you can get a free park map, take the Pennsylvania Turnpike to Exit 10. From there, drive south toward Somerset, where you will take SR 281 southwest to New Lexington. In New Lexington, at a "Y" intersection, SR 281 turns to the left. Go straight on SR 653 about 7 miles to the office, which is open Monday to Friday from 8 a.m. to 4 p.m. Other access points for the park are where the trail crosses main highways such as SR 31, US 30, and SR 271. Parking and water are available at these points.

Primitive camping is allowed for backpackers on the trail. Hikers must register with the park, and a small fee is required.

The address is Laurel Ridge State Park, RD 3, Box 246, Rockwood, PA 15557, (412) 455-3744.

Laurel Hill State Park is 3,935 acres of mature mixed oak and northern hardwood forest, open fields, pine plantations, a 65.5-acre lake, and 15 miles of streams. The park is in Somerset County. George Washington's troops camped here during the Whiskey Rebellion in 1794.

To reach the park, take the Pennsylvania Turnpike to Exit 10, and drive south toward Somerset. In Somerset, turn west onto SR 31 and continue toward Bakersville, about 7 miles. Watch for a directional sign and turn left onto LR 4001. The park is about 2 miles ahead. Stop at the visitors' center for a free map.

The park's day-use areas are open from dawn to dusk. Facilities at the park include 270 modern campsites. There are also group tenting facilities for up to 125 people. The visitors' center has historical, natural, and environmental exhibits. Environmental education programs are provided during the summer months. About 2,100 acres of the park are open for hunting, but hunting is not permitted in the area around the lake.

There is a small stand of virgin hemlocks on the Hemlock Hiking Trail; a self-guided nature trail is located off this trail. Check this area and the pine plantation for conifer-loving birds such as Black-throated Green Warbler and Magnolia Warbler.

The address is Laurel Hill State Park, RD 4, Box 130, Somerset, PA 15501, (814) 445-7725.

Kooser State Park is 250 acres of hemlock and oak forest with some open fields and meadows in Somerset County. The park is open from sunrise to sunset and has 45 campsites and nine cabins. Check brushy areas for Chestnut-sided Warbler and hemlocks for Magnolia Warbler. The address is Kooser State Park, RD 4, Box 256, Somerset, PA 15501, (814) 445-8673.

The other state parks along this ridge (Laurel Summit, Linn Run, and Laurel Mountain) have similar habitats and, presumably, similar birds.

Magnolia Warbler

JOHNSTOWN

Johnstown, population 28,134, is located in the Conemaugh River Gorge. The city is known for its history as an iron and steel-making center that relied on coal mines from the surrounding area. In recent years, the city's steel industry has been badly depressed. Tourism is becoming increasingly important with the development of the America's Industrial Heritage Project by the National Park Service. The elevation of the plateau surrounding Johnstown ensures that northern species will be seen in this area of southwestern Pennsylvania.

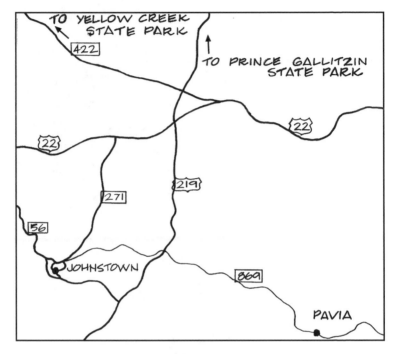

Johnstown

Gallitzin State Forest

The Gallitzin State Forest is more than 18,000 acres of various forest types in Cambria, Bedford, Indiana, and Somerset counties. The forest is named for Prince Demetrius Augustine Gallitzin, a Russian noble who became a Roman Catholic priest and served as a missionary to this area of Pennsylvania in the late 18th century. Several areas within the forest are of interest to birders.

The Dunlo Strip Mine Reclamation Area is more than 500 acres of open grasslands and shrubs in Cambria County. It is owned by the Commonwealth and managed by the Bureau of Forestry's Gallitzin District.

From Johnstown, take US 219 north to the St. Michael/Sidman exit. Take SR 869 east 2.2 miles to the intersection with SR 160. Turn left onto SR 160 and drive 0.1 mile, cross the railroad tracks, and turn right onto Seeseman Road. Drive 3.2 miles to Dunlo, where Seeseman Road becomes Pitcairn Avenue. At the stop sign, turn left and drive up the hill on Huff Street (LR 2005) to another stop sign. Turn right onto Pipeline Avenue, and drive about 1.4 miles to a dirt road on the left. This dirt road is the access to the site. The nasty looking ponds in the tipple area are worth checking for ducks, geese, and flycatchers. The area is gated on weekends and at night but is open from 7 a.m. to 6 p.m. Monday through Friday.

The district forester for the Gallitzin State Forest reports that Northern Harrier, Short-eared Owl, and Common Raven have been observed here in spring. In summer, an immature Bald Eagle was observed, and the area is good for other raptors.

Given the unusual bird life documented at other strip mine reclamation areas in the northwestern area of the Allegheny Plateau, this is a site that deserves more attention. If you visit, please share your records with the district forester.

The address is District Forester, Gallitzin State Forest, P.O. Box 506, Ebensburg, PA 15931, (814) 472-8320.

Within the Babcock Division of the Gallitzin State Forest are the Clear Shade Wild Area and the Bog Special Management Unit, which cover more than 5,000 acres of forest and contain two notable trails. The area is located on SR 56, east of Windber.

The John P. Saylor Memorial Trail is dedicated to the memory of Congressman John P. Saylor, who represented the Johnstown area from 1949 to 1973. He was an active member of the Insular Affairs Committee, was a coauthor of the Wilderness Act, and sponsored efforts to create several national parks.

The trail begins and ends at the Babcock Picnic Area, 4.5 miles east of Windber on SR 56. The picnic area is closed from December to May, but access to the park is allowed all year. The Saylor Trail consists of a northern loop (12 miles) and a southern loop (6 miles). Primitive camping is permitted. Free maps are available from the Gallitzin District Forest office; there is a large wooden map at the trailhead.

The trail winds through hardwood forest, forested wetlands, hemlock areas, and shrub-scrub wetlands. The tract of state land through which the trail winds is more than 5,000 acres. An interpretive brochure gives a fascinating account of the history of the area and an overview of the habitats and vegetation on the trail.

Note: Wells currently are inoperable. If you are backpacking or hiking in the area, you must boil or treat any water from springs or creeks.

Bog and Boulder Trail is a 2-mile trail through an unusual habitat in the Allegheny Plateau. To reach the trail from Johnstown, drive east on SR 56 about 15 miles to the forest headquarters building. Just past this building, which is on the left, you will see the parking area sign on the right. The sign is parallel to the road and is easy to miss. From the east, the trail is 9.3 miles from Pleasantville, also on SR 56.

Prior to 1900, this area was virgin timber, primarily Eastern Hemlock with Sugar Maple, Beech, Red Oak, and Black Cherry. Between 1898 and 1913, the Babcock Lumber Company logged off the area. In this poorly drained area, the cutting of the old-growth forest permitted the ground surface to become so saturated with water that new tree growth was extremely slow. The result is open bog-like areas with wetland shrubs and plants. From an observation tower, visitors to the Bog and Boulder Trail get a good view of the succession from bog to forest.

Birds in the area have not been well inventoried, but this may be a hot spot waiting to be discovered. Look for Alder Flycatcher, Swainson's Thrush, Hermit Thrush, Solitary Vireo, Black-throated Green Warbler, Blackburnian Warbler, and other species that prefer wetlands.

On a June 1993 Juniata Valley Audubon Society field trip, during drizzle and fog (and a severe Elm Spanworm infestation), we saw the following birds on the trail: Yellow-billed Cuckoo, Downy Woodpecker, Northern Flicker, Least Flycatcher, Great Crested Flycatcher, Blue Jay, American Crow, Black-capped Chickadee, Hermit Thrush, Cedar Waxwing, Solitary Vireo, Red-eyed Vireo, Black-throated Green Warbler, Ovenbird, Common Yellowthroat, Canada Warbler, Scarlet Tanager, Rose-breasted Grosbeak, Indigo Bunting, Rufous-sided Towhee, Chipping Sparrow, Field Sparrow, Dark-eyed Junco, and Brown-headed Cowbird.

The Gallitzin State Forest District Forester hopes to manage the tract with wildlife in mind and is interested in receiving lists of species recorded by birders. Contact him for more details: Mr. Gary Scott, District Forester, Gallitzin State Forest, P.O. Box 506, Ebensburg, PA 15931, (814) 472-8320.

The Charles F. Lewis State Forest Natural Area is 384 acres of deep, narrow gorge in the Clark Run watershed. The area is named for the first president of the Western Pennsylvania Conservancy and is an appropriate memorial to an outstanding conservationist. The forest is primarily oak and "hardwood cove trees" such as Tuliptree, Basswood, and Sugar Maple. A portion of this forest was damaged by forest fires more than 40 years ago; the resulting snags are good for woodpeckers. There also are many Mountain Laurel in the area.

The 2-mile Clark Run Trail goes through the site, which is located 1 mile south of the village of Cramer on SR 403. There is a parking lot on the north side of the road. From Johnstown, take SR 403 northwest about 5 miles to the area; the parking lot is on your right.

The area is open 24 hours a day, but camping is not permitted. Free maps are available from the district forester. **Note:** this area has been designated a reptile and amphibian protection area. Do not take, catch, or kill any reptile or amphibian. Both rattlesnakes and copperheads have been found here—be careful not to disturb them.

As with other sites in this state forest, please share your records. For more information, contact the District Forester, Gallitzin State Forest, P.O. Box 506, Ebensburg, PA 15931, (814) 472-8320.

Powdermill Nature Reserve

Owned by the Carnegie Museum of Natural History in Pittsburgh, the Powdermill Nature Reserve is more than 2,000 acres of mixed hardwood forest located 3 miles south of Rector in Westmoreland County. The reserve is a research field station for the museum, and visitors are restricted to the trails and area near the nature center. Hours and days that the reserve is open vary seasonally; call in advance to plan a trip.

To reach Powdermill, take US 30 east from Ligonier a half mile to SR 381. The reserve is about 6 miles from this intersection. An excellent guide to the birds of the reserve and surrounding area is *The Birds of the Ligonier Valley* by Robert C. Leberman. It can be purchased through the Carnegie Museum in Pittsburgh.

Neither camping nor picnicking is permitted at the reserve. There is a nature museum and education center, where exhibits feature local natural history. The big attraction at Powdermill for birders is the presence of breeding warblers such as Northern Parula, Cerulean, Kentucky, and Hooded Warblers. Check fields in the Ligonier Valley for Bobolinks, Grasshopper Sparrows, Savannah Sparrows, and other grassland species. The nearby mountain ridges are good for more "northern" species such as Winter Wren, Hermit Thrush, and Dark-eyed Junco.

The address is Powdermill Nature Reserve, Star Route South, Rector, PA 15677, (412) 593-6105. The address for the Carnegie Museum is 4000 Forbes Avenue, Pittsburgh, PA 15213, (412) 622-3131.

BLUE KNOB STATE PARK

Blue Knob State Park is 5,614 acres of mountainous forests and fields in northern Bedford County. The park is named for Blue Knob: At 3,146 feet, it is the second highest mountain in the Commonwealth, and it is located on a on a spur of the Allegheny Front. There are several beautiful views of the Ridge and Valley Province from this park. The park is within 25 miles of Johnstown, Altoona, and Bedford. To reach the park, take the Pennsylvania Turnpike to Exit 11 at Bedford. Drive north on US 220 to SR 869 west. Follow signs through the small town of Pavia. The office is a half mile past Pavia. Stop here for a free map.

Blue Knob has 17 miles of trails and 40 campsites. Picnicking is permitted, but there is no food concession. There is an organized group camp with facilities for 92 people. Most of the park is open to hunting in the fall and winter and during spring turkey season, so birders will want to take appropriate precautions or visit this park on Sundays during hunting season.

Because of its high elevation, Blue Knob has birds usually found further north. The park is especially good for migrants. Ruffed Grouse are active in the park in spring.

The address is Blue Knob State Park, RD 1, Box 449, Imler, PA 16655-9407, (814) 276-3576.

PRINCE GALLITZIN STATE PARK

Prince Gallitzin State Park is 6,249 acres of lake (1,600 acres), lakeshore, wetlands, mowed fields, wildlife food plots, brushy fields, and mixed hardwood forests. To reach the park, take US 219 north from Johnstown to Carrolltown. Take SR 4015 to Patton and turn right onto SR 36. Drive through town to the intersection with SR 1021 and turn left. At Nagle's Crossroad, SR 1021 veers to the left. Take SR 1026 to the right to reach the park office where you can get a free map.

Prince Gallitzin is open during daylight hours. In addition, the park has 437 campsites and ten modern cabins. An organized group camping area can accommodate 120 people. There are 9 miles of trails; three trails are self-interpretive. One trail, through a beech/maple forest on the western shore of the lake features poems with a forest theme.

Because of its diverse habitats, Prince Gallitzin is a good park for birding. Birds observed in spring have included Common Loon, Pied-billed Grebe, Double-crested Cormorant, Tundra Swan, Wood Duck, American Wigeon, Redhead, Lesser Scaup, Green-winged Teal, Blue-winged Teal, Gadwall, Ring-necked Duck, Oldsquaw, Bufflehead, Common and Red-breasted Merganser, and Common Moorhen.

In May, check the lake's shoreline for Semipalmated Plover, Greater Yellowlegs, Solitary Sandpiper, Spotted Sandpiper, Semi-palmated Sandpiper, and Least Sandpiper. Bonaparte's and Ring-billed Gulls have been observed in late spring. Acadian, Willow, and Least Flycatchers have been recorded in late spring.

The wetlands areas at Prince Gallitzin are excellent. A good observation point is the bridge over Slate Lick Run. American Bittern have been observed in late spring. Sora and Virginia Rail are confirmed breeders. An exciting observation in late May 1992 was two King Rail heard calling from a marshy area for several days.

Cliff Swallows have nested at the marina area in recent years.

Check grassy fields on the western side of the park (also reclaimed surface mines in the area) for Field, Vesper, Savannah, Grasshopper, and Henslow's Sparrows.

Winter birds have included American Tree Sparrow, White-throated Sparrow, Lapland Longspur, Snow Bunting, and Evening Grosbeak.

The address is Prince Gallitzin State Park, RD 1, Box 79, Patton, PA 16668, (814) 674-1000.

CLARION

Clarion, population 6,457, is the county seat of Clarion County and the home of Clarion State University. Economic activities in the area around Clarion include surface mining for coal, drilling for both oil and gas, dairy farming, and tourism. Nearby Cook Forest State Park is one of the most popular parks in the state system.

"The Strips"

"The Strips," reclaimed strip mines, are local hot spots for birds such as Northern Harrier, Short-eared Owl, Bobolink, Eastern Meadowlark, and grassland sparrows.

The Curllsville Strips between Curllsville and Rimersburg, off Route 2011, is an area of grasslands and a pond. Short-eared Owls have bred here in recent years. During the summers of the atlas project, these birds were found only at five reclaimed surface mines in Clarion and Jefferson counties and at Tinicum, near Philadelphia. Horned Lark also have nested in these areas. Northern Harrier and Rough-legged Hawk have been seen in winter.

To reach the Curllsville Strips, travel south on SR 68 from Clarion, about 8 miles to the intersection of Route 2007. Turn left and drive east on Route 2007 1.2 miles, toward Curllsville. At the intersection of Routes 2007 and 2011, in Curllsville, turn right on 2011 across the creek. Go 2.5 miles and turn left on Up Church Road (TR442). Continue 0.4 mile farther to a dirt road that goes straight while the township road curves right. This dirt road loops through the grassland habitat and returns to SR 2011 in 1.7 miles. Because this road is through private property, do your birding from the car.

The Mount Zion Strips are located near Knox. This area is approximately 800 acres of reclaimed surface mines. The area is included in the Clarion Christmas Bird Count, and a grassland breeding bird survey is done annually for the Pennsylvania Game Commission. Further study of the area was conducted by Kirk Piehler for his West Virginia University master's thesis, "Habitat Relationships of Three Grassland Sparrow Species on Reclaimed Surface Mines in Pennsylvania."

Short-eared Owls have nested here in recent years and have been recorded in all seasons. The area is also good for grassland sparrows such as Henslow's, Vesper, Savannah, and Grasshopper Sparrows in the spring and summer. In summer look for Upland Sandpiper, which occasionally breed here, and Dickcissel, which nested in 1988. Bobolink and Eastern Meadowlark are common.

To reach the Mount Zion Strips, drive south of Clarion on Route 68 to I-80, exit 9. Travel west on I-80 to exit 7 and take SR 3007 south across the Clarion River at Canoe Ripple Bridge, at 2.1 miles. As SR 3007 ascends the hill, take the first dirt road (TR 425) to the left, at 1.1 miles. Be careful; this is at the crest of a hill. At the next intersection, 1.1 miles, a "Y", turn left onto another dirt road. Begin checking the surrounding fields for Eastern Meadowlark and Eastern Kingbird. At 0.4 mile farther on this road, locked gates on both sides of the road prohibit driving through the reclaimed surface mines owned by C & K Coal Co., but walking is permitted. Park off the road, but do not block the gates.

Kahle Lake

Owned by the Pennsylvania Fish and Boat Commission, Kahle Lake is 254 acres of lake, marginal wetlands, farm fields, and more or less undisturbed second-growth forests. The area below the breast of the dam is good for spring wildflowers. The lake itself is known for migratory waterfowl, Common Loon, Tundra Swan, and Common Snipe in the spring. Other spring migrants include Pied-billed Grebe, Double-crested Cormorant, Bonaparte's Gull, and Forster's Tern. Osprey and Bald Eagle have been recorded in the summer, and both Yellow-billed and Black-billed Cuckoos are numerous when there is a Gypsy Moth outbreak in the area. Fall migrants include Bufflehead,

Hooded Merganser, and Red-breasted Merganser. Lapland Longspur and Snow Bunting have been sighted in winter.

To reach Kahle Lake, drive west from Clarion on SR 322 to Shippenville (4 miles) and turn left onto SR 208. Drive southwest on SR 208 for 9.7 miles to Lamartine, where you will turn right at the Salem Lutheran Church. At 0.5 mile, turn left onto a dirt road. The lake is ahead on the right. Picnicking is permitted at the lake, but camping is not. The site is open 24 hours a day, all year.

Kahle Lake's address is Kahle Lake, c/o Pennsylvania Fish and Boat Commission, P.O. Box 349, Franklin, PA 16322, (814) 437-5774.

Beaver Creek Wetlands/Wildlife Project

The Clarion Conservation District has acquired approximately 700 acres of ponds, wetlands, abandoned farmlands, second-growth woods, and evergreen plantations for recreational and educational use. To reach the area, drive northwest from Clarion on SR 322 to Shippenville, where you will turn south (left) onto SR 208. About 2 miles west of Knox, you will see ponds on both sides of the road. A parking lot is on the right. The site is open 24 hours a day, all year, but camping is not permitted.

The county plans to construct a nature center here. At present, educational programs are available in conjunction with Clarion University or the Seneca Rocks Audubon Society. The area is included in the Clarion Christmas Bird Count; other projects include a fish-stocking study by the Pennsylvania Fish and Boat Commission and annual Breeding Bird Surveys. A bird checklist is being compiled by members of the Seneca Rocks Audubon Society. Please share your data.

Wood Duck, Canada Goose, and Eastern Bluebird breed at the site, which is also good for neotropical migrants in the summer. In the fall look for Barred and Great Horned Owls, and Eastern Screech-Owl.

The address for the project is Beaver Creek Wetlands/Wildlife Project, Clarion Conservation District, P.O. Box 468, Clarion, PA 16214, (814) 266-4070.

COOK FOREST STATE PARK

Cook Forest State Park, 6,422 acres of forests, has some of the largest stands of virgin White Pine and Eastern Hemlock in Pennsylvania. Many of the trees are 200 to 350 years old and stand nearly 200 feet tall. The park was created by the state legislature in 1927. This is one of the few state parks where you can enjoy cultural activities as well as birding. During the summer months, plays, musicals, and other entertainment are presented at the Verna Leith Sawmill Theater every weekend. The theater is located in the Sawmill Center for the Arts, which also offers craft classes.

To reach the park, take Exit 13 from I-80 and drive north on SR 36 directly to the park. The park office is on the right just after you cross the Clarion River on SR 36. Stop at the office to pick up a brochure, map, and bird checklist with 186 species. From the west, leave I-80 at Exit 8, and take SR 66 north to Leeper. Turn right onto SR 36 and drive about 7 miles southeast to the park.

Cook Forest State Park offers a wide range of outdoor activities. Hiking through the park on the 27-mile network of trails is very popular. Several of the trails such as Indian Trail and Seneca Trail are very steep; do not attempt them unless you are in good physical condition. One area, the Forest Cathedral, is easily reached on the Longfellow Trail from the nature center. The trees in this area are 200 to 350 years old. A one-mile, self-guiding trail near the Sawmill Center for Arts explains the history of the Civilian Conservation Corps. Also near the Sawmill is a paved trail that is wheelchair-accessible.

Camping is permitted in a family campground with 226 tent and trailer sites. Some of the sites are paved and are wheelchair-accessible. The park also has facilities for group camping and 24 rustic cabins. **Warning:** The park has a population of Black Bear. Both campers and picnickers should be careful to store food in car trunks and to dispose of garbage properly.

Canoeing is popular on the Clarion River, which is rated a beginners' river. Contact the Cook Forest Vacation Bureau for information about livery services.

Cook Forest State Park is notable for birds that love conifers: Barred Owl is common. Yellow-bellied Flycatcher is an uncommon

Red Breasted Nuthatch

migrant. Red-breasted Nuthatch and Brown Creeper are common.
Winter Wren is present in small numbers from spring to fall. Hermit
Thrush and Black-throated Blue Warblers are common from spring
to fall. Solitary Vireo, Northern Parula, and Blackburnian, Pine,
Prairie, and Canada Warblers are found from spring to fall. Yellow-
throated Warbler is rare, but has been recorded spring to fall.

Occasionally found in Cook Forest's conifers are Pine Grosbeak,
Red Crossbill, Pine Siskin, Evening Grosbeak, and Fox Sparrow.

Dark-eyed Junco is found in the park in all seasons and is a common nester.

The park's address is Cook Forest State Park, P.O. Box 120, Cooksburg, PA 16217, (814) 744-8407. For information about the Sawmill Center for the Arts, write to the center at P.O. Box 6, Cooksburg, PA 16217, (814) 927-6655. For information on lodging, private campgrounds, and other services and attractions contact the Cook Forest Vacation Bureau, P.O. Box 50, Cooksburg, PA 16217.

WARREN

Located on the Allegheny River, Warren has a population of 11,122 and is an oil and lumber town. Recreation is important in the Warren area because the Allegheny National Forest and Kinzua Dam are located nearby. From January 28 to March 27, 1992, a Great Gray Owl (Pennsylvania's second confirmed record) had birders from all over the mid-Atlantic region flocking to Warren.

Allegheny National Forest

Located in Warren, McKean, Forest, and Elk counties in northwestern Pennsylvania, the Allegheny National Forest (ANF) is 512,000 acres of mixed hardwood forest (primarily cherry and maple) in varying stages of succession, stream corridors, meadows, natural and constructed ponds, and the 12,000-acre Allegheny Reservoir. Extractive industries remain important to the local economies. For example, there are between 4,000 and 6,000 producing oil and gas wells in the Allegheny National Forest.

For an overview of the multiple-use management in the forest, hike the "Land of Many Uses Interpretive Trail." This trail begins at the Tracy Ridge Campground on SR 321. An interpretive brochure explains 15 different aspects of forest management, such as wildlife, timber harvesting, oil and gas production, and research.

The forest service calculates that there are more than 3 million visitor recreation days (a visitor recreation day is defined as one 12-hour visit) in the forest each year for recreation ranging from hunting and fishing to hiking and birding. In fact, half the population of the U.S. lives within a day's drive of the forest, so recreational use probably

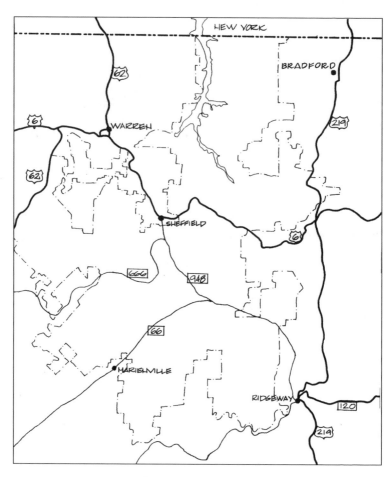

Allegheny National Forest

will continue to increase. There are four district offices in the forest: Marienville, Ridgway, Bradford, and Sheffield. Any of these offices can provide maps and other materials, or visitors can pick up information at the Kinzua Point Information Center at the intersection of SR 59 and Longhouse Scenic Drive, 9 miles east of Warren. Small maps are free, but larger, more detailed maps cost $2 and are well worth the price. There are plenty of informative signs directing visitors to the major recreation areas. A fishing hotline, (814) 726-0164, gives lake conditions. An excellent guide to the forest is *Allegheny National Forest Hiking Guide* by Bruce Sundquist, Carolyn Wielacher Yartz, and Jack Richardson, published by the Allegheny Group of the Sierra Club, P.O. Box 8241, Pittsburgh, PA 15217.

Facilities at the forest are numerous. There are 17 campgrounds, some of which are suitable for trailers, motor homes, or tents. Several are primitive sites for hike-in camping only. Other facilities include 170 miles of hiking trails, nine picnic areas, four swimming beaches, eight boat launches, and a marina. Fishing, hunting, boating, swimming, waterskiing, mountain biking, hiking, and winter sports such as ice-fishing, snowmobiling, and cross-country skiing are popular.

The forest is managed for timber harvesting, in addition to recreation. Visitors also will see (and smell) both active and inactive oil and gas wells. When new timber leases are opened and new wells are drilled, some forest roads may be closed to the public. Signs will inform you if hiking is permitted on roads closed to vehicles. Birders should be very careful in these areas. I avoid them altogether—the noise and activity tend to make birding unproductive.

The ANF provides a breeding habitat for many birds, including some threatened and endangered species. Birds observed during the Breeding Bird Atlas project include Great Blue Heron; Green-backed Heron; Canada Goose; Wood Duck; American Black Duck; Mallard; Hooded and Common Mergansers; Turkey Vulture; Sharp-shinned and Cooper's Hawks; Northern Goshawk; Red-shouldered, Broad-winged, and Red-tailed Hawks; American Kestrel; Ruffed Grouse; Wild Turkey; Killdeer; Spotted Sandpiper; American Woodcock; Black-billed and Yellow-billed Cuckoos; Eastern Screech-Owl; Great Horned, Barred, and Northern Saw-whet Owls; Common Nighthawk; Chimney Swift; Ruby-throated Hummingbird; Belted Kingfisher; Yellow-bellied Sapsucker; Pileated Woodpecker; Eastern Wood-Pewee; Acadian, Least, and Great-crested Flycatchers; Eastern Kingbird; Purple Martin; Tree Swallow; Northern Rough-winged Swallow; Bank, Cliff, and Barn Swallows; Common Raven; Black-capped Chickadee; Tufted Titmouse; Red-breasted and White-breasted Nuthatches; Brown Creeper; Carolina Wren; Winter Wren; Blue-Gray Gnatcatcher; Eastern Bluebird; Veery; Swainson's, Hermit, and Wood Thrushes; Gray Catbird; Brown Thrasher; Cedar Waxwing; Solitary, Yellow-

Winter Wren

throated, Warbling, and Red-eyed Vireo; Blue-winged, Nashville, Yellow, Chestnut-sided, Magnolia, Black-throated Blue, Yellow-rumped, Black-throated Green, Blackburnian, Pine, Prairie, Cerulean, and Black-and-white Warblers; American Redstart; Worm-eating Warblers; Ovenbird; Northern and Louisiana Waterthrushes; Mourning Warbler; Common Yellowthroat; Hooded and Canada Warblers; Yellow-breasted Chat; Scarlet Tanager; Northern Cardinal; Rose-breasted Grosbeak; Indigo Bunting; Rufous-sided Towhee; Field, Vesper, Savannah, Grasshopper, Swamp, and White-throated Sparrows; Dark-eyed Junco; Bobolink; Eastern Meadowlark; Northern Oriole; Purple and House Finch; Pine Siskin; and American Goldfinch.

The Allegheny Reservoir, also known as Kinzua Dam, is located at the northwestern edge of the ANF. The reservoir was completed in

1965 by the Army Corps of Engineers for flood control of the Allegheny River. There are 11 campgrounds on the shores of the reservoir; several are hike-in only. Access to the reservoir is from SR 59 in Warren.

Bald Eagle and Osprey have been recorded at the reservoir in all seasons. Double-crested Cormorant have been observed occasionally. Migrants such as Common Loon, Tundra Swan, Snow Goose, and mergansers are seen in both spring and fall.

The Sheffield District is the northwest quadrant of the forest. Heart's Content Scenic Area, one of the best-known sites in this district, is 121 acres of virgin Eastern Hemlock, White Pine, beech, Sugar Maple, and Black Cherry. Some of the trees are 400 years old. To reach the Heart's Content trailhead, take FS 18 north from Sheffield about 18 miles. The 1.25-mile Heart's Content Scenic Trail goes through the area; interpretive brochures are available for the trail. Swainson's Thrush has bred in this area. Look for Rusty Blackbirds and Winter Wrens near streams in winter.

The address is Sheffield District Ranger, U.S. Forest Service, Sheffield, PA 16347, (814) 968-3232.

The Bradford District is the northeastern quadrant of the forest. The ranger station for this district is located at the junction of SR 321 and SR 59. Longhouse Scenic Drive on Forest Route 262 follows the shoreline of the Kinzua Bay on the Allegheny Reservoir.

Beginning at the Dewdrop Campground (4 miles south of the junction of SR 59 and SR 262) is the Campbell Mill Interpretive Trail. An interpretive brochure available at the trailhead points out 34 numbered trees, shrubs, and geologic features.

Unfortunately, there are no bird checklists for this district. Share your records with the district ranger.

The address is Bradford District Ranger, U.S. Forest Service, Kinzua Heights, Star Route, Bradford, PA 16701, (814) 362-4613.

The Marienville District is the southwest quadrant of the ANF. Of special interest to birders is the Buzzard Swamp Wildlife Management Area. From Marienville, take FR 128 south to FR 157 and turn left. Just ahead on the left is the Songbird Sojourn Trail, a 1.6-mile self-guided interpretive trail that includes 26 stops that focus on birds' use of vegetation and habitats.

A bird checklist in the trail brochure lists 222 species recorded in the Buzzard Swamp area with the assistance of the Seneca Rocks Audubon Society. Birds observed at the swamp include birds typical to the region and some exciting migrants: Double-crested Cormorant; Snow Goose; Gadwall; Northern Pintail; American Wigeon; Redhead; Common Goldeneye; Hooded, Common, and Red-breasted Mergansers; King and Virginia Rails; Sora; Common Moorhen; American Coot; Upland Sandpiper; Greater and Lesser Yellowlegs; Willet; Wilson's Phalarope; Least Sandpiper; Northern Saw-whet Owl; Olive-sided Flycatcher; Eastern Wood-Pewee; Yellow-bellied, Acadian, Alder, Willow, and Least Flycatchers; Eastern Phoebe; Great Crested Flycatcher; Eastern Kingbird; Marsh and Sedge Wrens; American Pipit; 36 warbler species; Rusty Blackbird; Summer and Scarlet Tanagers; Rose-breasted, Pine, and Evening Grosbeaks; Hoary and Common Redpolls; Red and White-winged Crossbills; Savannah, Grasshopper, Henslow's, Sharp-tailed, Vesper, Lark, Clay-colored, Harris', Lincoln's, and Swamp Sparrows; Lapland Longspur; and Snow Bunting.

Note: Do not enter posted areas set aside for waterfowl propagation.

The address is Marienville District Ranger, U.S. Forest Service, Marienville, PA 16239, (814) 927-8628.

The Ridgway District is the southeastern quadrant of the forest. SR 948 and SR 66 are the main roads through this district. Unfortunately, there are no bird checklists available for this district.

A natural area that may be of interest is the Twin Lakes Trail. The trailhead for this trail is near the Twin Lakes Recreation Area on Forest Road 191. Access is from SR 66, south of Kane. Research at the Kane Experimental Forest Station in the early 1990s documented breeding Northern Goshawks in this general area.

The address is Ridgway District Ranger, U.S. Forest Service, Montmorenci Road, Ridgway, PA 15853, (814) 776-6172.

Cornplanter State Forest

Cornplanter State Forest is 1,256 acres of mature timber, old fields, aspen bottom, and an area that was heavily impacted by a tornado. The forest is named after the Seneca Chief Cornplanter, who lived near the area in the late 18th and early 19th centuries.

To reach the forest, take I-80 to Exit 13, Brookville. Drive northwest on SR 36 to Tionesta, cross the Allegheny River, and turn right on the first paved road to the right. The state forest land is one mile ahead. The trailhead for the Lashure Trail and Hunter Run Trail is located just ahead. These trails are self-guided interpretive trails; pick up a map/brochure at the trailhead.

To the right of the road is the 64-acre Woodcock Management Area. Although the stream bottom area is managed for American Woodcock, other species including Ruffed Grouse and Wild Turkey thrive here as well.

The address is Cornplanter State Forest, Pennsylvania Bureau of Forestry, 323 North State Street, North Warren, PA 16365, (814) 723-6951.

Chapman State Park

Chapman State Park, located in Warren County, is 805 acres of mixed hardwood forest, old-growth fields, a 68-acre lake, 3 acres of marshland, streams, and mowed lawns. Chapman has a 12-mile system of trails, including a Bluebird Trail. Several of these connect to trails in adjacent sections of the Allegheny National Forest and SGL 29.

To reach the park, take US 6 south from Warren 4 miles to Chapman Dam Road in Clarendon. Turn right and continue 5 miles to the park. Pick up a free map and checklist of common birds at the park office.

Facilities at Chapman, which is open daily from 8 a.m. to sunset, include 83 primitive campsites, a food concession, and picnic tables. The park office has available a variety of brochures from the Department of Environmental Resources and the Bureau of State Parks. From Memorial Day to Labor Day, environmental interpretive programs are offered. Schedules can be picked up at the office.

The park management plan lists 119 species observed in the park, including 21 confirmed breeders. Park staff reports that Northern Pintail recently has bred at the park. Check with the office for details.

The address is Chapman State Park, RD 2, Box 1610, Clarendon, PA 16313, (814) 723-5030.

BENDIGO STATE PARK

Located on the East Branch of the Clarion River about 50 miles southeast of Warren, Bendigo State Park is 100 acres of hardwood forest, predominantly birch, cherry, and maple. The park is 4 miles north of Johnsonburg on LR 1004 (Glen Hazel Road) and is adjacent to the 23,136 acres of SGL 25, a section of Elk State Forest, and Elk State Park.

Facilities at the park include a pool and picnic tables. This park originally was developed by the town of Johnsonburg, was improved by the Works Progress Administration in the 1930s, and became a state park in 1949.

A checklist of 148 birds is available at the park. It includes migratory species such as Common Merganser and Wood Duck. Fox Sparrow has been recorded in the fall. Birds recorded on the nearby SGL include Blue-winged Teal, Common Merganser, American Coot, and White-winged Crossbill in spring. Northern Harrier, Northern Goshawk, and Red-shouldered Hawk also have been recorded in the spring, and the area is good for Wild Turkey in the fall.

The address of Bendigo State Park is P.O. Box A, Johnsonburg, PA 15845, (814) 965-2646.

ELK STATE PARK

Elk State Park is located on the shore of the East Branch Reservoir on the Clarion River. The park is 3,192 acres, including a 1,160-acre lake, and is mostly forested. The park is open year-round, 24 hours a day. To reach Elk State Park, drive north from Johnsonburg 9 miles on LR 1001 (Glen Hazel Road).

A bird checklist of 138 species recorded at the park is available at the office. Migratory waterfowl can be seen on the lake during spring and fall migration. Osprey has been recorded in the spring and fall, and Greater Yellowlegs and Belted Kingfisher have been recorded in the fall. Evening Grosbeak and Pine Siskin are irregular winter visitors.

The park's address is Elk State Park, P.O. Box A, Johnsonburg, PA 15845, (814) 965-2646.

MOSHANNON STATE FOREST

The Moshannon State Forest is 190,000 acres of many varied habitats in Clearfield, Elk, Cameron, and Centre counties. Access is from many points; free maps are available from the forest office.

The Quehanna Trail (75 miles) and numerous side trails pass through the forest, which also includes three state parks: Parker Dam, S.B. Elliott, and Black Moshannon. One of the most primitive areas in the state is the 50,000-acre Quehanna Wild Area. Vehicle traffic is limited in this area, and there are no cabins. Maps of the many trails in this area also are available from the forest office. Several shallow impoundments are excellent for migrating waterfowl, and migrations of warblers in spring can be terrific.

The address is Moshannon State Forest, District Forester, P.O. Box 952, Clearfield, PA 16830, (814) 765-3741.

Parker Dam State Park

Parker Dam State Park is 968 acres of wetlands, a 20-acre lake, pine and spruce plantations, and mixed hardwoods located 17 miles north of Clearfield in Clearfield County. To reach the park, take Exit 18 off I-80 and drive north on SR 153 for about 10 miles. The access road is on the right.

The park is open daily from dawn to dusk. There are 110 campsites, 50 with electric hookups; 16 primitive cabins are available for rental. Three areas are available for group camping. A food concession is operated in summer. The park has a nature center and a museum with exhibits about the Civilian Conservation Corps (CCC).

The western trailhead of the Quehanna Trail System is located at Parker Dam. There are eight trails in the park itself; the Beaver Dam Trail begins near the park office and passes several beaver dams.

Great Blue Heron is common in summer. In fall, Cedar Waxwing is a common migrant. Park staff reports that Northern Shrike is a rare winter visitor.

The address is Parker Dam State Park, RD 1, Box 165, Penfield, PA 15849, (814) 765-0630.

S.B. Elliott State Park

S.B. Elliott State Park is 128 acres of second-growth oak and mixed hardwood forest and swamp just north of I-80, Exit 18, in Clearfield County. The park serves as a trailhead for the Quehanna Trail and has 25 campsites for tents or trailers and primitive cabins built by the CCC.

The address is S.B. Elliott State Park, RD 1, Box 165, Penfield, PA 15849,(814) 765-0630.

Black Moshannon State Park

Black Moshannon State Park is 3,394 acres of upland second-growth hardwoods, scrub-shrub wetlands, and a 250-acre lake, bog, and swamp in Centre County. To reach the park, take US 220 south from Exit 23 on I-80 to Julian. Follow the signs to the park. From the west, take SR 504 east from Philipsburg.

First-time visitors to Black Mo, as it is known to local residents, often wonder why the lake's water is the color of tea: This is because of the tannin released by rotting vegetation.

The park has 80 modern campsites, 13 primitive cabins, and five modern cabins. There are several trails, including the Bog Trail, which is a boardwalk through a large bog at the upper end of the park's lake. This trail is accessible to wheelchairs. Of special interest on this trail are carnivorous plants: Northern Pitcher Plant (*Sarracenia purpurea*), Round-leaved Sundew (*Drosera rotundifolia*), and Swollen Bladderwort (*Utricularia inflata*).

Both beavers and Eastern Black Bear are found in this park.

A nature center with environmental exhibits offers interpretive programs for families during summer months. Check at the park office for a schedule. Special programs for groups can be arranged.

More than 3,000 acres of the park is open to hunting. Be careful; consult a park map for more information.

Black Moshannon has a bluebird trail; Tree Swallow is abundant. When lake levels are low, the exposed mudflats are good for shorebirds, especially during migration. In spring and fall, migrant waterfowl are notable.

The address is Black Moshannon State Park, RD 1, Box 183, Philipsburg, PA 16866, (814) 342-1101.

"GOD'S COUNTRY"

The north-central region of Pennsylvania is sparsely populated and wildly popular with hunters and anglers, who gave it the nickname "God's Country." The area also is known as the Northcentral Highlands and includes Potter, Cameron, Clinton, Lycoming, and Tioga counties. The plateau is deeply carved by streams here, so the effect is of mountains and valleys. Nearly 1.5 million acres of the land here is owned by the Commonwealth, as state forests, state game lands, or state parks. There are 15 state parks in the Allegheny Plateau region of these five counties.

Sizerville State Park

Sizerville State Park is 385 acres of deciduous hardwood forest with some pine stands and two trout streams in Cameron and Potter counties, about 75 miles northwest of Lock Haven. Sizerville is surrounded by 460,617 acres of State Forest Lands and is near several tracts of State Game Lands. The park is a good base for exploring these nearby areas.

To reach the park, take SR 120 from Lock Haven to Emporium. In Emporium, take SR 155 north to the park. Stop at the park office for a free map. A bird checklist is under development; check at the park office to see if it has been published.

The park has 23 modern campsites (half available by reservation and half on a first-come, first-served basis), picnic facilities, a food concession in summer, and more than 3 miles of trails. A nature center features exhibits about the natural history of the area. Environmental education programming by the park naturalist is available from Memorial Day to Labor Day.

In spring, migrant warblers pass through the park. Look for Chestnut-sided, Magnolia, Black-throated Blue, Yellow-rumped, and Blackburnian Warblers. Some spend the summer. Other summer birds include breeding Pileated Woodpecker, Eastern Screech-Owl, Broadwinged Hawk, Ruffed Grouse, Wild Turkey, and Ruby-throated

Hummingbird. Winter birds are typical deciduous/pine forest species, including Yellow-bellied Sapsucker. During invasion years, look for Pine Siskin and Evening Grosbeak.

The address is Sizerville State Park, RD 1, Box 238A, Emporium, PA 15834, (814) 486-5605.

Sinnemahoning State Park

Sinnemahoning State Park is 1,920 acres of wooded mountains, abandoned farms, wetlands, and open water in Cameron and Potter counties. To reach the park, take SR 872 north about 8 miles from the junction of SR 120 and 872. Stop at the park office for a free map and checklist.

The park is open daily from 8 a.m. to sunset and has 35 campsites. Food is not available at Sinnemahoning, but picnic facilities are numerous.

The big attraction at Sinnemahoning is a pair of Bald Eagles who usually appear in late May and remain until late August. They do not breed here. In recent years, park staff have led weekend eagle watch tours on a pontoon boat. These are very popular—arrive early to sign up for a tour. While you are waiting for the tour to begin, walk to the head of the lake and check for ducks and waterfowl. Volunteers set up spotting scopes and conduct an informal program featuring the eagles on weekends and holidays in summer. Osprey is fairly common in spring and summer, occasional in fall.

The address is Sinnemahoning State Park, RD 1, Box 172, Austin, PA 16720, (814) 647-8401.

RENOVO

The area surrounding Renovo, population 1,526, is called Pennsylvania's "Black Forest" because of the dense tree cover, rugged terrain, and sparse population. In fact, the entire population of Clinton County is only 37,182; nearby Potter County is larger than Clinton County but has a population of only 16,717. The area is known for its lumber industry; most of the forests in the area are second-growth. They were clear cut in the late 19th and early 20th centuries.

Ole Bull State Park

Ole Bull State Park is a small park of mixed hardwoods, pine plantations, bottom land, beaver dam ponds, and wetlands on the shores of Kettle Creek in Potter County. The park is named for a Norwegian violinist who attempted to establish a community of immigrants here in 1852. Unfortunately, the person who sold the land for the settlement to Bull reserved all but the steep hillside acreage for himself. Unable to farm the land, most of the settlers moved on to Minnesota and Wisconsin.

Hunting is not allowed in most of the park, and that is important in this area. During hunting season, birders can take advantage of Ole Bull State Park while the hunters enjoy the remainder of the county. Another good time to visit Ole Bull is in early May when Trailing Arbutus and Trillium are blooming and warbler migration is at its peak.

To reach the park, drive north from Renovo 26 miles on SR 144. The park is open daily from dawn to dusk. Facilities here include a 0.75-mile nature trail, interpretive displays at the visitors' center, picnic tables and pavilions, and 81 tent and trailer campsites in two campgrounds. In addition to the nature trail, the park has the Daugherty Loop Trail the trailhead for the 85-mile Susquehannock Trail. An interpretive naturalist is on duty during the summer months; regular programs are scheduled. The park also has published a brochure, "Where Forest Meets Stream," that provides an overview of the habitats found here.

A free bird checklist available at the park office includes 107 species including breeding species such as Common Merganser; Wood Duck; Great Crested Flycatcher; Common Raven; Red-breasted Nuthatch; Brown Creeper; Veery; Magnolia, Black-throated Green, Blackburnian, Pine, and Black-and-white Warblers; American Redstart; Canada Warbler; Rose-breasted Grosbeak; and White-throated Sparrow.

In spring, the park is good for migrants, mostly woodland birds with an occasional Common Loon or White-winged Scoter on the creek. Many migrants also pass through the park in the fall. The park is updating its bird records and would appreciate receiving lists from birders.

Blackburnian Warbler

The park's address is Ole Bull State Park, HCR 62, Box 9, Cross Fork, PA 17729, (814) 435-2169.

Nearby State Parks

The following state parks have primarily forested habitats. Look for these birds known to nest in the Northern Tier: Chestnut-sided Warbler, Magnolia Warbler, Black-throated Blue Warbler, Yellow-rumped

Warbler, Black-throated Green Warbler, Blackburnian Warbler, Black-and-white Warbler, American Redstart, Ovenbird, Northern Waterthrush, Canada Warbler, White-throated Sparrow, and Dark-eyed Junco. **Note:** some are widely scattered in the area.

Prouty Place State Park is 10 acres of forest located 25 miles west of Galeton off SR 44. The park is open from mid-April to mid-December. The address is Prouty Place State Park, c/o Lyman Run State Park, RD 1, Box 136, Galeton, PA 16922, (814) 435-6444.

Cherry Springs State Park is 48 acres of field and forest. The park is the home of the Woodsmen's Carnival, held annually in early August. Woodsmen compete for cash prizes in tree felling, log rolling, and other activities. There is a small airfield, constructed in 1935 by the CCC, adjacent to the park. The address is Cherry Springs State Park, c/o Lyman Run State Park, RD 1, Box 136, Galeton, PA 16922, (814) 435-6444.

Lyman Run State Park is 595 acres of forest-covered mountains and a 45-acre lake with wetlands at its upper end. To reach the park, take SR 6 east from Coudersport and turn right onto LR 2004. There are 50 campsites, and the 83-mile Susquehannock Trail goes through the park. Nearly half of the park is open to hunting. The address is Lyman Run State Park, RD 1, Box 136, Galeton, PA 16922, (814) 435-6444.

Patterson State Park, 10 acres, is a forested tract 25 miles west of Galeton. From Sweden Valley on SR 6, take SR 44 south to the park. The address is Patterson State Park, c/o Lyman Run State Park, RD 1, Box 136, Galeton, PA 16922, (814) 435-6444.

Denton Hill State Park, 700 acres, is a ski concession on SR 6 between Coudersport and Galeton with downhill and cross-country skiing. The address is Denton Hill State Park, P.O. Box 367, Coudersport, PA 16915, (814) 435-2115.

Sproul State Forest

The Sproul State Forest is 290,000 acres of forest from seedling/ sapling areas to mature second growth. There also are wetlands and open areas, including pipeline rights-of-way. Free maps are available at the district office, 4 miles west of Renovo on SR 120, or by mail. Backpack camping is permitted. Wild Turkey is abundant in the area.

The address is Sproul State Forest, HCR 62, Box 90, Renovo, PA 17764, (717) 923-1450.

Kettle Creek State Park

Kettle Creek State Park is 1,793 acres of bottom land, mixed hardwoods, and wetlands, Kettle Creek Lake, and the larger Kettle Creek Reservoir. To reach the park, drive southwest from Renovo on SR 120 about 5 miles to Westport. Turn right onto LR 4001 and drive 7 miles north to the park.

The park has 71 campsites available from April to December and a food concession in the summer months. Picnicking is permitted. An interpretive naturalist provides programs and staffs the nature center located at the lower campground during the summer months. There are many trails through the park and through the adjacent Sproul State Forest. A bird checklist with about 100 species is available at the park office. The park is attempting to update this list and would appreciate records from birders who visit.

A sampling of the species recorded includes Common Loon, Tundra Swan, Osprey, Blue-gray Gnatcatcher, Scarlet Tanager, and Indigo Bunting in spring. Birds recorded in summer include Pied-billed Grebe, Bufflehead, Common Merganser, Broad-winged Hawk, and Black-and-White Warbler.

The park's address is Kettle Creek State Park, HCR 62, Box 96, Renovo, PA 17764, (814) 923-0206.

Bucktail State Park is a 75-mile scenic drive park along Sinnemahoning Creek and the West Branch of the Susquehanna River from Emporium to Lock Haven on SR 120. The drive is mostly wooded, with a few small farms and villages. Most of the land in this park is privately owned—do your birding from your car, or ask permission to enter property. Check for migrating waterfowl in spring and fall.

The address is Bucktail State Park, c/o Sizerville State Park, RD 1, Box 238A, Emporium, PA 15834, (814) 486-5605.

GRAND CANYON OF PENNSYLVANIA

The Grand Canyon of Pennsylvania is also known as Pine Creek Gorge. It is located in southern Tioga County and extends about 47 miles south from Ansonia. The gorge, which reaches a maximum depth of 1,450 feet was created by glacial erosion. Two state parks are located on the shores of Pine Creek: on the east, Leonard Harrison State Park and on the west, Colton Point State Park. Turkey Path descends from Leonard Harrison State Park to the bottom of the gorge. The area is designated a National Natural Landmark.

Leonard Harrison State Park

Leonard Harrison State Park is 585 acres of conifer and hardwood forests with some open fields on the east rim of Pine Creek. To reach the park, drive west from Wellsboro on SR 660 about 10 miles. The road reaches a dead end at the park. Stop at the park's visitors' center for a free map, geology brochure, and bird list of 54 breeding species.

The park is open daily from 8 a.m. to dusk. There are 30 campsites, and picnics are allowed. A nature center features environmental, geologic, and historic exhibits. Programs are offered.

The park naturalist reports that the following birds breed in the area: Pileated Woodpecker; Least Flycatcher; Northern Raven; Redbreasted Nuthatch; Hermit Thrush; Eastern Bluebird; Veery; Yellow, Chestnut-sided, Magnolia, Black-throated Blue, Blackburnian, and Black-and-white Warblers; American Redstart; Ovenbird; Mourning Warbler (rare); and Common Yellowthroat. Osprey sometimes are seen flying through the canyon. A nesting pair of Bald Eagles has resided year-round in the gorge since 1987.

The address is Leonard Harrison State Park, RD 6, Box 199, Wellsboro, PA 16901, (717) 724-3061.

Colton Point State Park

Colton Point State Park is about 350 acres of conifer and hardwood forests with some small clear cuts on the west rim of the Pennsylvania Grand Canyon. To reach the park, take SR 6 west from Wellsboro to Ansonia. In Ansonia, take Colton Road to the park.

Colton Point is open daily from 8 a.m. until dusk. Facilities at the park include picnic tables and 25 campsites. Birds are similar to those found in Leonard Harrison State Park (see listing earlier in this chapter).

The address is Colton Point State Park, c/o Leonard Harrison State Park, RD 6, Box 199, Wellsboro, PA 16901, (717) 724-3061.

Tioga/Hammond Lakes National Recreation Area

Two large lakes about 60 miles northeast of Williamsport are managed for flood control in the Susquehanna watershed and recreation. Hammond Lake is located on Crooked Creek, and Tioga Lake is located on Mill Creek.

To reach the lakes, take I-15 north from Williamsport. The recreation area is just north of the village of Lambs Creek. Turn left to reach Hammond Lake, or continue to SR 287 and make a sharp left turn. Tioga Lake is on I-15.

Facilities at the recreation area include modern and primitive campsites, picnic areas, and a food concession. Free maps are available at the headquarters building.

There is an Osprey hacking tower at Hammond Lake. With luck, the species will someday breed here. Other birds seen during the summer include Bald Eagle; Osprey; Horned Lark; Cliff and Bank Swallows; Great Blue and Green-backed Herons; Bobolink; Eastern Meadowlark; Eastern Phoebe; several flycatcher species; raptors; Yellow, Hooded, and Black-throated Blue Warblers; Belted Kingfisher; Northern Oriole; and several vireos.

In winter Snowy Owls have been recorded.

The best place to watch birds is along the abandoned railroad grade. A hike along this trail gives a good view of riparian, swamp, forest, field, edge, and lake habitats. Such a diversity of habitats is good for a diversity of birds, especially in spring and fall migration.

The address is Hammond Lake, U.S. Army Corps of Engineers, RD 2, Box 68, Tioga, PA 16946.

Hills Creek State Park

Hills Creek State Park is 407 acres of hardwoods and pine plantation with a 137-acre lake. To reach the park, take SR 6 from either Mansfield or Wellsboro and follow directional signs from Whitneyville.

The park is open year round and has 110 tent/trailer campsites. There are 5 miles of trails. A nature center is open in the summer and offers a variety of programs. Migrant Osprey and Bald Eagle are seen here in spring and summer, and breeding Bald Eagle from nearby Grand Canyon of Pennsylvania sometimes wander into the park.

The address is Hills Creek State Park, RD 2, Box 328, Wellsboro, PA 16901, (717) 724-4246.

Little Pine State Park

Little Pine State Park is 2,158 acres of lake, stream, marsh, open meadow, thicket, evergreen plantation, and mature hardwoods in Lycoming County 15 miles north of Jersey Shore. From Jersey Shore, take SR 44 north to Waterville (approximately 11 miles). Turn right at the park sign and drive north on LR 4001 about 4 miles to the park office. Pick up a free map and bird list.

The park, open daily from sunrise to sunset, has a bluebird trail, 5 hiking trails, and a self-guided nature trail. There are 104 primitive campsites. A food concession operates in summer. A nature center is open on weekends during summer, and programs for all ages are offered.

Breeding birds include Wood Duck, Common Merganser, Barred Owl, Great Crested and Least Flycatcher, Prothonotary Warbler, and Swamp Sparrow.

The address is Little Pine State Park, HD 63, Box 100, Waterville, PA 17776-9705, (717) 753-8209.

SUSQUEHANNOCK STATE FOREST

Susquehannock State Forest is 262,000 acres of forested and associated habitats in Potter and Cameron counties. The 89-mile Susquehannock Trail system goes through a variety of habitats in the forest.

The Forest H. Dutlinger State Forest Natural Area is located in the Hammersley Wild Area on Hammersley Fork. This 1,521-acre wilderness includes a 158-acre stand of old-growth hemlock. To reach this area, take SR 144 to the village of Cross Forks; 4.5 miles south of the village, a dirt road intersects with the highway. Turn right (north) onto the dirt road and drive to where the road ends at Hammersley Fork. Use the footbridge to cross the stream and enter the wild area.

This area has not been well-censused for birds. Please share your records with the district forester. The address is Susquehannock State Forest, 8 East 7th Street, Coudersport, PA 16915, (814) 274-8474.

NORTHEAST NORTHERN TIER

The northeast corner of Pennsylvania is very sparsely populated and wild. Although the back roads can be a problem in winter, this region has yielded Snowy Owl, Red Crossbill, White-winged Crossbill, and other winter visitors in recent years. In summer, look for neotropical migrants.

World's End State Park

World's End State Park is 780 acres on Loyalsock Creek in Sullivan County. To reach the park, take US 220 east from Williamsport to Fairfield, then take SR 87 north to Forksville and turn right onto SR 154, which leads directly to the park.

The park has 12 miles of hiking trails. Environmental programs are offered in the summer.

Northern Parula is fairly common along Loyalsock Creek in World's End. Yellow-bellied Flycatcher has bred in the nearby Wyoming State Forest. Black-throated Green Warbler is very common, while Blackburnian, Black-throated Blue, Chestnut-sided, Yellow-rumped, and Canada Warblers and Northern Waterthrush breed in the area.

The address is World's End State Park, P.O. Box 62, Forksville, PA 18616-0062, (717) 924-3287.

Rickett's Glen State Park

Rickett's Glen State Park is 13,050 acres best known for its beautiful trails, waterfalls, and geology. There are two lakes and a large tract of hemlock forest. To reach the park, take Exit 35 from I-80 and follow SR 487 north to the park.

The address is Rickett's Glen State Park, RD 2, Box 130, Benton, PA 17814-8900, (717) 477-5675.

Mount Pisgah State Park

Mount Pisgah State Park is 1,302 acres of eastern hardwoods, conifers, open fields, lake, and lakeshore located in Bradford County. The park's 75-acre lake is Stephen Foster Lake and is named for the American composer who was a local resident. To reach the park, take US 15 north from Williamsport to SR 6 and turn right (east). Continue east on SR 6 to the village of West Burlington, and take LR 3019 north to the park.

White-throated Sparrow

The park is open daily. A food concession is operated in the summer, and picnics are permitted. A guarded pool is open from Memorial Day weekend to Labor Day. There are 11 miles of hiking trails—one of which, Mill Stream Nature Trail, is a self-guided interpretive trail. Most of the park is open to hunting; the free park map shows which areas are closed to hunting. The lake is popular with anglers in all seasons; ice-fishing is allowed when ice conditions are reliable.

A nature center houses environmental education displays. Park staff offers a variety of programs during the summer. Check at the park office for a schedule.

Birds in the park include migrating Osprey in the spring and migrating loons in the fall. Great Blue Heron is common, as is Eastern Bluebird. Red-tailed Hawk is common; an albino Red-tailed was a summer resident in recent years.

The address is Mount Pisgah State Park, RD 3, Box 362, Troy, PA 16947-9448, (717) 297-2734.

THE POCONOS (EASTERN GLACIATED PLATEAU)

The Poconos is the area between the Wyoming Valley (Wilkes-Barre and Scranton) and the Allegheny Front (the boundary with the Ridge and Valley Province). During the Illinois and Wisconsin Glaciations, this area of Pennsylvania was the southern terminus of glacial ice. Rocks picked up in Canada were deposited here when the ice retreated. Lakes, bogs, and swamps were created. The Pocono Plateau was so deeply carved by meltwater streams that numerous waterfalls were created. The area has been an important tourist area for many years.

The Lacawaxan River at the northern end of the Poconos is good for eagles in winter. To reach the river, take SR 6 west from Milford to LR 1003. Turn right on LR 1003 and drive toward Rowland. At the intersection with SR 590, turn right and drive along the river, being careful to pull completely off the road when looking for eagles.

A very good in-depth treatment of the area can be found in *The Poconos: An Illustrated Natural History Guide* by Carl S. Oplinger and Robert Halma.

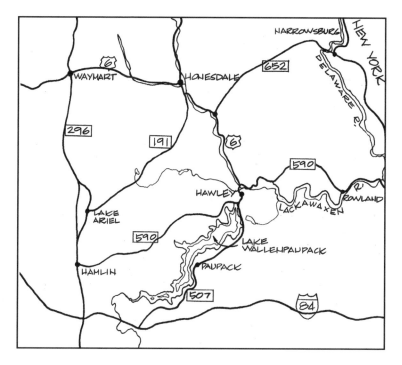

The Poconos

Promised Land State Park

Promised Land State Park is 5,808 acres of mixed hardwoods, pine plantation, two lakes, and wetlands in Pike County. Promised Land Lake is 422 acres; Lower Lake is 173 acres.

To reach Promised Land, drive north from Stroudsburg on SR 191 to SR 447. Turn right onto SR 447, and drive to Canadensis, where you will turn right onto SR 390. The park is on SR 390, about 10 miles north of Canadensis. Stop at the park office for a free map and list of 142 bird species recorded in the park. A "Pennsylvania Trail of Geology" brochure explains the glacial effects seen here.

Promised Land was settled by members of the Shaker religion in 1878; however, the rocky soils in the area were not well-suited for agriculture, and the group soon moved on. The park was opened to the public in 1905 and was expanded by the CCC in the 1930s.

Facilities at the park include 535 campsites, 12 family cabins, a food concession in summer, three swimming beaches, and 30 miles of trails, some of which are wheelchair-accessible. The park office has exhibits and dioramas. Seasonal guided walks are offered, and the Conservation Island Nature Trail is a self-guided, interpretive trail. Two areas, Bruce Lake Natural Area and Pine Lake Natural Area, are managed as undeveloped areas. Vehicles are not permitted in these areas.

Birds recorded in the park include American Bittern; Gadwall; American Wigeon; Canvasback; Lesser Scaup; Bufflehead; Osprey; Common Moorhen; Solitary, Yellow-throated, and Philadelphia Vireos; Yellow, Chestnut-sided, Cape May, Black-throated Blue, Yellow-rumped, Black-throated Green, Blackburnian, Cerulean, and Black-and-white Warblers; American Redstart; Ovenbird; Northern and Louisiana Waterthrushes; Common Yellowthroat; and Canada Warblers; Rusty Blackbird; and Pine Grosbeak.

The address is Promised Land State Park, RD 1, Box 96, Greentown, PA 18426, (717) 676-3428.

Dorflinger-Suydam Wildlife Sanctuary

Dorflinger-Suydam Wildlife Sanctuary is 600+ acres of open hay fields, oak-hickory forest, two lakes, and several small ponds near White Mills in Monroe County.

To reach the sanctuary, take I-84 to Exit 5 and follow SR 191 north to Hamlin Corners. Turn right onto SR 590 east. Continue on SR 590 to SR 6. Take SR 6 west through Hawley to the traffic light at White Mills. Turn right, and go up the hill to a stop sign. Follow the sanctuary signs to the entrance.

The site is also the location of the Dorflinger Glass Museum and is open Wednesday through Sunday from 10 a.m. to 4 p.m. There is a small charge for admission to both the museum and the sanctuary.

Several trails go through the sanctuary; the Blue Heron Trail is wheelchair-accessible.

Birds commonly observed here in spring include Green-backed Heron, Wood Duck, Common Merganser, Killdeer, Pileated Woodpecker, and Eastern Bluebird.

In summer, Canada Goose, Great Blue Heron, Tree and Barn Swallows, and Wood Thrush are common.

The address is Dorflinger-Suydam Wildlife Sanctuary, P.O. Box 21, White Mills, PA 18473, (717) 253-1185.

Lackawanna State Forest

The Lackawanna State Forest is 6,000 acres of mixed hardwoods and wetlands located in Lackawanna County southeast of Wilkes-Barre and Scranton. The Gifford Pinchot Trail through the forest's Thornhurst area is 23 miles long and open to primitive camping. A free permit is required; contact the district forest office for details.

To reach the trailhead, take Exit 35 from the Northeast Extension of the Pennsylvania Turnpike (SR 9). Take SR 940 east to Blakeslee. In Blakeslee, turn left onto SR 115 toward Wilkes-Barre. After crossing the Lehigh River, continue a mile and a quarter to LR 2040. Turn right onto LR 2040. Continue to the village of Thornhurst, where you will turn left onto LR 2016. The trailhead is on the right, 4 miles ahead.

To reach Thornhurst from Scranton, travel south on I-81 to Exit 49. Take SR 315 south one mile to Dupont. At the second traffic light in Dupont, turn southeast onto LR 2035, known locally as Suscon Road. The trailhead is on the left side of the highway, 11.1 miles from Dupont (about a mile past the Luzerne-Lackawanna County line).

The Thornhurst area of the Lackawanna State Forest is 6,000 acres of mixed hardwoods and wetlands. The area is open 24 hours a day, seven days a week. Free trail maps are available from the district forester.

Three areas near the trailhead worth checking are Bear Lake, Balsam Swamp, and Behler Swamp.

Birds that nest at Thornhurst include Black-crowned Night-Heron, Canada Goose, American Black Duck, Wood Duck, Common Merganser, Sharp-shinned and Cooper's Hawk, American Woodcock, Common Snipe, Barred and Northern Saw-whet Owl, Least Flycatcher, Wood Thrush, Hermit Thrush, Veery, Solitary Vireo, Yellow-throated Vireo, Warbling Vireo, and Red-eyed Vireo.

The address is Forest District Manager, Forest District No. 11, State Office Building, 100 Lackawanna Avenue, Room 401, Scranton, PA 18503-1923, (717) 963-4561.

Common Snipe

Lehigh Gorge State Park

Lehigh Gorge State Park is a 4,548-acre park on the banks of the Lehigh River. A 26-mile abandoned railroad grade is open to hiking but closed to motorized vehicles. The park is open from 8 a.m. to sunset every day.

There are three access points to the park: White Haven, Rockport, and Coalport. Take I-80 to Exit 40 to reach the White Haven, or northern end of the park. From the interchange, take PA 437 north to White Haven and turn right onto SR 940. At the White Haven Shopping Center, turn right and continue to the access area parking lot.

To reach Rockport, where the park office is located, take I-80 to Exit 40 and drive south on SR 940 to SR 4010, where you will turn left onto SR 4010. At SR 4014, turn left and travel into the village of Rockport, where you can visit the park office and pick up a free map and bird checklist.

The final access point is at Coalport. To reach this entrance to the park, take the Northeast Extension of the Pennsylvania Turnpike to Exit 34, and drive north on SR 209 about 6 miles to Coalport. Turn right onto SR 903, cross the river, and turn left onto Front Street, which becomes Coalport Road. The gate to the access area is ahead on the left.

The entire park is a deep gorge with steep walls and thick vegetation. Rock outcroppings and waterfalls make the hike interesting and beautiful. The major attraction of the river itself is white-water rafting. Most of the park also is open to hunting in the fall and winter.

Birds observed in the park include migrant waterfowl on the river in spring and fall. As of spring 1993, the park was conducting a survey of birds observed. Results will be used to produce a checklist.

The address is Lehigh Gorge State Park, RD 2, Box 56, Weatherly, PA 18255, (717) 427-8161.

Woodbourne Sanctuary

Woodbourne Forest and Wildlife Sanctuary is 652 acres of old-growth forest (hemlock with maple), swamp, bog, and successional fields located in Susquehanna County. It is owned by The Nature Conservancy. To reach the sanctuary, take US 6 west from Scranton to Tunkhannock. At the intersection with SR 29, turn right and travel north for 16 miles to Woodbourne.

The sanctuary is open daily during daylight hours. Camping is not permitted. A map of the sanctuary is available—a donation is requested. A free bird checklist records 143 species, of which 72 are breeders. Woodbourne is included in the Susquehanna County Christmas Bird Count and a breeding bird survey.

A self-guided, one-mile nature trail loops through fields, forest, the swamp, and along a stream. Numbered stops feature vegetation such as 300- to 400-year-old hemlocks, ferns, club mosses, and wildflowers such as Painted Trillium, Goldthread, Starflower, and Mountain Laurel.

In summer look for the following birds known to breed at Woodbourne: Wild Turkey, Great Horned Owl, Yellow-bellied Sapsucker,

Willow and Alder Flycatchers, Winter Wren, Hermit Thrush, Canada Warbler, Blackburnian Warbler, Northern Waterthrush, and Dark-eyed Junco.

In winter, Pine Grosbeak is a rare visitor.

The address is Woodbourne Forest Preserve, RD 6, Box 6294, Montrose, PA 18801, (717) 278-3384.

Yellow-bellied Sapsucker

Tobyhanna State Park

Tobyhanna State Park is 5,440 acres of coniferous forest, mixed hardwoods, a clearing with meadow edge, and a swamp at the shore of a 170-acre lake. To reach the park, take I-380 to Exit 8 then SR 423 north for 2 miles to the park entrance. Pick up a free map at the park office. The park is open from 8 a.m. to sunset daily and has 140 primitive campsites.

There are several trails in the park; a 5-mile trail encircles the lake (part is wheelchair-accessible), and a 2.75-mile trail crosses forest and swamp land.

Tobyhanna has a mix of habitats suitable for a wide range of birds. Most common spring species include American Woodcock, Wild Turkey, Ruffed Grouse, Killdeer, Cedar Waxwing, Ruby-throated Hummingbird, House Wren, Field Sparrow, and American Goldfinch. In summer Great Blue Heron, Canada Goose, Mallard, American Black Duck, Wood Duck, Ring-billed Gull, Belted Kingfisher, Wood Thrush, and Red-winged Blackbird are abundant.

Fall migrants include Green-winged and Blue-winged Teal, Bufflehead, Canada Goose, American Black Duck, and American Woodcock. In winter, Eastern Screech-Owl, Great Horned Owl, Barred Owl, Pileated Woodpecker, and Horned Lark have been observed.

The address is Tobyhanna State Park, P.O. Box 387, Tobyhanna, PA 18431, (717) 894-8336.

Gouldsboro State Park

Gouldsboro State Park, located adjacent to Tobyhanna State Park, is 2,800 acres of mixed hardwoods and softwoods, with interspersed swamp and pond edge and some open fields. There is a 250-acre lake at Gouldsboro. To reach the park, take Exit 6 from I-380 to SR 507 and drive 2 miles north to the entrance.

The park is open from 8 a.m. to sunset daily. A section of old SR 611 is used as a trail and is accessible to wheelchairs.

Birds here are similar to nearby Tobyhanna. Cooper's Hawk and Bald Eagle have been observed in summer, and numerous warblers migrate through in spring and fall.

The address is Gouldsboro State Park, c/o Tobyhanna State Park, P.O. Box 387, Tobyhanna, PA 18431, (717) 894-8336.

Big Pocono State Park

Big Pocono State Park is 1,306 acres of rugged mountain terrain with mixed hardwoods and softwoods and a dense laurel underbrush. To reach the park, take Exit 45 from I-80 and take SR 715 (follow the signs) past the Camelback Ski Area to the park.

The park is open from 8 a.m. to sunset daily. Facilities include four trails, including one that is wheelchair-accessible. A nature center features animal life.

The address is Big Pocono State Park, c/o Tobyhanna State Park, P.O. Box 387, Tobyhanna, PA 18431, (717) 894-8336.

Hickory Run State Park

Hickory Run State Park is 15,483 acres of varied habitats, including a small lake, that are good for an overview of Poconos wildlife.

To reach the park, take Exit 41 from I-80 and follow SR 534 south to the park. The park has 36 miles of hiking trails, a swimming beach, and visitors' center.

The park is best known for its immense boulder field, deposited 20,000 years ago when freeze-and-thaw action broke the rocks from the ridges at the north and south of the field. A "Pennsylvania Trail of Geology" brochure explains the process in detail. Pick up a free copy of the brochure at the park office.

Check swampy areas near Sawmill Trail for Alder Flycatcher (uncommon), Tree Swallow, Yellow Warbler, Common Yellowthroat, Canada Warbler, Swamp Sparrow, and Rusty Blackbird (uncommon).

The address is Hickory Run State Park, RD 1, Box 81, White Haven, PA 18661, (717) 443-9991.

Hermit Thrush

Browning Beaver Meadows

Browning Beaver Meadows is 78 acres of wetlands, beaver meadow, and wooded hillside owned by the Northeast Pennsylvania Audubon Society. The site is open by permission of NEPA only.

Birds observed in spring include Barred Owl, numerous warblers, and nesting Eastern Bluebird. In summer, Pied-billed Grebe; American Bittern; Wood Duck; Common Snipe; American Woodcock; American Kestrel; Hermit and Wood Thrush; Yellow-throated Vireo; and Blue-winged, Black-throated Blue, and Black-throated Green Warblers have been observed.

The address is Browning Beaver Meadow, RD 2, Box 319D, Lake Ariel, PA 18436, (717) 253-9250.

Chapter 4
Pittsburgh Plateau

 The Pittsburgh Plateau is the southwestern corner of Pennsylvania. The region is characterized by lower elevations than the Allegheny Plateau. Here, the gently rolling hills range from 700 to 1,600 feet. Rivers and streams drain into the Mississippi River watershed by way of the Allegheny River or the Monongahela River, which join in Pittsburgh to form the Ohio River. This region makes up 18% of Pennsylvania.

Soils are sedimentary with alluvial soils on flood plains. Average annual precipitation is about 40 inches. The average annual temperature is between 48° and 52° Fahrenheit, with an average July extreme maximum temperature of 90° and an average January minimum extreme of –6°. Forests in the region are mostly fragmented and are predominantly hardwoods of the Appalachian Oak Forest type.

In the past, this region was devoted to agriculture, especially dairy, and extractive industries such as surface mining for coal. Today's local economic activities include manufacturing, retailing, and tourism.

Birders will not find the more northerly species here, except during migration, because of the lower elevation of the region. In fact, this is the only place in Pennsylvania to expect the southern species, Summer Tanager, which was confirmed as a breeding species during the Breeding Bird Atlas Project only in Beaver, Washington, and Greene counties.

Carolina Wren, Red-bellied Woodpecker, Prairie Warbler, and Cerulean Warbler breed in appropriate habitats in the plateau. Abundant year-round residents of the Pittsburgh Plateau are Canada Goose, American Kestrel, Rock Dove, Mourning Dove, Red-headed Woodpecker, Carolina Chickadee, Tufted Titmouse, Northern Cardinal, House Finch, and House Sparrow. In winter, abundant residents include Ring-billed Gull and Dark-eyed Junco. Abundant breeding

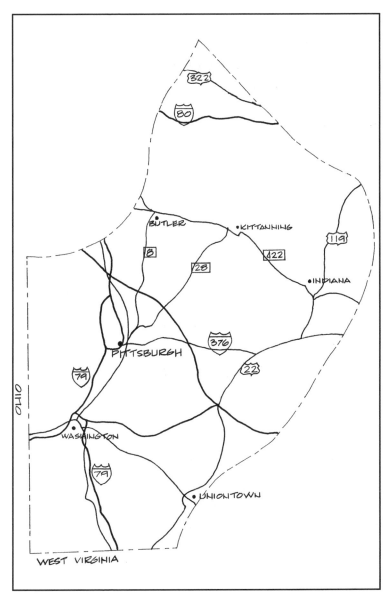

Pittsburgh Plateau

birds are Turkey Vulture, Eastern Wood-Pewee, Barn Swallow, Blue Jay, Wood Thrush, Red-eyed Vireo, Ovenbird, and Field Sparrow.

PITTSBURGH

Located at the "Golden Triangle" where the Allegheny and Monongahela rivers join to form the Ohio River, Pittsburgh has a population of 369,879 and is Pennsylvania's second largest city. Nearly all of Allegheny County is urban; the county's population is 1,336,449.

The word "Pittsburgh" was synonymous with "steel" in the not-so-distant past, but today many of the city's steel mills stand idle. The city is not dead, though; it is home to large companies such as Heinz and Westinghouse. Pittsburgh has two major universities—Pitt and Carnegie Mellon—and several smaller colleges. The city has several major hospitals and is well-known as a center for organ transplant research.

Birders will find much to enjoy in Pittsburgh, including breeding Peregrine Falcons in the heart of downtown, thanks to a successful project conducted for several years by the Pennsylvania Game Commission. Scan the skies above the Gulf Tower at 7th Avenue and Grant Street. Closed-circuit television in the lobby gives a view of the nestlings.

To report a rare bird alert, call the Audubon Society of Western Pennsylvania at (412) 963-6104. For tourism information, contact the Greater Pittsburgh Convention and Visitors' Bureau, 4 Gateway Center, Suite 514, Pittsburgh, PA 15219, (412) 281-7711 or (800) 366-0093.

The Carnegie

The Carnegie is a complex that includes an art museum, library, music hall, and the Carnegie Museum of Natural History. Although best known for its outstanding collection of dinosaurs, the museum has an excellent display of mounted birds from Pennsylvania and around the world. Admission is charged. The Carnegie is open Tuesday to Saturday, 10 a.m. to 5 p.m., and Sunday 1 p.m. to 5 p.m.

The Carnegie is located at 4000 Forbes Avenue, Pittsburgh, PA 15213, (412) 622-3131.

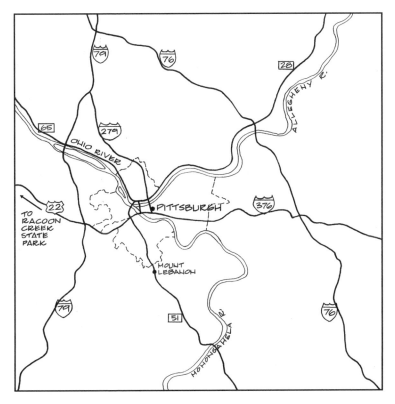

Pittsburgh

Pittsburgh Zoo

The Pittsburgh Zoo has a collection of more than 6,000 animals representing 483 species. Special exhibits include a Children's Farm, Niches of the World, Aqua Zoo, Asian Forest, African Savanna, and Tropical Forest. Admission is charged. The zoo is open daily from Memorial Day to Labor Day, 10 a.m. to 6 p.m. and Labor Day to Memorial Day, 9 a.m. to 5 p.m.

The Pittsburgh Zoo is located at Highland Park, Pittsburgh, PA 15206, (412) 665-3640.

Pittsburgh Aviary

The Pittsburgh Aviary is located at Allegheny Commons West and is accessible from downtown by the 16B, 16C, or 16D bus. To reach the aviary by car, take the Fort Duquesne Bridge across the Allegheny River to Allegheny Avenue. At Western Avenue, turn right and drive to the aviary, ahead on the left. The aviary is open seven days a week from 9 a.m. to 4:30 p.m.; it is closed on Thanksgiving, Christmas, and New Year's Day. The collection features birds from around the world.

The address is The Aviary, Allegheny Commons West, Pittsburgh, PA 15212, (412) 321-1 FLY.

North Park

North Park is located in the North Hills region of Pittsburgh, 13 miles north of the Golden Triangle. To reach the park, take I-79 to the Wexford Exit. From there, take SR 910 to Pearce Mill Road where you will turn right and enter the park.

The park is 3,300 acres of deciduous and evergreen forests with several small ponds, two lakes, several wetlands areas, fields in various stages of succession, and many streams. Picnicking is allowed, and food is available at private concessions. North Park is included in the Pittsburgh Christmas Bird Count.

The park has more than 30 miles of trails through varied terrain. The Lake Shore Drive and South Ridge Drive trails are paved and accessible to wheelchairs. There is a Braille Trail near the Latodami Nature Center.

The park has numerous picnic pavilions, a golf course, basketball courts, baseball diamonds, and a variety of other recreational facilities. Free maps and bird checklists are available at the park office.

The Latodami Nature Center is open for a variety of nature programs and has a variety of nature displays. Check at the park office for a calendar of events. Special programs are available for groups. The center's staff leads nature hikes every Thursday morning from 10 a.m. to noon.

More than 200 species of birds have been recorded in North Park. Research projects in recent years have focused on cavity nesters, especially Wood Duck, Great Horned Owl, Eastern Screech-Owl, American Kestrel, and Eastern Bluebird.

The park's two lakes are good for migrating waterfowl in spring and fall. The Rachel Carson Trail is good for passerine species at any time of year.

The park's address is North Park Administration Building, Pearce Mill Road, Allison Park, PA 15101, (412) 935-1766. The nature center's address is Latodami Nature Center, 575 Brown Road, Wexford, PA 15090, (412) 935-2170.

Point State Park

Point State Park is 36 acres of lawn and trees at Pittsburgh's Golden Triangle—the point where the Allegheny and Monogahela rivers join to form the Ohio River. The park is an easy walk from downtown. Park in one of the garages there because cars are not permitted inside the park. The entrances to the park are on Commonwealth Place, directly across the street from the Hilton. The park is open daily from 7 a.m. to 11 p.m. Most of the sidewalks are wheelchair-accessible.

A 150-foot high, computer-controlled fountain is the focal point of the park. The fountain, which sits in a 200-foot basin, is especially dramatic at night when it is lit. Lucky air passengers on certain approaches to Pittsburgh International Airport get a spectacular view of the fountain.

Just behind the fountain is the outline of the original Fort Duquesne. The park is the home of the Fort Pitt Museum, which features exhibits on Pittsburgh's frontier period. In summer, the museum is open Tuesday to Saturday, 10 a.m. to 4:30 p.m., and Sunday, noon to 4:30 p.m. It is closed on Mondays and Tuesdays during the winter.

Fifty birds have been recorded at the park. During migration, this park is a good vantage point for checking the rivers for ducks and geese. At other times of the year, Point State Park is a lovely place for a lunchtime walk. Picnics are allowed, but there is no food concession. Look for city birds such as Mallard, Northern Cardinal, Northern Mockingbird, American Robin, and Song Sparrow. Downtown Pittsburgh has a nesting pair of Peregrine Falcons, thanks to reintroduction efforts of the Pennsylvania Game Commission. These birds sometimes are seen from the park.

In winter check the open water of the river for Common Golden-eye. In August and September hundreds of Common Nighthawks are attracted to the lights of Three Rivers Stadium across the Allegheny and can be seen from the Point.

The park's address is Point State Park, 101 Commonwealth Place, Pittsburgh, PA 15222, (412) 471-0235. The museum's address is Fort Pitt Museum, c/o Point State Park, (412) 281-9284.

South Park

South Park is 2,000 acres owned by Allegheny County in the South Hills suburbs of Pittsburgh. The park is primarily deciduous forest with open fields, pine groves, small streams, and several small ponds.

To reach the park from downtown Pittsburgh, take I-279 to the Liberty Bridge. Cross the bridge, go through the Liberty Tunnel (Pittsburghers call it the Liberty Tubes), and make a left on to SR 51. At the intersection with SR 88 (Library Road), turn right and drive on SR 88 for about 6 miles to the park.

The park is open 7 days a week from sunrise to midnight. There are more than 25 miles of trails, mostly horse trails. A 0.75-mile wheel-chair-accessible trail is planned. A small nature center and headquarters features exhibits on beavers, trees, fossils, and snakes. The park publishes an annual schedule of programs such as "Birds of Prey," "Nature's Pharmacy," and "Mushroom Mania." South Park also publishes fact sheets on natural history topics.

Birds at the park are typical of suburban parklands. Abundant species are Red-tailed Hawk, woodpeckers (including several Pileated), and Blue Jay. Great Blue Heron, Belted Kingfisher, Red-bellied Woodpecker, Rose-breasted Grosbeak, and Rufous-sided Towhee are less abundant but are present from spring to fall. On winter nights, both Eastern Screech-Owl and Great Horned Owl can be heard.

The address is South Park, S. Park Administration Building, Buffalo Drive, Library, PA 15129, (412) 835-4810.

Beechwood Farms Nature Reserve

Beechwood Farms is 134 acres of fields, thickets, and a pond owned by the Audubon Society of Western Pennsylvania. Forty acres

Rufous-sided Towhee

have been set aside for research on native plants. The reserve is located in Allegheny County, about 8 miles from Pittsburgh.

To reach Beechwood Farms, take SR 28 east from downtown Pittsburgh to Exit 5B, where you will take SR 8 north. Drive 0.5 mile to a traffic light, and turn right onto Kittanning Street. Continue 4.4 miles to Beechwood Farms.

The reserve's trails are open from dawn to dusk daily. Other facilities, including a library, nature center, bookstore, and gift shop are open Tuesday through Saturday from 9 a.m. to 5 p.m. and on Sunday from 1 p.m. to 5 p.m. There are 5 miles of trails; an excellent series of brochures and booklets has been developed to use on the trails. Some are designed especially for children. Field trips, programs for youth and adults, and workshops for teachers are scheduled.

In spring and summer watch for Broad-winged Hawks; a pair has nested here in recent years. At the pond, look for Great Blue Heron, Green-backed Heron, Spotted Sandpiper, and Belted Kingfisher. In brushy areas of multiflora rose along Meadowview Trail, Yellow-breasted Chat and Prairie Warbler have nested. More than 30 species of warblers migrate through Allegheny County; Beechwood Farms is a lovely place to look for many of them.

The address is Beechwood Farms Nature Reserve, 614 Dorseyville Road, Pittsburgh, PA 15238, (412) 963-6100.

Hillman State Park

Hillman State Park is an undeveloped park of 3,780 acres located near Florence. To reach the park, take US 22 to SR 168 north. Drive north on SR 168 to Florence and turn right onto SR 4004. The park is ahead on the left.

The more information about birds and other wildlife the park staff has as this site is being developed, the more likely it is that future park facilities will be planned to accommodate birds (and birders!). If you bird here, please share your lists with the staff.

The address is Hillman State Park, c/o Pennsylvania Game Commission, RD 2, Box 206, Waynesburg, PA 15370, (412) 627-6356.

Ryerson Station State Park

Ryerson Station State Park, located in Greene County, is 1,164 acres including the 62-acre Ronald J. Duke Lake. The park is near the site of historic Fort Ryerson, built in 1792 as a place of refuge from Indian raids.

To reach the park, take I-79 to Morrisville (Exit 3) and then take SR 21 to the park (about 25 miles). Enter the park on LR 3022 and drive to the left at the "Y" intersection just below the breast of the dam. Stop at the park office for a free map.

The park's habitats include woodlands, mowed fields, old fields, brush, 64-acre R.J. Duke Lake, and two acres of wetlands. There are 10 miles of trails; one short trail near the park office is paved and is accessible to wheelchairs. The Fox Feather Trail is a self-guided nature trail. The park also has 50 campsites for tents or trailers and an organized group camping area. Fishing, hunting, boating, swimming, and picnicking are permitted. The park is open daily from dawn to dusk.

A nature center provides a variety of programs and has exhibits on recycling and other environmental or natural topics. Campfire programs are provided at the amphitheater on Saturday and holiday

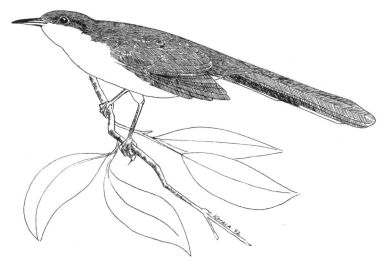

Yellow-billed Cuckoo

evenings during the summer. Many brochures and fact sheets can be obtained at the nature center. Unfortunately, the park does not have a bird checklist. Please share your records with the staff.

Osprey visit the park during spring migration, and Great Blue Heron is a year-round resident. Look for both Black-billed and Yellow-billed cuckoo, especially during a Gypsy Moth outbreak.

This park is a good place to look for 3 of the *Empidonax* species. Acadian Flycatcher ("peet-seet") breeds throughout Greene County; check wooded areas along North Fork or any of the small streams that feed the lake. In more open, brushy areas, listen for Willow Flycatcher ("fitz-bew"). The habitat is also appropriate for Least Flycatcher ("chebek"). In Greene County, the Carolina Chickadee is *the* chickadee. Orchard and Northern Orioles both breed in this area.

Note: The Summer Tanager is a breeding species throughout Greene County. Check open oak forests in the park and surrounding areas.

The park's address is Ryerson Station State Park, RD 1, Box 77, Wind Ridge, PA 15380, (412) 428-4254.

Keystone State Park

Keystone State Park is 1,169 acres of forest, fields, streams, marsh, and 78-acre Keystone Lake located about 30 miles east of Pittsburgh in Westmoreland County. To reach the park, take US 22 east to SR 981. Turn right and drive south on SR 981 to Derry Road (the third left). Take Derry Road about 2 miles to the park office, where you can pick up a free map.

The park is open daily from dawn to dusk. Night fishing is permitted. There are 100 tent/trailer campsites, a food concession, and picnic facilities. A nature center provides historical and environmental programs from spring to fall. There are 4 miles of trails through a variety of habitats, including a bluebird trail. The park is the site of acid mine drainage research.

In spring, look for migrating waterfowl including Common Loon, Common Goldeneye, and Bufflehead. Osprey also have been seen during migration. Other birds recorded at the park have included Pied-billed Grebe; Great Blue Heron; Great Egret; Green-backed Heron; Bonaparte's Gull; Spotted Sandpiper; Acadian and Great Crested Flycatchers; Northern Rough-winged, Tree, and Barn Swallows; Rufous-sided Towhee; and Orchard Oriole.

The address is Keystone State Park, RD 2, Box 101, Derry, PA 15627, (412) 668-2939 or 668-2566.

Raccoon Creek State Park

Raccoon Creek State Park is located in southern Beaver County, about 25 miles from downtown Pittsburgh. The park is made up of mixed deciduous forests, pine plantations, wetlands, streams, and two lakes. Raccoon Creek Lake is 101 acres, and a smaller lake is 4 acres. The park is large—7,323 acres—and is well-known for its wildflower reserve. In the 1800s the park was the site of Frankfort Mineral Springs, a nationally known health spa. A self-guided interpretive trail that begins at the park office leads to the spring.

To reach Raccoon Creek, take US 22 from Pittsburgh to US 30. The park is located on US 30 about 7 miles west of Imperial. Stop at the park office for a map, free bird checklist, and wildflower reserve brochure.

The park has facilities for organized group camping, family camping, primitive camping, picnicking, boating, swimming, hiking, hunting, and fishing. Raccoon Creek also has 10 modern cabins, a lodge that sleeps nine, and a large recreation lodge that is suitable for group meetings or family reunions. There is no food concession in the park, but there are stores nearby. The park is open daily from 8 a.m. to sunset.

Raccoon Creek operates a nature center from April to November at the wildflower reserve. The park is included in the Raccoon Creek State Park Christmas Bird Count and has a bluebird trail. Five miles of trails at the wildflower reserve meander through a variety of habitats. More than 500 species of wildflowers have been identified here; the best times to visit are from late April to mid-May and from August to October. The spring wildflower season coincides with bird migration. The Audubon Trail is best for migrating warblers because it is above a 20-foot cliff and offers a vantage point above the tree tops.

Note: When visiting this park in the spring wear shoes suitable for wetlands walking. Many of the trails go through wet areas.

Birds recorded in the park include Common Loon, Pied-billed Grebe, and Horned Grebe (rare) during both spring and fall migration. Waterfowl seen during migration have included Tundra Swan, Snow Goose (rare), Canada Goose, Wood Duck, Green-winged Teal, American Black Duck, Mallard, Northern Pintail, Blue-winged Teal, Northern Shoveler, Gadwall (rare), American Wigeon, Canvasback (rare), Redhead (rare), Ring-necked Duck, Tufted Duck, Greater Scaup, Lesser Scaup, Oldsquaw, Common Goldeneye, Bufflehead, Hooded Merganser, Common Merganser, and Red-breasted Merganser.

Eleven birds of prey have been recorded, and American Coot are common migrants in spring, uncommon in fall. Ring-billed and Herring Gulls are occasional migrants, while Bonaparte's Gull and Common Tern are rare migrants. Four species of owl are year-round residents; Eastern Screech-Owl is the most common.

Eastern Wood-Pewee is common in spring through fall, and Least and Acadian Flycatchers are uncommon. Check the appropriate habitats.

Seven thrushes have been observed. Swainson's is a common migrant but is uncommon in summer. Veery, Gray-cheeked Thrush, Hermit Thrush, and Wood Thrush also spend the summer in the park.

Thirty-three warblers have been observed, most during migration. In early May, look for the following: Blue-winged, Golden-winged, Tennessee, Orange-crowned, and Nashville Warblers; Northern Parula; Yellow, Chestnut-sided, Magnolia, Cape May, Black-throated Blue, Yellow-rumped, Black-throated Green, Blackburnian, Yellow-throated, Prairie, Bay-breasted, Blackpoll, Cerulean, and Black-and-white Warblers; American Redstart; Prothonotary and Worm-eating Warblers; Ovenbird; Northern Waterthrush; Kentucky, Connecticut, and Mourning Warblers; Common Yellowthroat; Hooded, Wilson's, and Canada Warblers; and Yellow-breasted Chat.

The address is Raccoon Creek State Park, RD 1, Box 900, Hookstown, PA 15050, (412) 899-2200, office; (412) 899-3611, nature center.

UNIONTOWN

Uniontown, population 12,034, is the county seat of Fayette County and is in the heart of coal mining county. The industry is not as prevalent as it was, but it still is important to the local economy. Uniontown is a good base for day trips to Friendship Hill, Fort Necessity, and the Laurel Highlands region of the Allegheny Plateau (see Chapter 3).

Friendship Hill National Historic Site

Friendship Hill is a 662-acre historic site about 50 miles south of Pittsburgh near Point Marion. The site is the former country estate of Albert Gallatin, an 18th century entrepreneur who served as Secretary of the Treasury under Presidents Jefferson and Madison.

To reach the site, take SR 21 from Uniontown west to SR 166 and continue south to Friendship Hill. Stop at the historic house/visitors' center to get a free map and bird checklist of 152 species. (**Note:** The checklist includes 29 "probable" species. The park staff is interested in updating the checklist, so birders should report any unusual sightings.) A bookstore/gift shop is operated at the visitors' center. Exhibits explain the life of Albert Gallatin.

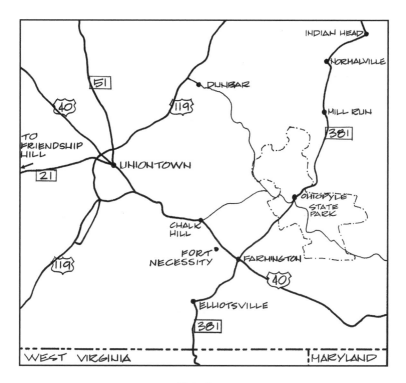

Uniontown

The site's habitats include deciduous forest, meadows, a wetland constructed to treat acid mine drainage, and streams. The site is bounded by the Monongahela River. There are 8 miles of trails through both woods and meadows; none is wheelchair-accessible.

Common Loon is a common spring migrant. Other common spring migrants are Horned and Pied-billed Grebe. The Red-necked Grebe is a rare migrant. In spring, check the river for migrant waterfowl. In summer, listen for Northern Bobwhite. Brown Thrasher and Wood Thrush are common, while Hermit and Swainson's Thrush and Veery are uncommon. Rusty Blackbird is an uncommon migrant. Evening Grosbeak, Common Redpoll, and Pine Siskin are occasional winter visitors.

The address is Friendship Hill National Historic Site, RD 1, Box 149-A, Point Marion, PA 15474, (412) 725-9190.

Fort Necessity National Battlefield

The original Fort Necessity was built by George Washington in 1754. A reconstruction of the fort has been built at Fort Necessity National Battlefield, located 11 miles east of Uniontown on US 40. The park is administered by the National Park Service and is 902 acres of scrubby open fields and mixed deciduous forest.

The park is open daily from 9 a.m. to 5:30 p.m. It has approximately 5 miles of trails, but none is wheelchair-accessible. Free maps are available at the visitors' center, which features historic displays. There is a bookstore. The park does not have a bird checklist, so report your sightings to the park staff.

The address is Fort Necessity National Battlefield, RD 2, Box 528, Farmington, PA 15437, (412) 329-5512.

KITTANNING

Kittanning, population 5,120, is the county seat of Armstrong County. It is located on the eastern bank of the Allegheny River, and a beautiful little park extends along the riverbank. This is a good place to look for migrating waterfowl. Three Rails-to-Trails projects in the area have converted abandoned railroad rights-of-way into trails worth exploring.

Crooked Creek Lake

Located south of Kittanning in Armstrong County, Crooked Creek Lake is owned by the U.S. Army Corps of Engineers and is operated primarily for flood control of the Allegheny and Ohio Rivers. Habitats include the lake and its surrounding shoreline, open fields, woodlands, marshes, thickets, and wildlife food plots.

To reach the lake take US 422 from Kittanning to SR 66. Drive south on SR 66 about 5 miles to LR 2019, which loops through the recreation area.

Crooked Creek lake has five trails and an observation blind behind the environmental learning center. Programs are offered on various

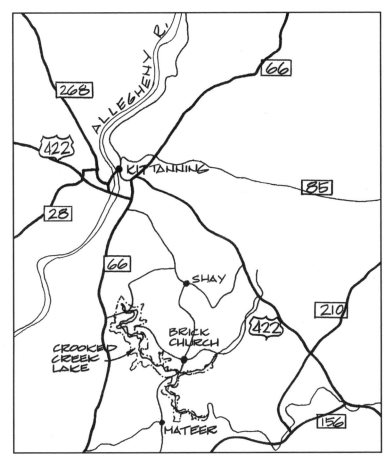

Kittanning

environmental, interpretive, and water safety topics. The environmental learning center has both historic and wildlife exhibits.

The lake is included in the Buffalo Creek Valley Christmas Bird Count. A free bird checklist is available.

Birds observed at Crooked Creek have included numerous Great Blue Herons, migrating waterfowl, Osprey (three nesting platforms are installed for when the birds decide to stay), and Bald Eagle.

In May 1989, an American White Pelican was photographed at Crooked Creek.

The address is Crooked Creek Lake, RD 3, Box 323A, Ford City, PA 16226, (412) 763-3161.

Roaring Run Trail

Roaring Run Trail, located in Armstrong County along the bank of the Kiskiminetas River, is a 3.5-mile Rails-to-Trails project owned by the Roaring Run Watershed Association. To reach the trail, drive from Kittanning south on SR 66 to Apollo. In Apollo take Cask Avenue to Canal Road and travel 0.5 mile to the parking area.

The trail, closed to motor vehicles, is open 365 days a year. This 3.5-mile Rails-to-Trails project is accessible to wheelchairs for the first 1.5 miles. A steep, wooded hillside borders the trail on one side, while the Kiskiminetas River is on the other side.

From the trail, birders can get a good look at migrating waterfowl on the river in spring. Raptors are often seen in this area. Ruffed Grouse, Wild Turkey, Belted Kingfisher, and Pileated Woodpecker are common. The address is Roaring Run Trail, Roaring Run Watershed Association, P.O. Box 40, Spring Church, PA 15686, (412) 478-1233.

Armstrong Trail

Armstrong Trail is a 52-mile long Rails-to-Trails project in Armstrong County. The trail extends from Schenley to East Brady on the east bank of the Allegheny River. Access is at numerous points.

The trail is open 24 hours a day but is closed to motorized vehicles. It passes through swamps, fields, meadows, woods, and urban areas. With its clear view of the river and passage through many different habitats, this may be a hot spot waiting to be discovered. Bald Eagle have been observed in spring, summer, and winter.

The address is Armstrong Trail c/o Armstrong County Tourist Bureau, 402 East Market Street, Kittanning, PA 16201, (412) 548-3226.

Great Shamokin Path-Cowanshannock Branch

Great Shamokin Path-Cowanshannock Branch is a 4.2-mile trail from Yatesboro to NuMine. From Kittanning, take SR 85 east to

Yatesboro. Turn right at the ball field and right again at the next intersection. There is a parking lot beside the small lake.

The path is owned by Cowanshannock Creek Watershed Association and is always open to nonmotorized travel. The path goes along Cowanshannock Creek and through woods, fields, wetlands, and marshes. There are lakes at both ends—Devil's Washbasin at Yatesboro and White Lake and Wetland at NuMine. This is a relatively new trail and may yield interesting discoveries.

The address is Great Shamokin Path-Cowanshannock Branch, Cowanshannock Creek Watershed Association, P.O. Box 307, Rural Valley, PA 16249.

INDIANA

Indiana, population 15,174, is the county seat of Indiana County and the home of Indiana University of Pennsylvania. The area around the town is devoted to surface mining for coal and agriculture. Indiana County is known as "The Christmas Tree Capital of the World." There is an Amish community north of Indiana in the Smicksburg area.

Yellow Creek State Park

Yellow Creek State Park is a 3,140-acre park in Indiana County. The park includes Yellow Creek Lake, a 720-acre impoundment. Yellow Creek is one of the best birding spots in the Commonwealth, and the Todd Bird Club has maintained excellent records of 243 birds observed in the park. The club leads bird hikes every week at the park. Contact the park office for details.

To reach the park, drive east from Indiana on US 422 about 9 miles to SR 259. Turn right onto SR 259. The park office is just ahead on the right. Stop at the park office and pick up a free map. Park staff will allow visitors to look at a copy of the bird inventory included in the park's management plan; however, a checklist is not available.

The park has facilities for boating, swimming, and picnicking. A nature center is open from Memorial Day to Labor Day. A food concession is operated in the summer months. The park is extremely popular with anglers; in the spring Laurel Run is stocked with trout and becomes crowded. In winter, ice-fishing is popular. There are

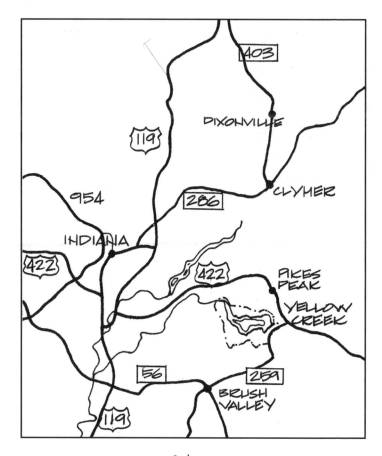

Indiana

three trails: Laurel Run Trail is a half-mile self-guided interpretive loop along the creek, Ridgetop Trail is 2 miles through a variety of habitats, and Damsite Trail is 2.5 miles that includes a good view of the lake.

Camping is not permitted at the park, but there are two commercial campgrounds nearby. Contact the Indiana County Tourist Bureau, Wayne Avenue and Sixth Street, Indiana, PA 15701, or phone (412) 465-2661, extension 230, for more information.

Check the marshy area to the right of SR 259 between the park office and the beach area for American Bittern, Virginia Rail, Sora, and Common Moorhen. Any area with a clear view of the lake is good for waterfowl in spring. A scope is useful because this is a large lake.

During spring migration, Marsh Wren has been seen in the small marsh between Little Yellow Creek and the first parking area for the beach facilities. This marsh is also good for Common Snipe. In winter, the beach area is good for Horned Lark. In spring and fall look for American Pipit. A Bald Eagle was seen during the fall 1993 migration.

Beyond the swimming beach, an observation blind with informative posters about waterfowl identification overlooks the lake. During migration the lake is excellent for waterfowl—28 species have been recorded: Tundra Swan, Snow Goose, Brant, Canada Goose, Wood Duck, Green-winged Teal, American Black Duck, Mallard, Northern Pintail, Blue-winged Teal, Northern Shoveler, Gadwall, American Wigeon, Canvasback, Redhead, Ring-necked Duck, Greater Scaup, Lesser Scaup, Oldsquaw, Black Scoter, Surf Scoter, White-winged Scoter, Common Goldeneye, Bufflehead, Hooded Merganser, Common Merganser, Red-breasted Merganser, and Ruddy Duck.

Grampap's Cove and Gramma's Cove are good for waterfowl, and shorebirds such as Solitary and Spotted Sandpipers are common.

A spruce/pine plantation at the top of the hill was the winter resort for Long-eared Owls in 1983. While checking for kinglets and nuthatches in winter, scan the trees carefully for owls.

Passerine species recorded in the park include Brown Creeper; Veery; Gray-cheeked, Swainson's, Hermit, and Wood Thrushes; Northern and Loggerhead Shrike; White-eyed, Solitary, Yellow-throated, Warbling, Philadelphia, and Red-eyed Vireos; 35 warbler species; and the following sparrows: American Tree, Chipping, Clay-colored (rare), Field, Vesper, Savannah, Fox, Song, Lincoln's, Swamp, White-throated, and White-crowned.

Rarities such as Purple Gallinule, Hudsonian Godwit, Red Knot, Franklin's Gull, and Swainson's Warbler also have been recorded here. This park's bird list is extensive and outstanding because a dedicated band of excellent birders visits the park weekly.

The park's address is Yellow Creek State Park, RD 1, Box 145-D, Penn Run, PA 15765, (412) 463-3850.

Keystone Dam

Keystone Dam, owned by utility companies, is administered by the Pennsylvania Fish and Boat Commission. In spring, it is good for migrating waterfowl and warblers, and in late summer and fall for shorebirds.

To reach the lake, drive west from Indiana on US 422 to Elderton. Turn right onto SR 210 and drive about 3 miles to the breast of the dam. From SR 210, you can scan the lake. Bring a scope.

The boat launch located near the village of Atwood is good for shorebirds and waterfowl. All six swallow species have been seen here. The marshy area on Jefferson Street (a dirt road) is good for Wood Duck and Mallard. When water levels are low, this is another place to check for shorebirds.

The best location for shorebirds is at the end of another dirt road that turns to the left one mile further up SR 210. White-rumped, Baird's, and Stilt Sandpipers have been observed here. A steep path to the right of this area leads to a good view of the lake. Here birders have seen Great Egret, Black-crowned Night-Heron, and Double Crested Cormorant. Virginia Rail is also possible.

Another spot worth checking is to the left of the Silver Canoe Campground. Look for a "Keystone Lake—West Side" sign. Willow Flycatcher, Yellow Warbler, and Swamp Sparrow breed here. In spring, American Woodcock perform nuptial displays.

Blue Spruce County Park

Blue Spruce County Park is 420 acres of mixed hardwoods and a 12-acre lake owned by Indiana County. The park is located 6 miles north of Indiana on SR 110, near the town of Ernest. Follow directional signs for either Blue Spruce Lodge or Lakeside Center.

The park is open daily from sunrise to sunset and has 6 miles of trails and a visitors' center. Educational programs are offered; examples of past programs are "Birds of Prey," "Topographic Map Reading," and "Woodworking for Wildlife."

Unfortunately the park does not have a bird checklist. Please share your records.

The address is Blue Spruce County Park, RD 2, Box 157-J, Indiana, PA 15701, (412) 463-8636.

Chapter 5
Ridge and Valley Province

The Ridge and Valley Province in Pennsylvania extends from the Allegheny Front diagonally to the New Jersey border. This region makes up about 23% of Pennsylvania. The western boundary of the region runs roughly parallel to Route 220; the eastern boundary is the Great Valley. The region is characterized by rounded mountain ridges with elevations ranging from 390 feet in the valleys to 2,700 feet at the mountaintops. Rivers and streams flow into the Susquehanna, Potomac, and Delaware watersheds.

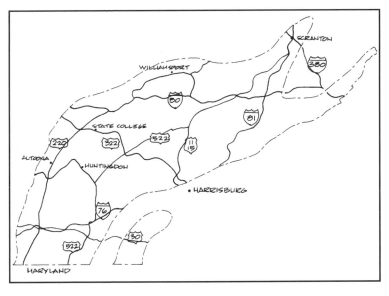

Ridge and Valley Province

Black-capped Chickadee

The average annual temperature of the region is 50° Fahrenheit, with a January average of 26°F and a July average of 72°F. The average annual precipitation ranges from 38 to 42 inches, with more precipitation in the eastern section of the region than in the west. Snowfall varies from an average of 50 inches per year in the northern section of the region to 40 inches in the south.

Abundant year-round residents of the Ridge and Valley Province include Canada Goose, American Kestrel, Rock Dove, Mourning Dove, Black-Capped Chickadee, Tufted Titmouse, Northern Mockingbird, Northern Cardinal, Dark-eyed Junco, House Finch, and House Sparrow.

An abundant winter visitor is the Ring-billed Gull. In summer, birders will have no trouble finding the following breeding birds: Turkey Vulture, Eastern Wood-Pewee, Barn Swallow, Blue Jay, Wood Thrush, Red-eyed Vireo, Ovenbird, and Field Sparrow.

The American Black Duck is an abundant spring and fall migrant, while Sharp-shinned Hawk, Broad-winged Hawk, and Red-tailed Hawk are the most abundant of the 15 birds of prey that have been recorded during fall migration.

In winter, check agricultural fields in this region for Horned Lark (common), American Tree Sparrow (common), Lapland Longspur (rare), and Snow Bunting (rare).

Table 5-1
Raptor migration in fall through Pennsylvania

Species	Migration
Northern Goshawk	late Oct. and Nov.
Cooper's Hawk	late Sept. to mid-Nov.
Sharp-shinned Hawk	late Aug. to early Nov.; peak in October
Red-tailed Hawk	late Aug. to early Dec.; peak in early Nov.
Red-shouldered Hawk	October to mid-Nov.
Broad-winged Hawk	late Aug. to early Oct.; peak in mid-Sept.
Rough-legged Hawk	early Oct. to early Dec.
Golden Eagle	late Sept. to early Dec.
Northern Harrier	mid-Aug. to mid-Dec.; peak in late Oct., early Nov.
Osprey	late Aug. to early Nov.; peak in mid-Sept.
Peregrine Falcon	mid-Sept. to mid-Nov.; peak in mid-Oct.
Merlin	late Aug. to early Dec.; peak in mid-Oct.
American Kestrel	late Aug. to early Nov.; peak in mid-Sept.

Source: Hawk Mountain Sanctuary

BEDFORD

Bedford, population 3,137, is the county seat of Bedford County. It is located at the site of Fort Bedford, built in 1758. US 30 follows the route of Forbes Road, built by Gen. John Forbes during the French and Indian War. Exit 11 of the Pennsylvania Turnpike (I-70/76) is located at Bedford; motels and restaurants are numerous.

The mountains around Bedford are wooded except where timbering operations have salvaged trees killed by a combination of Gypsy Moth infestations and drought. The valleys are largely agricultural. There are more than a dozen covered bridges in Bedford County; for a map, contact the Bedford County Tourist Information Center, 37 East Pitt Street, P.O. Box 1771, Bedford, PA 15522, (814) 632-1771.

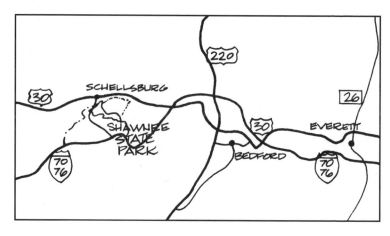

Bedford

Shawnee State Park

Located near Schellsburg, 10 miles west of Bedford on US 30, Shawnee State Park is 4,290 acres of rolling hillside forests, fields, and lakeside wetlands along 451-acre Shawnee Lake. The park is open daily from 8 a.m. to sunset and has 12 miles of trails through a variety of habitats. In summer, a food concession operates near the guarded swimming beach. There are 265 campsites that can accommodate tents or trailers. Hunting is permitted on more than 3,000 acres of this park—make sure you pick up a map at the park office if you visit in fall, winter, or spring.

In spring, the park is good for migrating waterfowl. Common Loon; Pied-billed, Horned, and Red-necked Grebe; Tundra Swan; Gadwall; American Wigeon; Blue-winged Teal; Wood Duck; Canvasback; Ring-necked Duck; Lesser Scaup; Bufflehead; Oldsquaw; Red-breasted Merganser; and Ruddy Duck all have been observed. Double-crested Cormorant also has been recorded.

A sampling of other birds observed in spring includes Virginia Rail; Sora; American Coot; Greater Yellowlegs; Spotted Sandpiper; Short-billed Dowitcher; Dunlin; Ring-billed and Bonaparte's Gulls; and Common, Forster's, Caspian, and Black Terns.

Excellent warbler flights pass through the park in early May. Look for the following: Golden-winged, Nashville, Yellow, Chestnut-sided, Black-throated Blue, Yellow-rumped, Black-throated Green, Pine, Prairie, Cerulean, and Black-and-white Warblers; American Redstart; Louisiana Waterthrush; and Common Yellowthroat; and Hooded, and Wilson's Warblers.

Note: Birders who also are interested in historic architecture and antiques will find much to admire around Schellsburg.

The address is Shawnee State Park, P.O. Box 67, Schellsburg, PA 15559, (814) 733-4218.

Hooded Warbler

Reynoldsdale State Fish Hatchery

Reynoldsdale State Fish Hatchery, located 12 miles northwest of Bedford on SR 56 in New Paris, is worth checking for an occasional Black-crowned Night-Heron. Belted Kingfishers consider the hatchery a fast-food joint. The address is Reynoldsdale Fish Cultural Station, RD 1, Box 50, New Paris, PA 15554, (814) 839-2211.

Warrior's Path State Park

Warrior's Path State Park is 334 acres of old fields, wood lots, wetlands, and a freshwater bog. The park, located in Bedford County, is bordered by a large bend in the Raystown Branch of the Juniata River. To reach Warrior's Path, take SR 26 north from Everett about 13 miles to Saxton. Turn onto 913 east. Drive 1 mile to a traffic light and turn right onto Eighth Street. The park access road is one mile ahead. Free maps are available at the park office.

The park gate is closed November 1 to April 15. From April 15 to October 30, the park is open from 8 a.m. to sunset.

The park has 3 miles of hiking trails and facilities for picnics. There is a bluebird trail. Fishing in the river is popular. Hunting is not permitted in most of the park.

Osprey have been seen at the park during spring migration. In summer, Eastern Bluebird and Great Blue Heron are common. Fall migrants have included Cooper's Hawk, Red-shouldered Hawk, and Northern Goshawk.

The park's address is Warrior's Path State Park, c/o Trough Creek State Park, RD 1, Box 211, James Creek, PA 16657-9702, (814) 658-3847.

ALTOONA

Altoona, population 51,881, is located in Blair County. The city was founded by the Pennsylvania Railroad in 1854 when railroad lines were built to connect eastern Pennsylvania and Pittsburgh. As a company town, Altoona prospered, but in recent years the railroad repair shops have cut back on employment. Sadly, new industries have been much smaller, so the population has declined. The city is situated at

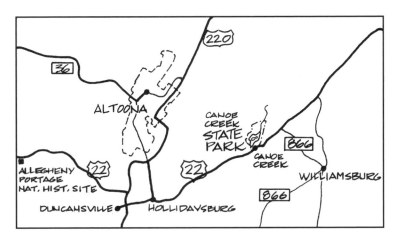

Altoona

the base of the Allegheny Front, and views from many of Altoona's neighborhoods are gorgeous. The Gospel Hill flag, visible from nearly anywhere in the city, is lit at night and attracts Common Nighthawks.

America's Industrial Heritage Project is being developed as a multi-site national park that will explain the cultural history of the area. Tourists who come to learn about railroading, steelmaking, and coal mining will find natural beauty as well.

Fort Roberdeau

An 18th century fort reconstructed to celebrate the Bicentennial, Fort Roberdeau is bordered by a hardwood forest and open fields owned by Blair County. To reach the park, take Pleasant Valley Boulevard north to Kettle Street in Altoona. Turn right at the inter-section, and proceed through Sinking Valley to the park, 8.7 miles. A large sign directs visitors to the park, which is on the left.

Programs focus on the history of the site, but a newly constructed nature center has a bird observation window. Picnicking is permitted, but food is not available in the park. Field trips for groups or schools are arranged in cooperation with the Juniata Valley Audubon Society. The park is the site of a Pennsylvania Society for Ornithology Special

Areas Project. Eventually a bird checklist should become available. Check at the park office for more information.

In winter, Common Snipe is sometimes found at springs in the valley. The farms in Sinking Valley also are good for Horned Lark in winter.

The address is Fort Roberdeau Park, RD 3, Box 391, Altoona, PA 16601, (814) 946-0048.

Valley View Park

Located just behind Valley View Nursing Home in Altoona, this park is 45 acres of forest and fields with a small stream and pond. To reach it, take US 220 to the 17th Street Exit. Take Pleasant Valley Boulevard (old US 220) north 1.4 miles and turn right at the park sign. Valley View Park is very new, and facilities still are being added as funds become available. Because of the nearby nursing home, everything is being done to make the park as accessible to the handicapped as possible.

Facilities include picnic pavilions with tables designed for wheelchair users and a playground. Bird records for the park are sparse; please share your records.

The address is Valley View Park, c/o Blair County Court House, 423 Allegheny Street, Hollidaysburg, PA 16648, (814) 946-4779.

Canoe Creek State Park

Canoe Creek State Park is 958 acres of old farm fields, woodlands, wetlands, two streams, and a 155-acre lake. The park is located in Blair County, about 12 miles east of Altoona. To reach the park, take the Frankstown Road Exit off US 220 to US 22. Turn left, and drive east about 7 miles to the Turkey Valley Road (there is a sign on US 22). Turn left and proceed about a half mile to the park entrance. Stop at the park office for a free map. Ask about the availability of a bird checklist; this park is a Pennsylvania Society for Ornithology "Special Areas Project" that has recorded 153 species. One of the results of these projects is the development of checklists.

The park is open year-round from 8 a.m. to sunset. Facilities include eight modern cabins, hundreds of picnic tables, a swimming beach, and a food concession in summer. A nature center is open during the summer, and programs featuring environmental education, history of the area, and other subjects are offered. The park has 6 miles of hiking trails, 5 miles of bridle trails, and a bluebird trail. It is included in the Culp Christmas Bird Count.

About 550 acres of the park are open to hunting in the fall and winter. Canoe Creek is also very popular with anglers; the lake is stocked with trout, bass, muskellunge, and other species. A boat concession rents rowboats and canoes.

This park is the site of caves where a colony of endangered Indiana Bats hibernates in winter. Although entrance to the bat cave is forbidden, the park staff occasionally provides informative "bat walks" on summer evenings. Check at the nature center for a schedule.

In spring, Canoe Lake is wonderful for migrant waterfowl. In late March, look for Common Loon, Pied-billed Grebe, Horned Grebe, Tundra Swan, Canada Goose, American Wigeon, Ring-necked Duck, Lesser Scaup, Bufflehead, Hooded Merganser, Common Merganser, and Ruddy Duck. In addition, Osprey and Bald Eagle are common migrants. A scope is useful for viewing birds on the lake. The park is also good for wildflowers in mid-May; Yellow Lady's Slipper grows along the Limestone Trail. My family always takes a walk on Mothers' Day to see them.

Later in the spring, Least Bittern, Sora, and Virginia Rail migrate through. Stand quietly on the bridge where Mary Ann's Creek enters into the lake on the west side of the park and scan the edge of the cat-tail marsh.

Summer residents include American Kestrel, Tree Swallow, Eastern Bluebird, Blue-gray Gnatcatcher, Golden-winged Warbler (check at the second fishing access on Canoe Creek, on the east side of the park).

Fall migrants include many warblers. Marsh Wren is a rare fall migrant.

Wintering birds include Eastern Screech-Owl, Red-bellied Woodpecker, Cedar Waxwing, Winter Wren, American Tree Sparrow, Swamp Sparrow, and, rarely, Snow Bunting.

The park's address is Canoe Creek State Park, RD 2, Box 360, Hollidaysburg, PA 16648, (814) 695-6807.

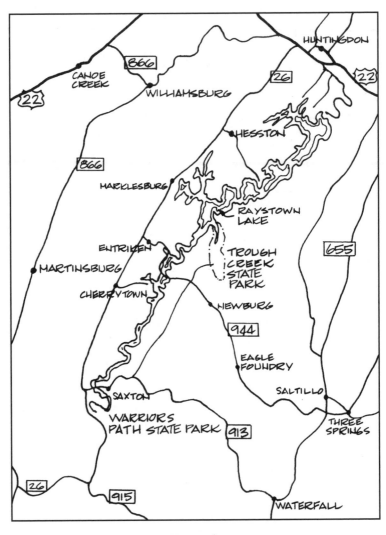

Huntingdon

HUNTINGDON

Huntingdon, population 6,843 is the county seat of Huntingdon County and the heart of "Lake Raystown Country." Tourism is becoming increasingly popular here, and there are two large state prisons nearby. Visit willingly or unwillingly. Huntingdon is also the home of Juniata College.

Raystown Lake

Raystown Lake is nearly 30,000 acres of flood-control project operated by the U.S. Army Corps of Engineers. The lake itself is 30 miles long and encompasses 8,300 acres. There are 19 public day-use areas and a resort concession at Raystown Lake. Access is from numerous points on SR 26 south of Huntingdon. Free maps are available at all public access points.

In recent years, Bald Eagle has been observed here in winter. The lake is excellent for migrating waterfowl in March and April—especially in sheltered backwater areas. Waves of warblers also migrate through in spring.

Shorebirds migrate through in summer: Lesser Yellowlegs, Solitary Sandpiper, Western Sandpiper, Least Sandpiper, Pectoral Sandpiper, and Short-billed Dowitcher.

The area is good for raptors in all seasons, and both Black and Turkey Vultures can be observed here.

The address is Raystown Lake, Manager's Office, Corps of Engineers, RD 1, Box 222, Hesston, PA 16647, (814) 658-3405.

Trough Creek State Park

Trough Creek State Park is 541 acres of mostly wooded, mountainous habitat on the banks of Trough Creek in southern Huntingdon County.

To reach the park, take SR 26 south from Huntingdon to SR 994. Cross the bridge over the upper end of Raystown Lake and continue to the intersection with SR 3031. Turn left. The park office is straight ahead. Pick up a free map and brochure of the geology of the park. Trough Creek Drive is to the left and goes through the park.

Facilities include 32 campsites for tents or trailers, picnic tables, and 16 miles of hiking trails. The Rhododendron Trail passes through beautiful growths of Rhododendron (look for Black-throated Blue Warbler) and passes Rainbow Falls—be sure to have a camera. Balanced Rock, at the Raven Rock Trail, is another site worth recording on film. In spring, this park is a wildflower hot spot.

Birds observed here include Red-shouldered, Broad-winged, and Red-tailed Hawks; Common Raven; Brown Creeper; Blue-gray Gnatcatcher; Swainson's Thrush; Ovenbird; and numerous warblers, especially during migration.

The address is Trough Creek State Park, RD 1, Box 211, James Creek, PA 16657, (814) 658-3847.

Stone Valley Recreation Area

Stone Valley Recreation Area is located about 8 miles south of State College (take Route 26 south to Pine Grove Mills where the road turns left and continue about 4 miles; turn left onto SR 1029 and go 1.7 miles to the east entrance to Stone Valley on the left side of the road). The 700-acre area is owned by the Pennsylvania State University, which uses it for research, instruction, and recreation. Cabins and boats are available for rent. Numerous picnic tables are available; Pine Warblers are common from May to August in the pine trees throughout the picnic area.

Habitats include hardwoods, conifers, a 72-acre lake, fields, wetlands, and streams. Ten hiking trails offer good access to these habitats. The recreation area is surrounded by 6,000 acres of undeveloped land.

Because of its diversity of habitats, Stone Valley is an excellent location for birding. A checklist of 233 birds has been compiled by the Shaver's Creek Environmental Center (see listing later in this chapter). Stone Valley Lake is especially good during both spring and fall migration when Common Loon, Horned Grebe, Pied-billed Grebe, Blue-winged Teal, Wood Duck, Greater and Lesser Scaups, Hooded Merganser, Ring-necked Duck, Osprey, Spotted Sandpiper, and Solitary Sandpiper may be seen. Other migrants include Yellow-bellied Sapsucker, Northern Waterthrush, and Yellow-rumped Warbler.

American Woodcock

Two pairs of Barred Owl nest in the boggy area at the north end of the lake. Other nesting species near the lake include Green-backed Heron, Wood Duck, and Belted Kingfisher. In wooded areas look for Broad-winged Hawk, Pileated Woodpecker, Great Crested Flycatcher, and Chestnut-sided Warbler.

In the fields above the Civil Engineering Lodge, look for Eastern Bluebird, Golden-winged Warbler, Black-throated Green Warbler, Chestnut-sided Warbler, Prairie Warbler, Louisiana Waterthrush, American Redstart, Scarlet Tanager, and Rose-breasted Grosbeak.

Winter birds include Horned Lark, Evening Grosbeak, Pine Siskin, Dark-eyed Junco, White-throated Sparrow, and, rarely, Pine Grosbeak, Red Crossbill, Common Redpoll, and Snow Bunting.

The address for Stone Valley is Stone Valley Recreation Area, 257 Recreation Building, The Pennsylvania State University, University Park, PA 16802, (814) 863-0762.

Woodcock Management Demonstration Area. An area of the Ironstone Trail was studied in the 1940s as Woodcock habitat. Recently, Penn State established this area as the Woodcock Management Demonstration Area. Where the Ironstone Trail crosses the East Entrance Road, pick up a descriptive flyer from the mounted box and proceed through five habitat types (White Oak stand, old field forest, feeding and resting cover, old farmstead, and clear cut). Male American Woodcock arrive at this location as early as the first week of March. Courtship displays continue through April and into May.

Shaver's Creek Environmental Center. Located at the Stone Valley Recreation Area, Shaver's Creek Environmental Center was developed by Penn State to give its students in the Department of Leisure Studies practical experience. Shaver's Creek features a nature center with good hands-on displays of local wildlife and habitats. A well-stocked bird feeding station is operated year-round and provides good opportunities for photographing birds.

Shaver's Creek maintains the Lake Trail. Its habitats include coniferous forest, deciduous forest, open fields, and streams; a boardwalk section passes through the marsh at the eastern end of the lake (look for Cedar Waxwing in all seasons). Begin the trail at the parking area adjacent to the nature center.

Shaver's Creek operates a bookstore where a checklist of 233 birds, maps of the hiking trails, and a good variety of nature books are available.

Shaver's Creek also operates the Raptor Center, which is licensed by Pennsylvania Game Commission to rehabilitate injured, ill, or orphaned birds of prey. The Raptor Center has an excellent display of raptors (including Bald Eagle, Golden Eagle, and Barred Owl, among others) that cannot be released into the wild. Visitors find these raptors good for identification studies and for introducing children to birds of prey. Raptors can be "adopted" for a donation.

Shaver's Creek offers a wide variety of programs, including bird breakfasts: early morning walks followed by a pancake breakfast featuring real maple syrup from Shaver's Creek's trees. Memberships are available, and members receive a quarterly newsletter, program guide published three times a year, and a discount at the bookstore.

The center's address is Shaver's Creek Environmental Center, 203 Henderson Building South, The Pennsylvania State University, University Park, PA, (814) 863-2000.

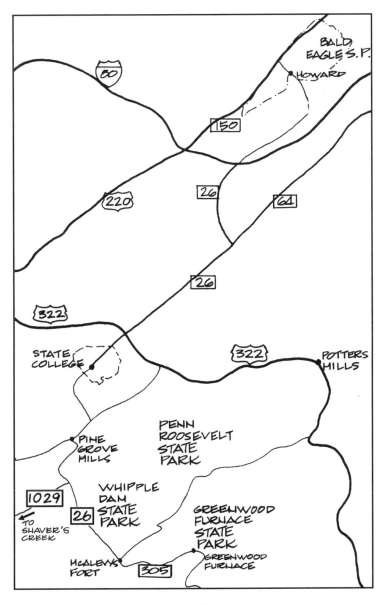

State College

STATE COLLEGE

State College, population 38,047, is best known as the home of Penn State and its Nittany Lions. The community also has several high-tech industries and is a typical college town with many fine restaurants and shops. The university has several museums, including one devoted to mineral industries—a fossil-lover's mecca. The Frost Entomological Museum on campus has 250,000 insect specimens, including some live ones. Also of interest is the huge flower garden, near the stadium, where new varieties are tested and candidates for All-America Rose designation are evaluated.

Greenwood Furnace State Park

Greenwood Furnace State Park, located in Huntingdon County, is 349 acres of wetlands, a 6-acre lake, mature forest, and mowed and unmowed fields. To reach the park, from State College take SR 45/26 south Pine Grove Mills. Turn left onto SR 26 and continue to McAlevy's Fort, where you will veer left onto SR 305 and proceed about 5 miles to the Greenwood Furnace. Pick up a free map at the park office.

Facilities at the park, which is open daily from 8 a.m. to sunset, include 50 campsites, a food concession open in the summer, and several miles of trails, including the Greenwood Spur of the Mid-State Trail, the Tuscarora Link, and a small bluebird trail. A beautiful trail encircles the lake. The visitors' center features historical/cultural displays and programs about the iron-making community that occupied this site.

Osprey are sometimes seen in the summer here, as are Great Blue Heron and Northern Oriole.

Although many birds have been seen in the park, the staff does not have a formal list. The park would welcome volunteers to help it inventory birds and to expand and monitor its bluebird trail.

The address is Greenwood Furnace State Park, RD 2, Box 118, Huntingdon, PA 16662, (814) 667-3808.

Bear Meadows Natural Area

Bear Meadows is 325 acres of bog in the Rothrock State Forest. A trail around the area is easily hiked, but shoes will get wet. Rhododendron thickets, Mountain Laurel, Balsam Fir, and Red and Black Spruce encircle the wetlands. Northern Pitcher Plant, Round-leaved Sundew, and Tree Huckleberry grow here.

To reach Bear Meadows, drive east from State College on US 322 to Boalsburg. From the traffic light at the Pennsylvania Military Museum, continue 1.9 miles and turn right. (Watch for the turn to the Tussey Mountain Ski Area.) At 0.6 mile veer to the right. Stay on this road, Bear Meadows Road, until you get to a "Y" intersection. Veer to the right to enter the natural area.

In summer, look for breeding species such as Canada Warbler more commonly found much farther north. We once saw an obviously sick bat struggling to hang onto a branch in broad daylight here. A Cooper's Hawk swept past and caught the bat as it fell to the ground. This natural area is also good for insects, especially dragonflies, and Eastern Black Bear, especially during blueberry season.

Free maps are available from the forestry office. The address is Bear Meadows Natural Area, c/o Rothrock State Forest, P.O. Box 403, Huntingdon, PA 16652, (814) 643-2340.

Penn Roosevelt State Park

Penn Roosevelt State Park is a 75-acre park in a very isolated area of the Seven Mountains region of Centre County. To reach the park take SR 322 from State College to Potter's Mills, 13 miles. From Potter's Mills continue on SR 322 for 2.5 miles and turn left (this is the second left) onto Crowfield Road. Drive 3.2 miles to a "Y" intersection where Boal Gap Road joins from the right. Continue straight 1 mile to the park. The park can also be accessed from Bear Meadows; follow Bureau of Forestry signs.

The park has a 3.5-acre lake, 15 primitive campsites for tents only, and is always closed to hunting. I have never had to share this park with another human when I have gone there during the week.

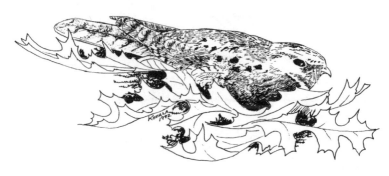

Whip-poor-will

The best times to visit this park are in spring for waves of migrating warblers, and in summer when Wood Thrush sing during the day, Veery at dusk, and Whip-poor-will later at night.

The address is Penn Roosevelt State Park, c/o Greenwood Furnace State Park, RD 2, Box 118, Huntingdon, PA 16662, (814) 667-3808.

Detweiler's Run Natural Area

Detweiler's Run Natural Area is a beautiful, isolated area of the Rothrock State Forest. The big attraction here is breeding birds that are not easily found elsewhere in central Pennsylvania. The area is located on a dirt forest road that may be difficult to travel in winter.

To reach the site from Bear Meadows, (see listing earlier in this chapter), take Bear Meadows Road to the intersection with Detweiler Run Road and turn left. Detweiler's Run Natural Area is located to the right of this road, but the entire area is good for birding.

The Mid-State Trail runs through the area and primitive camping is allowed, so this would be a good place for a birding/backpacking trip. Parking is available at Greenwood Furnace State Park, but check in with the park office before leaving your car overnight. Free maps of Rothrock State Forest are available from the forestry office. A bird checklist is not available. The area is included in the State College Christmas Bird Count.

The area is a hemlock/white pine forest with an undergrowth of rhododendron. Standing Stone Creek runs parallel to the road.

In spring, look for migratory warblers in this area. Birds that breed here include Acadian Flycatcher; Winter Wren; Veery; Wood Thrush; Red-eyed Vireo; Black-throated Blue, Black-throated Green, Black-burnian, and Black-and-white Warblers; American Redstart; Worm-eating Warbler; Ovenbird; Hooded and Canada Warblers; and Scarlet Tanager. Several of these birds are otherwise rare breeders in central Pennsylvania.

The address is Detweiler's Run Natural Area, c/o Rothrock State Forest, P.O. Box 403, Huntingdon, PA 16652, (814) 643-2340.

Whipple Dam State Park

Whipple Dam State Park is 244 acres of primarily forested habitat and a 22-acre lake located 10 miles south of State College in Huntingdon County.

To reach the park, take SR 45 south from State College to Pine Grove Mills. Turn left at the traffic light onto SR 26. At Whipple Road, turn left and continue 0.5 mile to the park.

Birds are similar to those in the surrounding Rothrock State Forest.

The address is Whipple Dam State Park, c/o Greenwood Furnace State Park, RD 2, Box 118, Huntingdon, PA 16662, (814) 667-3808.

Bald Eagle State Park

Bald Eagle State Park is a 5,900-acre park owned by the U.S. Army Corps of Engineers and leased by the Commonwealth of Pennsylvania. The park is located in Centre County, midway between Lock Haven and Milesburg. Habitats at Bald Eagle are varied: deciduous forests, marsh, swamp, old fields, scrub brush, ponds, and a 1,730-acre deep-water lake. The park is included in the Bald Eagle Christmas Bird Count.

To reach the park from the east, take I-80 to Exit 26 and go north on US 220 to SR 150. Turn left onto SR 150, and continue about 13 miles to the park. From the west take I-80 to Exit 23, and take SR 150 north about 10 miles to the park.

The park is open daily from 8 a.m. to sunset. There are 100 modern and 70 primitive campsites. Picnics are allowed, and there is a food concession open during the summer. There are eight hiking trails, one of which is designed to attract butterflies.

In spring, Bald Eagles migrate through Bald Eagle. In fall, Bald Eagles and, rarely, Golden Eagles migrate through, along with geese, ducks, and shorebirds. Eastern Bluebird, Great Horned Owl, Eastern Screech-Owl, Red-tailed Hawk, American Kestrel, and Canada Goose nest at the park.

The address is Bald Eagle State Park, RD 1, Box 56, Howard, PA 16841-9607, (814) 625-2775.

Poe Valley State Park

Poe Valley State Park is 620 acres of mixed forest, stream, a 25-acre lake, and about an acre of forested wetland. The park is located in southeastern Centre County in the 198,000-acre Bald Eagle State Forest.

Poe Valley is remote. All roads that lead to the park are gravel state forest roads. Access is not guaranteed in winter. To reach the park, take SR 45 from State College toward Milheim, about 21 miles. About one mile west of Milheim, there is a sign that directs you to the right on LR 445. Follow the signs on this road to LR 2012, and then to the park. Free maps are available.

Day-use areas in the park are open from 8 a.m. to sunset. There are 78 campsites with primitive facilities. There is a swimming beach where a food concession is operated in the summer. A nature center also is open in summer, and the park naturalist can provide guided walks and slide programs. Exhibits feature the lumber/railroad history of the area and artesian spring hydrogeology.

Birds in the park include Pied-billed Grebe and Great Blue Heron in summer, accipiter species, Red-tailed Hawk, Ruffed Grouse, Wild Turkey, Spotted Sandpiper, Great Horned Owl, Barred Owl, Eastern Screech-Owl, Belted Kingfisher, Pileated Woodpecker, Blue-gray Gnatcatcher, Northern Waterthrush, Scarlet Tanager, and Northern Oriole.

The address is Poe Valley State Park, c/o Reed's Gap State Park, RD 1, Box 276A, Milroy, PA 17063, (814) 349-8778.

Poe Paddy State Park

Poe Paddy State Park, 25 acres, is located at the confluence of Big Poe Creek and Penn's Creek in southeastern Centre County. The park is 4 miles east of Poe Valley State Park on the gravel Big Poe Road. Signs direct visitors to Poe Valley and warn travelers: "Travel at own risk." I have not had problems on this road in summer, but winter travel can be tricky. Long after main highways have been plowed, this road will remain snow-covered.

The park is located at the site of a lumbering community that flourished in the 1880s and 1890s. The stream, Penn's Creek, that runs through the park is nationally known as a trout stream. The site's beauty has long been appreciated; in the early 1900s an excursion train ran from Milroy to Poe Paddy.

Facilities at the park include two small Adirondack lean-tos and 43 tent and trailer campsites. The campground is primitive. Two areas are set aside for group camping. The Mid-State Trail traverses the park. Poe Valley Nature Trail is a self-guided interpretive trail. The Poe Valley State Park naturalist provides guided walks and other programs by advance arrangement. The park is open from 8 a.m. to sunset.

Habitats at the park are riverine, about 5 acres of forested wetlands, and mixed deciduous/coniferous forest.

Most common woodland species can be observed here. Birds are similar to those found at nearby Poe Valley, with the exception of waterfowl. Osprey and Bald Eagle have been reported along Penn's Creek.

The address is Poe Paddy State Park, c/o Reed's Gap State Park, RD 1, Box 276A, Milroy, PA 17063; Poe Valley: (814) 340-8778; Reed's Gap: (814) 667-3622.

Reed's Gap State Park

Reed's Gap State Park is 220 acres of mixed deciduous and coniferous forest through which Honey Creek, a small trout stream, flows. The park is located in Mifflin County's New Lancaster Valley. To reach the park, take US 322 from State College east about 20 miles to Milroy. In Milroy take LR 1001 to LR 1002, which leads directly to the park. The park is about 7 miles from Milroy. Free maps are available at the park office. **Warning:** Many Amish people live in this area. Be careful to watch for horse-drawn buggies on the road.

Reed's Gap is the trailhead for the Reed's Gap Spur of the Mid-State Trail, and the park has 5 miles of trails, including a 1.1-mile self-guided nature trail. The park also has 14 campsites for tents only. Hunting is prohibited in much of the park. There is a swimming pool and a food concession.

Birds in the park include Barred Owl, Eastern Screech-Owl, Red-tailed Hawk, Red-shouldered Hawk, Turkey Vulture, Pileated Wood-pecker, Downy Woodpecker, Northern Flicker (yellow-shafted), Ruffed Grouse, Chipping Sparrow, Barn Swallow, Black-and-white Warbler, and Eastern Phoebe.

The address is Reed's Gap State Park, RD 1, Box 276A, Milroy, PA 17063, (814) 667-3622.

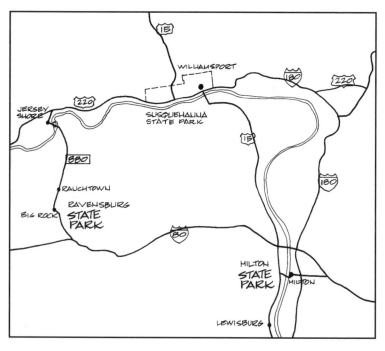

Williamsport

WILLIAMSPORT

Located on the West Branch of the Susquehanna River, Williamsport, population 31,933, is the county seat of Lycoming County. Historically, it was the center of the lumbering industry in north-central Pennsylvania. Lumber barons' homes are referred to as "Millionaires' Row." Today the claim to fame is the Little League World Series held here annually.

An exciting recent development is the reintroduction, by hacking, of two Peregrine Falcons on the Commonwealth Bank Building in downtown Williamsport. The best view of the birds is from the Center City parking deck. If you visit Williamsport, be sure to be on the lookout for returning Peregrine Falcons and report any sightings. Volunteers from Lycoming Audubon Society (see Appendix 2) have assisted with the project and have monitored the birds.

Susquehanna State Park

Susquehanna State Park is 20 acres along the north shore of the West Branch of the Susquehanna River at Williamsport. The park provides access to the river for viewing waterfowl during migration. The address is 454 Pine Street, Williamsport, PA 17701, (717) 326-1971.

Montour Preserve

The Montour Preserve is a 966-acre recreation facility in Montour County owned by Pennsylvania Power and Light (PP&L). The preserve includes 165-acre Lake Chillisquaque, an emergency cooling water supply for a large coal-fired electric generating plant, and mixed deciduous woodlands, pine plantations, fields, wet meadows, and ponds.

To reach the preserve, take I-80 to Exit 33. From there, drive north on SR 54 to Washingtonville, following the signs to the preserve.

The preserve has 10 trails, ranging in length from 0.25 mile to 4.25 miles. The Goose Woods Trail is wheelchair-accessible and has a wood chip surface. A Braille Trail provides a multisensory nature experience. There are self-interpretive nature displays at the visitors' center; the exhibits feature birds of prey, mammals of Pennsylvania, lake life, and Native American artifacts. A "discovery corner" is designed for children. Feeding stations are operated at the visitors' center, at two observation blinds, and along the Goose Woods Trail. The preserve publishes a quarterly newsletter that gives information about public programs on natural and cultural history, wildlife, music, and arts and crafts.

PP&L has published several free booklets featuring birds. These are available at the nature center. "Bluebird Trail" is a booklet that explains nine stops on the preserve's Bluebird Trail through fields and edges. This trail is good for Eastern Bluebird as well as American Kestrel and Tree Swallow. Another publication, "Common Birds of Montour Preserve," is a very nice beginner's guide to birding and includes a checklist of 224 bird species observed at Montour between 1972 and 1985.

Some examples of birds at the preserve are Common Loon, Bald Eagle, and Osprey during the spring migration. In fact, both spring and fall migrations are exciting at this site; look for both waterfowl and warblers. Rarities spotted here have included Red-necked Grebe, Double-crested Cormorant, Glossy Ibis, Greater White-fronted Goose, Ruddy Duck, Black-bellied Plover, Ruddy Turnstone, Sanderling, and Red-necked Phalarope.

The fly ash basin at the Montour Steam Electric Power Plant also is good for migrants. To reach the fly ash basin, drive south from the visitors' center about 2 miles on LR 1003.

Call or write in advance of your visit for a permit to use one of the observation blinds. The address is PP&L Montour Preserve, RD 1, Box 292, Turbotville, PA 17772, (717) 437-3131.

Lewisburg "Cellblock C"

Lewisburg Federal Penitentiary, Cellblock C, is a birding hot spot you can't visit. And wouldn't want to. It is of interest, though, because this is the only known site where the Eurasian Jackdaw has bred in the western hemisphere.

The jackdaws were first noticed in 1985 by a tower guard at the prison. The pair remained through the winter and were recorded on the Lewisburg Christmas Bird Count. The birds continued to do time at the prison until 1987 when an ill fledgling was discovered on the grounds and taken to the Philadelphia Zoo's veterinary lab. Unfortunately, the young bird died the same day it was found. It is now a specimen at the Academy of Natural Sciences in Philadelphia.

The parent birds attempted nesting again in 1988, and again the young died. In 1991, the pair fledged 2 young. The pair was again seen in 1992.

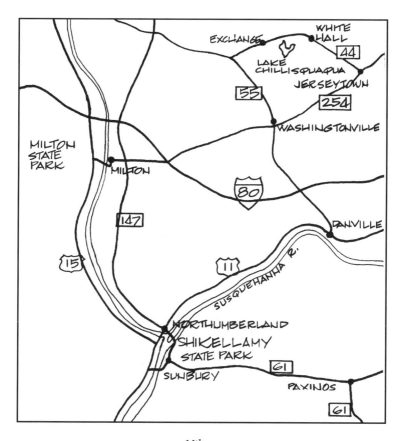

Milton

Shikellamy State Park

Shikellamy State Park is 131.5 acres in two locations: on Packers Island located where the North Branch and the West Branch of the Susquehanna meet and on the west shore of the West Branch off US 11, 7 miles north of Selingsgrove. The island portion of the park is largely parking lot and marina (with year-round restaurant and summer snack bar), but it makes a good access point for viewing waterfowl migration in the early spring and again in the fall. The riverbank is cemented into bulkheads or stabilized by riprap, so this is not a good site for shorebirds. One outstanding sighting here was of a Sabine's Gull in September, 1981. This species has been recorded only six times in Pennsylvania.

To reach the Packers Island portion of the park, take SR 147 north from Sunbury or south from Northumberland.

The address is Shikellamy State Park, Bridge Avenue, Sunbury, PA 17801, (717) 286-7880.

Milton State Park

Milton State Park is an 83-acre island on the Susquehanna River between Milton and West Milton in Northumberland County 14 miles upstream from Shikellamy State Park. The southern half of this park is wooded; mowed fields make up the northern half. This is another good place to view migrating waterfowl on the river in spring and fall.

The address is Milton State Park, c/o Shikellamy State Park, Bridge Avenue, Sunbury, PA 17801, (717) 286-7880.

R.B. Winter State Park

R.B. Winter State Park is 695 acres of White Pine/Hemlock forest, open hardwoods, small cold-water lake, mountain stream, and scattered wetlands. The park is in Union County, about 18 miles west of Lewisburg on SR 192.

The park has 60 primitive campsites and is open for day-use from 8 a.m. to sunset daily. A food concession is operated from Memorial

Day to Labor Day. In summer a nature center offers interpretive and environmental education programs. Exhibits at the visitors' center feature both environmental and historical themes.

The park's birds include migrant Great Blue Heron, Bufflehead, Common Merganser, Osprey, American Woodcock (occasional), Black-throated Green Warbler, Black-and-white Warbler, Yellow-bellied Sapsucker, and Fox Sparrow.

Breeding birds include Eastern Phoebe, Ruby-throated Hummingbird, Cliff Swallow, Common Yellowthroat, Bay-breasted Warbler, Yellow-rumped Warbler, Blackburnian Warbler, Belted Kingfisher, Veery, Wood Thrush, American Tree Sparrow, and Chipping Sparrow.

Winter birds include Pine Siskin, Golden and Ruby-crowned Kinglets, Evening Grosbeak, Common Redpoll (rare), and Red Crossbill (rare).

Year-round residents include Barred Owl; Cooper's and Sharp-shinned Hawk; Pileated Woodpecker; Brown Creeper; Red- and White-breasted Nuthatches; Cedar Waxwing; and White-throated, American Tree, and Song Sparrows.

The address is R.B. Winter State Park, RD 2, Box 355, Mifflinsburg, PA 17844, (717) 966-1455.

Sand Bridge State Park

Sand Bridge State Park is a very small picnic grove of 1.5 acres located in Union County 10 miles west of Lewisburg on SR 192. The park is open year round from sunrise to sunset for day-use only . Sand Bridge's habitat is mixed forest with little understory. Rapid Run flows through the park.

Year-round residents in the park include Barred Owl, Pileated Woodpecker, Broad-wing Hawk, Brown Creeper, Red- and White-breasted Nuthatches, Common Raven, Dark-eyed Junco, and Tufted Titmouse. In summer, look for Turkey Vulture, Blackburnian Warbler, Wood Thrush, Eastern Phoebe, and Rufous-sided Towhee.

The address is Sand Bridge State Park, c/o R.B. Winter State Park, RD 2, Box 355, Mifflinsburg, PA 17844, (717) 966-1455.

McCall Dam State Park

McCall Dam State Park is 6.7 acres of second-growth White Pine and Hemlock forest with some mowed fields. The park is located on White Deer Creek in the Bald Eagle State Forest at the western entrance to R.B. Winter State Park.

To reach the park, drive west from Lewisburg on SR 192 to R.B. Winter State Park. From there, take a forestry road to McCall Dam, about 4 miles. Pick up a map at the R.B. Winter park office.

The park is open year-round from sunrise to sunset daily. Camping facilities are open to organized groups only. Picnics are permitted; food is not available at the park.

Birds listed on the park's avian inventory include Barred Owl, Cedar Waxwing, Whip-poor-will, Great-crested Flycatcher, Hermit Thrush, Black-throated Green Warbler, and Blackburnian Warbler.

The address is McCall Dam State Park, c/o R.B. Winter State Park, RD 2, Box 355, Mifflinsburg, PA 17844, (717) 966-1455.

WILKES-BARRE/SCRANTON

Located in a prong of the Ridge and Valley Province that extends into the Allegheny Plateau in northeastern Pennsylvania, Wilkes-Barre, population 47,523, and Scranton, population 81,805, almost entirely fill the urbanized, industrial Wyoming Valley. Wilkes-Barre is the county seat of Luzerne County, and Scranton is the county seat of Lackawanna County.

North of Scranton, Archbald Pothole State Park is home of the largest pothole in Pennsylvania—and one of the smallest state parks. The pothole is 42 feet wide and 38 feet deep; the state park is 153 acres. The address is Archbald Pothole State Park, c/o Lackawanna State Park, RD 1, Box 230, Dalton, PA 18414, (717) 945-3239.

Frances Slocum State Park

Frances Slocum State Park is 1,035 acres of mixed hardwoods, pine, hemlock, and old fields in Luzerne County. The park is north of Wilkes-Barre. To reach it, drive north on SR 309 about 5 miles to

Carverton Road, then north one mile on Eighth Street, then west one mile on Mount Olivet Road.

The park is open daily from 8 a.m. to sunset. It has 100 campsites and facilities for picnics. There is a food concession and 4.5 miles of trails. A visitors' center offers programs on environmental education and has exhibits on Native American culture and wetlands.

The park's management plan lists 207 bird species.

The park's address is Frances Slocum State Park, 565 Mount Olivet Road, Wyoming, PA 18644, (717) 696-3525.

Nescopeck State Park

Nescopeck State Park is an undeveloped tract of 3,000 acres of old field, open field, bottomland forest, upland forest, hemlock ravines, open cattail marsh, ponds, alder marsh, and swampy woods. In other words, Nescopeck has something for every bird.

To reach the site, currently managed by the Pennsylvania Game Commission, take SR 309 north from Hazleton. At the intersection with Honey Hole Road (LR 3040), turn right. Stay on Honey Hole Road—you will pass under I-80 and pass the back entrance to Beech Mountain Estates on the right. Where the road bears to the left, there is a small PGC sign. Continue 4 miles ahead to a former residence now used by staff. You can park here.

The park has no facilities but is always open. It has been the subject of a Pennsylvania Society for Ornithology Special Areas Project (SAP) conducted by Alan Gregory, who reports 142 species observed here (130 during the SAP).

Notable spring species include Common Loon, Pied-billed and Horned Grebes, American Bittern, Red-shouldered Hawk, and Barred Owl. Fields along Nescopeck Creek are used by American Woodcock for spring courtship flights. In summer, four flycatcher-species breed here (listen!): Acadian ("Pit-see"), Least ("Che-bek"), Willow ("Fitz-bew"), and Alder ("Fee-bee-o"). Blackburnian Warbler also breeds.

In fall, the park is outstanding habitat for warbler migration. Olive-sided Flycatcher and Marsh Wren have been observed. In winter, the site has held Pine Grosbeak, Common Redpoll, Pine Siskin, and Evening Grosbeak in recent years.

There are no office facilities at this park yet. For more information and a free copy of his SAP data, contact Alan Gregory, P.O. Box 571, Conyngham, PA 18219-0571.

Carbon County Environmental Education Center

Carbon County Environmental Education Center (CCEEC) is located at the 6,500-acre Mauch Chunk Lake Park 5.2 miles west of Jim Thorpe. The center is owned by Carbon County. To reach CCEEC, take SR 309 south from Tamaqua for a half mile, then turn left onto Owl Creek Road (SR 3012). Drive 5.2 miles on Owl Creek Road to the intersection with SR 902 and continue past the intersection for a half mile to CCEEC, located in a barn on the right. There is a sign.

The center is open daily from 8 a.m. to 4:30 p.m. Camping is permitted at Mauch Chunk Lake Park. Food is available. The center's diverse habitats include mature second-growth forests, lake, streams, evergreen plantations, and fallow fields. There is an observation blind at one edge of the lake.

The center provides programs for the general public, schools, and organizations and features hands-on exhibits, collections, and live specimens. It also operates a wildlife rehabilitation program. Memberships are available; members receive a quarterly newsletter and discounted rates for special events.

In spring, many warbler species and a good variety of waterfowl migrate through the site. Great Blue Heron, Green-backed Heron, and Black-crowned Night-Heron, and Cooper's and Rough-legged Hawks have been observed.

Summer breeders include Wood Duck, Eastern Screech-Owl, Belted Kingfisher, Pileated Woodpecker, Brown Creeper, Blue-gray Gnatcatcher, Eastern Bluebird, Yellow Warbler, Pine Warbler, Hooded Warbler, and Rose-breasted Grosbeak.

Fall migrants include Snow Goose; American Wigeon; and Common, Red-breasted, and Hooded Mergansers. Osprey and Bald Eagle also have been observed.

In winter, visitors include Red-breasted Nuthatch, Pine Grosbeak, Pine Siskin, and Evening Grosbeak.

The address is Carbon County Environmental Education Center, 625 Lentz Trail, Jim Thorpe, PA 18229, (717) 645-8597.

HAWK MOUNTAIN SANCTUARY

Hawk Mountain Sanctuary is a 2,200-acre birding hot spot of international importance. It is not uncommon to find yourself sharing a rock with a birder from another country. Hawk Mountain also is internationally important as an example of what can be accomplished when an individual, in this case Rosalie Edge, decides to protect birds. The sanctuary is an inspiring place to visit, not only to witness the miracle of hawk migration in the fall, but also to witness the miracle of a place where research and education continue to be a tribute to that courageous woman. All birders should be grateful to the members of the Hawk Mountain Sanctuary Association, who provide the financial resources that make this place so special.

I literally became a birder 20 years ago at Hawk Mountain. My grandmother took my husband and me to visit the sanctuary shortly after we were married, and one look at a Merlin through a pair of binoculars changed my life. Take someone you love to Hawk Mountain!

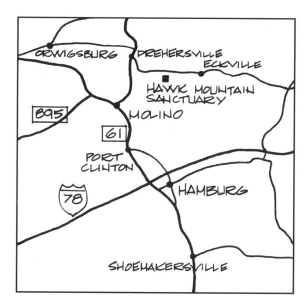

Hawk Mountain Sanctuary

To get there, drive north from Reading on SR 61 to Molino, where you will turn right onto LR 895. Drive 2 miles to Drehersville. Turn right onto LR 2108 and drive up the mountain to the sanctuary headquarters where you will pay a small fee for the privilege of sitting on a rock while you watch birds of prey migrate in the fall or for the privilege of exploring the hiking trails and watching forest species during the other seasons. (See page 119 for highlights of fall raptor migration.)

While in the headquarters, recently expanded, take time to read the information about the exhibits and get a refresher course in hawk identification by studying the mounted specimens overhead. A feeding station is operated year-round, and a short trail leads to an observation blind.

The sanctuary also operates an excellent bookstore and small gift shop. Two books of special interest are published by the sanctuary: *Hawks Aloft,* by Maurice Broun, the sanctuary's first curator, tells the story of the fight to protect birds of prey and the early years of establishing the sanctuary; *The Mountain and the Migration: A Guide to Hawk Mountain,* by James Brett, explains the migration. The latter book also includes a checklist of plants and animals, including 238 birds recorded at the sanctuary, the Pine Swamp, and the Little Schuylkill River since 1934.

The address is Hawk Mountain Sanctuary, Route 2, Kempton, PA 19529, (610) 756-6961.

Beltzville State Park

Beltzville State Park is 2,972 acres of forest, fields, wetlands, streams, pond, and 947-acre lake in Carbon County.

To reach the park, take the Northeast Extension of the Pennsylvania Turnpike to Exit 34. The park is just ahead on SR 209. Stop at the park office for a free map and bird checklist of 215 species.

The park is open year-round from 8 a.m. to sunset. Picnicking is permitted, and there is a food concession. There are 11 miles of trails and an observation blind off Ground Pine Trail. A visitors' center provides cultural, historical, and natural programs. Exhibits feature a variety of topics including wetlands and bluebirds.

Bird species observed here include migrants such as Common Loon and Horned Grebe, Greater and Lesser Scaup, Bufflehead, Yellow-bellied Sapsucker, Swainson's Thrush, American Pipit, and a wide variety of vireos, warblers, and sparrows. Summer residents include Wood Duck; Whip-poor-will; Least, Acadian, and Willow Flycatchers; Purple Martin; Cliff Swallow; Veery; Yellow, Pine, and Black-and-white Warblers; Vesper, Savannah, and Grasshopper Sparrows; and Orchard and Northern Orioles.

The address is Beltzville State Park, RD 3, Box 3720, Lehighton, PA 18235, (610) 377-0045.

Tuscarora State Park

Tuscarora State Park is 1,716 acres of mostly hardwood forest and a 92-acre lake. The north side of the lake is developed with a guarded beach for swimming in summer. Birding is better on the south side of the lake, away from crowds.

To reach the park, take I-81 to Exit 38. Take SR 54 east to Barnesville and turn right onto LR 1015. Continue to a "T" intersection with SR 1018. The park office is to the right, but the entrance to the parking areas is to the left. Pick up a free map at the park office.

Facilities at the park, which is open daily during daylight hours, include a food concession and boat-launch ramp. Birds at this park are similar to nearby Locust Lake Park (see below).

The address is Tuscarora State Park, RD 1, Box 1051, Barnesville, PA 18214, (717) 467-2404.

Locust Lake State Park

Locust Lake State Park is located at the western end of Locust Valley in Schuylkill County. It is 1,144 acres of northern hardwood forest, hedgerows, abandoned fields, wetlands, and 52-acre Locust Lake. The majority of the park—all but 60 acres—is forested.

To reach the park, take I-81 to Exit 37, and take LR 1011 to Locust Lake Road and enter the park. Pick up a free map and bird checklist at the park office. The park has 282 campsites, a camp store/boat rental concession open from Memorial Day to Labor Day, and swimming beach. An environmental interpretive program offers guided hikes, slide presentations, and crafts and games. Special programs can be arranged by contacting the park naturalist.

There are several trails of interest to birders. A bicycle trail, which is accessible to wheelchairs, encircles the lake. The Ridge Trail goes through a wetlands area, a mature forest, and a young woodland area, and parallels Locust Creek for several hundred feet. The Hemlock Trail follows the stream through a mature hemlock stand. Oak Loop Trail traverses a mature deciduous forest. **Warning:** Much of the park is open to hunting in the fall, winter, and early spring.

Birds recorded at the park include uncommon migrant Pied-billed Grebe in both summer and fall; Northern Harrier is common in summer. Spotted Sandpiper and American Woodcock can be seen in spring and summer. Eastern Screech-Owl and Great Horned Owl are common. Brown Creeper is common in fall and winter. Twenty warbler species have been recorded. Check the wetlands for Northern Waterthrush and areas along the stream for Louisiana Waterthrush. Rose-breasted Grosbeak and Indigo Bunting also can be found in the park from spring to fall.

The address is Locust Lake State Park, c/o Tuscarora State Park, RD 1, Box 1051, Barnesville, PA 18214, (717) 467-2772.

TUSCARORA STATE FOREST

The Tuscarora State Forest is 91,700 acres including the Frank E. Masland, Jr., Natural Area; the Hemlocks Natural Area; the Tuscarora Wild Area; the Hoverter & Sholl Box Huckleberry Natural Area; and four state parks: Col. Denning, Fowlers Hollow, Little Buffalo, and Big Spring. The forest is very primitive. The Tuscarora Trail goes through the area.

Free maps are available from the Pennsylvania Bureau of Forestry. A brochure featuring the Frank E. Masland, Jr., Natural Area is of interest and has a map of the 1,270-acre tract of old second-growth forest. Another brochure features the Iron Horse Trail constructed in 1981 by the Youth Conservation Corps. A third brochure provides a map and information about the Hemlocks Natural Area, a tract of virgin hemlocks.

Also of interest is a "Tuscarora State Forest Auto Tour" brochure that has a map and directions for a 26-mile, 12-stop tour that begins at the district's headquarters near Blain and ends at a pioneer cemetery near Landisburg. Several of the scenic overlooks on this tour are good for fall raptor migration. Even better are Hollow Road Overlook, the Mountain Road Overlook, the Big Knob Tower, and the Flat Rock Trail Overlook in Col. Denning State Park.

The forest is excellent for migrant warblers in spring in addition to fall raptors. In winter, Barred and Great Horned Owls are found.

The address is Tuscarora State Forest, District Forester, P.O. Box 67, Blain, PA 17006, (717) 563-3191.

Colonel Denning State Park

Colonel Denning State Park is 273 acres of woodland with a 3.5-acre lake located in Cumberland County. The park is named for a Revolutionary War veteran who developed and manufactured an improved wrought iron cannon for the Continental Army stationed at Washingtonburg Forge, now Carlisle Barracks.

To reach the park from Carlisle, take SR 641 west to Newville and turn right onto SR 233. The park is 8 miles north of Newville. Free maps are available at the park office.

The park is open daily from 8 a.m. to sunset; the swimming beach is open from 11 a.m. to 7 p.m. daily between Memorial Day and Labor Day. Picnicking is permitted, and there is a food concession near the swimming beach. There are 52 primitive campsites at the park. Hunting is permitted in most of the park.

There are more than 18 miles of hiking trails in the park, which also is a trailhead for the 105-mile Tuscarora Trail. The Doubling Gap Nature Trail is a self-guided trail through a wetlands area. Of special interest to birders is the Flat Rock Trail that begins near the park office and continues 2.5 miles to the Flat Rock Overlook, which is good for raptor migration in the fall.

A nature center at the park is open from Memorial Day to Labor Day and provides environmental education, nature, and historical programs and exhibits.

Birds recorded in the park in spring include Brown Thrasher, Cedar Waxwing, American Tree Sparrow, Chipping Sparrow, and Red-winged Blackbird. Summer birds include both Red- and White-breasted Nuthatch, Belted Kingfisher, Red-headed and Pileated Woodpecker, Great Crested Flycatcher, American Redstart, Louisiana Waterthrush, Canada Warbler, Scarlet Tanager, Rose-breasted Grosbeak, and Eastern Meadowlark. In fall and winter, look for Red-bellied Woodpecker, Red- and White-breasted Nuthatch, Brown Creeper, and Rufous-sided Towhee.

The address is Colonel Denning State Park, 1599 Doubling Gap Road, Newville, PA 17241, (717) 776-5272.

Waggoner's Gap. Another good nearby location for hawk watching is Waggoner's Gap on SR 74 north of Carlisle. To reach Waggoner's Gap from Colonel Denning, take SR 233 north to Landisburg and turn right on to SR 850. At Bridgeport, the road becomes SR 74. Drive to the summit of Tuscarora Mountain and park near the transmitter station. A short hike up the trail to the right will bring you to a sandstone bench. Migrating raptors are typical of the Appalachian Mountains.

Fowler's Hollow State Park

Fowler's Hollow State Park is located in the 30,000-acre Tuscarora State Forest in Perry County.

To reach the park, drive northwest from Carlisle on SR 74 to Bridgeport (about 11 miles). At the "Y" intersection in Bridgeport take LR 3017 (the left arm of the "Y") and continue to Landisburg. Continue on SR 233 to another "Y". Take the left arm, LR 850, to the intersection with SR 274 in Loysville. Turn left onto SR 274 and proceed to Blain. At the east end of town, turn left onto LR 3008 and cross the bridge over Fowler Hollow Run. Turn right onto LR 3004, Fowler's Hollow Road, and proceed 7 miles to the park.

Free park maps are available at the park, though there is no office. Fowler's Hollow has 18 primitive campsites and is open for day use from sunrise to sunset 365 days a year. Picnics are permitted, but there is no food concession.

Habitats at the park include Hemlock and mixed oak forest with an understory of red maple, hickory, and ash. Fowler's Hollow is a good trailhead for hiking in the Tuscarora State Forest.

The park's management plan inventory of birds includes 55 species. Look for Whip-poor-will, Eastern Wood-Pewee, Black-throated Blue Warbler, and Yellow-breasted Chat.

The address is Fowler's Hollow State Park, c/o Col. Denning State Park, 1599 Doubling Gap Road, Newville, PA 17241, (717) 776-5272.

Big Spring State Park

Big Spring State Park is a 45-acre state park in the Tuscarora State Forest. To reach the park, take the Pennsylvania Turnpike, I-76, to Exit 14. From there, drive north on SR 75 about 12 miles to a "Y" intersection with SR 274. Take the right arm of the "Y", SR 274, to the park.

Sherman Creek runs through the park. The big spring for which the park is named is the second largest spring in Pennsylvania. The park is the trailhead for the Iron Horse Trail and other trails in the Tuscarora State Forest.

Birds in the park are similar to those in nearby Col. Denning State Park.

The address is Big Spring State Park, c/o Col. Denning State Park, 1599 Doubling Gap Road, Newville, PA 17241, (717) 776-5272.

LITTLE BUFFALO STATE PARK

Little Buffalo State Park is 830 acres of fields, forest, and an 88-acre lake in Perry County. To reach the park, take US 322 west from Harrisburg to the Newport exit. Then take SR 34 south through Newport to the park's access road on the right. Stop at the park office for a free map. A bird checklist is not available.

The park is open daily from 8 a.m. until sunset. Picnicking is permitted, and there is a food concession in the summer. The park also has a historic grist mill that is operated during warm weather (check at the visitors' center for a schedule). A covered bridge and historic 18th century tavern are also of historic interest. About 300 acres of the park are open for hunting. Fishing, including ice fishing, is popular at Little Buffalo.

The park has about 7 miles of trails. A 1.5-mile self-guided interpretive trail begins near the visitors' center. The exercise trail below the breast of the dam is excellent for Eastern Bluebird. An occasional Bald Eagle is seen in the park, which is 12 miles from the hacking towers on the Susquehanna River. In spring, Osprey is seen, and in fall grebes, coots, and Redhead and Ring-necked Duck migrate through the park along with other waterfowl. Turkeys are common in winter.

The address is Little Buffalo State Park, RD 2, Box 256, Newport, PA 17074, (717) 567-9255.

Swatara State Park

Swatara State Park is an undeveloped park of 3,451 acres in Schuykill and Lebanon counties. The park is located at Swatara Gap, between Second and Blue Mountains. A "Pennsylvania Trail of Geology" brochure interprets the landscape of the area and provides details about the Swatara Gap Fossil Site, located along SR 72 where I-81 crosses Swatara Creek.

To reach the park, exit I-81 at SR 443. Drive south on SR 443, the western boundary of the park.

The management plan for Swatara lists 143 species. Please forward copies of your lists to the park office. As plans are made for developing the park, such information may prove very useful.

The address is Swatara State Park, c/o Gifford Pinchot State Park, 2200 Rosstown Road, Lewisberry, PA 17339, (717) 432-5011.

Second Mountain Hawk Watch

Second Mountain Hawk Watch is located at Fort Indiantown Gap Military Reservation in Lebanon County. An organized hawk watch has been conducted here since 1984. The count in 1992 was just more than 10,900 birds.

To reach the site, take I-81 to Exit 29 (Fort Indiantown Gap). At approximately one-quarter mile, you will see a yellow-and-black "Second Mountain Hawk Watch" sign. Follow the directions to the summit. **Warning:** It is very important to follow the signs to the lookout. Fighter pilots and other military personnel on maneuvers have to wait until birders who wander from the approved route are escorted out of the way by military police. This can be expensive at best and dangerous at worst.

The hawk watch itself is 1.5 acres of mountaintop deciduous forest. Plans are in the works to construct a visitors' center here with exhibits and information about hawk identification.

Hawk flights are typical for the region. In recent years, Gyrfalcon and Swainson's Hawk have been observed (very rare). Most common are Broad-winged Hawk in September and Sharp-shinned and Red-tailed in October. (See Table 5.1, page 119.)

For more information, contact Second Mountain Hawk Watch, c/o Morris Cox, RD 1, Lot 2, Annville, PA 17003.

BUCHANAN STATE FOREST

The Buchanan State Forest is named in honor of James Buchanan, the only Pennsylvanian ever to serve as president of the United States. The area has five main tracts in Franklin, Fulton, and Bedford counties, and covers 70,386 acres. A free map of the forest is available from the district headquarters. The habitat of the Buchanan Forest is primarily oak forest.

The Tuscarora Trail and many local trails go through the forest. Picnic areas are designated for day-use only, from 8 a.m. to sunset, but the remainder of the forest is unrestricted. Areas of special interest to birders are the Cowan's Gap and Buchanan's Birthplace State Parks and the following natural and wild areas: Sweet Root Natural Area, Pine Ridge Natural Area, Martin Hill Wild Area, and Redbud Valley Nature Center. The Sidling Hill area was used as a CCC camp during the Great Depression and as a quarters for conscientious objectors during World War II.

Sweet Root Natural Area

This site is located near Chaneysville in southern Bedford County. To reach the site, take US 30 east from Bedford to SR 326. Turn right onto SR 326 and drive toward Chaneysville. Just north of Chaneysville, there is a sign and parking lot for Sweet Root.

A marked trail leads to one of only 13 pockets of virgin timber found in the early twentieth century when foresters surveyed the Commonwealth. It has been protected since 1921. The area has trees up to three feet in diameter. The endangered Eastern Wood Rat is found in dry, rocky outcroppings at the mountain tops. Look for birds normally found in deep woods and isolated places.

Cowan's Gap State Park

Cowan's Gap State Park is 1,085 acres of mixed hardwood forest, wetlands, and a small lake fed by Little Aughwick Creek. The park is located in Franklin County, about 14 miles from the Pennsylvania Turnpike's Exit 14. At that exit, take SR 75 south to Richmond Road, turn right, and follow the signs to the park. The park office is on Aughwick Road near Cowan's Gap Lake. Stop there for a map and bird checklist.

The park is open daily from 8 a.m. to sunset. Its facilities include ten modern cabins, 260 campsites with modern comfort stations, and numerous picnic tables. A food concession is operated during the summer. A nature center, also open during the summer, features historic and natural history exhibits. Various programs and escorted hikes are offered. Check at the center for a schedule.

Cowan's Gap has 10 miles of hiking trails. A portion of the Lakeside Trail is accessible to wheelchairs. The Twin Springs Trail is a self-guided nature trail. The 105-mile Tuscarora Trail passes through the park.

About half of the park is open to hunting, but the area around the shore is restricted. A bird feeding station is operated near parking lot number 3, on the south side of the lake.

Birds observed in the park include Common Loon, Horned Grebe, Pied-billed Grebe, Double-crested Cormorant (rare), and Tundra Swan during spring and fall migration. In early April look for Ring-necked Duck, White-winged Scoter, Oldsquaw, Bufflehead, and Red-breasted Merganser. Yellow-crowned Night-Herons have been seen in summer. Both Turkey and Black Vultures are summer residents in this area. Many raptors have been recorded during fall migration.

Spotted Sandpipers have been seen in spring, usually in mid-May. An American Avocet was photographed here after a hurricane in September 1971. Both Yellow-billed and Black-billed Cuckoos are summer residents. Yellow-bellied Sapsucker is a spring and fall migrant, while Red-bellied Woodpecker is a year-round resident. Great Crested and Acadian Flycatchers are summer residents, as is Eastern Wood-Pewee.

Common Ravens are year-round residents. Brown Creeper and Red-breasted Nuthatches are migrants. Blue-gray Gnatcather is a summer resident, as is Yellow-throated Vireo. Twenty-three warbler species have been recorded, most during migration. Resident warblers include Black-and-white Warbler, Worm-eating Warbler, Ovenbird, Louisiana Waterthrush, Common Yellowthroat, and American Redstart.

Scarlet Tanager is a summer resident, as is Rose-breasted Grosbeak. Common Redpoll and Pine Siskin occasionally visit in winter.

The park's address is Cowan's Gap State Park, HC 17266, Fort Loudon, PA 17223-9801, (717) 485-3948.

Buchanan's Birthplace State Park

Buchanan's Birthplace State Park is 18.5 acres of mixed hardwoods and white pine along a mountain stream. The park is located in Franklin County near Cove Gap. To reach the park, take US 30 to Fort Loudon. From there, take SR 75 south to SR 16, turn right onto SR 16 and follow the signs to the park.

Buchanan's Birthplace features a large pyramid monument to President James Buchanan, picnic facilities, and restrooms. Free park maps are available at the park and at nearby Cowan's Gap State Park. With the exception of waterfowl and shorebirds, birds are similar to those found at nearby Cowan's Gap State Park.

The park's address is Buchanan's Birthplace State Park, c/o Cowan's Gap State Park, HC 17266, Fort Loudon, PA 17224, (717) 485-3948.

Tuscarora Summit, or The Pulpit

Tuscarora Summit, also known as The Pulpit, is a good location for fall raptor migration. An organized count has been conducted daily during migration for 20 years. To reach the area, located in Fulton County, take US 30 west from Chambersburg to the summit of Tuscarora Mountain, about 25 miles. At the summit there is an inn, where you will park. A marked path leads to the lookout.

Raptors recorded at The Pulpit include Black Vulture, Turkey Vulture, Osprey, Bald Eagle, Northern Harrier, Sharp-shinned Hawk, Cooper's Hawk, Northern Goshawk, Red-shouldered Hawk, Broad-

Northern Goshawk

winged Hawk, Red-tailed Hawk, Rough-legged Hawk, Golden Eagle, American Kestrel, Merlin, and Peregrine Falcon.

Flights are typical for the Ridge and Valley Province in Pennsylvania. Expect to see large numbers of Broadwings in September and Sharpies and Red-tails in October. In 1992, 5,207 raptors were observed at this site.

Pine Ridge Natural Area

This 568-acre tract about one mile southeast of Chaneysville on LR 2002 is Resettlement Lands, or small farms purchased by the federal government during the Depression to encourage families to resettle on more productive land. As a result, the area is characterized by abandoned fields and pastures reforested with pine plantations. Look for pine-loving species such as Northern Parula.

Martin Hill Wild Area

This 11,500-acre tract also is located in southern Bedford County south of Rainsburg on SR 326. Access to the heart of the area is by a road that requires four-wheel drive vehicles or by hiking in on one of the trails. This is one of the most wild areas in southern Pennsylvania. The area was harvested in the late 1800s but second-growth forests are nearly 100 years old, so the wilderness character of the tract is hospitable to wildlife including Bobcat, Black Bear, White-tailed Deer, and Wild Turkey.

Redbud Valley Nature Center

This 514-acre tract was purchased by Edmund Kerper, an attorney and naturalist, in 1934. Kerper's dream was to create a sanctuary for songbirds. He planted trees, flowers, and shrubs to attract wildlife to his property. In the 1970s, Youth Conservation Corps and other youth groups constructed trails, stream crossings, and outdoor learning stations here.

The address for the four previous sites is Buchanan State Forest, District Forester, RD 2, Box 3, McConnellsburg, PA 17233, (717) 485-3148.

DELAWARE WATER GAP NATIONAL RECREATION AREA

From just below where Cummins Creek enters the Delaware River, about 5 miles north of Milford, Pennsylvania, the Delaware Water Gap National Recreation Area extends south along both the Pennsyl-

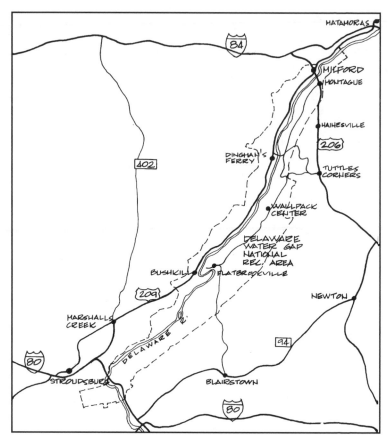

Delaware Water Gap National Recreation Area

vania and New Jersey shores of the river to the Delaware Water Gap south of East Stroudsburg.

Visitors' centers for the area are located in New Jersey at Kittatinny Point, just off I-80 at Exit 53, and in Pennsylvania at Dingman's Falls, just off SR 209. Stop at one of these centers to pick up a free map and bird checklist of 263 species.

Migration is especially exciting in this area. The Delaware Valley is a corridor for numerous species. Warblers are the highlight of late April and early May; 37 species have been recorded. Warblers that stay in the area for the summer include Blue-winged, Golden-winged, Brewster's, Lawrence's, and Nashville Warblers; Northern Parula; Yellow, Chestnut-sided, Magnolia, Black-throated Blue, Black-throated Green, Blackburnian, Pine, Prairie, Cerulean, and Black-and-white Warblers; American Redstart; Prothonotary and Worm-eating Warblers; Ovenbird; Northern and Louisiana Waterthrushes; Kentucky Warbler; Common Yellowthroat; Hooded and Canada Warblers; and Yellow-breasted Chat.

A canoe trip down the river in summer may yield Pied-billed Grebe, American Bittern, Great Blue Heron, Great Egret, Snowy Egret, Green-backed Heron, Mute Swan, Wood Duck, American Black Duck, Hooded Merganser, or Common Merganser. Numerous outfitters rent canoes.

From August to November, hawks and other raptors can be seen. In winter, visitors from the north include Snow Goose, Common Goldeneye, Bufflehead, Horned Lark, Gold-crowned and Ruby-crowned Kinglets, American Tree Sparrow, Fox Sparrow, Snow Bunting, Common Redpoll, and Evening Grosbeak. Less common but worth looking for are Lapland Longspur, Rusty Blackbird, Pine Grosbeak, Red Crossbill, and White-winged Crossbill.

The Delaware River is one of few places in the East where Bald Eagles spend the winter. The National Park Service recommends taking River Road north from Shawnee. Stop at Smithfield Beach and the Dingman's Ferry Bridge to look for eagles. The stretch of river between Poxono Island and Depew Island is particularly good.

The nearby Lacawaxan River is another good place for eagles. To reach the river, take SR 6 west from Milford to LR 1003. Turn right on LR 1003 and drive toward Rowland. At the intersection with SR 590, turn right and drive along the river, being careful to pull completely off the road when looking for eagles.

The address is Delaware Water Gap National Recreation Area, Bushkill, PA 18324. A tape-recorded message provides reports on weather and river conditions: (914) 252-7100.

Pocono Environmental Education Center

Pocono Environmental Education Center (PEEC) is located between Stroudsburg and Milford on SR 209 in the Delaware Water

Gap National Recreation Area. PEEC, formerly a honeymoon resort, is a 38-acre residential center that offers workshops for teachers, families, individuals, and groups. Many of PEEC's workshops are approved for in-service credits for teachers in Pennsylvania and other states. Registration fees are very reasonable and include lodging, meals, and programming. For example, a three-day birding weekend scheduled for April 1993 cost $79.

The center is the largest facility of its kind in the Western Hemisphere. PEEC also offers field trips for schoolchildren. The campus is surrounded by 200,000 acres of public lands.

Many of PEEC's workshops feature birds, and several are devoted entirely to birding. For example, "In Search of Eagles" is a weekend devoted to censusing wintering Bald Eagles on the Delaware River. "Warbler Weekends" are held in the spring; daytime walks are complemented by evening programs. "Hawk Watch Weekends" were scheduled in September, October, and November in 1993. A weeklong "Field Ornithology Workshop" also was held in 1993. Special programs for beginners and experienced birders are available. Write to PEEC for a brochure, "Bird Watching Weekends."

The highlight of the birding year at PEEC is the spring warbler migration in late April and early May. Thirty-seven warbler species have been recorded. In the fall, raptors are common migrants. Wintering Bald Eagles are joined by Common Merganser, Common Goldeneye, Rough-legged Hawk, Red-breasted Nuthatch, and Fox Sparrow.

Memberships in "Friends of PEEC" are available. Members receive a discount at the center's bookstore/gift shop, invitations to special events, and a quarterly newsletter.

The address is Pocono Environmental Education Center, RD 2, Box 1010, Dingman's Ferry, PA 18328, (717) 828-2319.

Delaware Valley Raptor Center

Delaware Valley Raptor Center (DVRC) is a private, nonprofit organization dedicated to protecting birds of prey. DVRC owns a 1600-acre sanctuary open to members only. However, membership dues are modest, and new members are always welcome. In addition to admission to the sanctuary, members receive a very informative journal twice a year, and invitations to a summer picnic and a fall hawk-watch field trip.

Most importantly, DVRC operates a raptor rehabilitation center. The center received 82 raptors for treatment in the 1992 season. Of those, 43% were returned to the wild. Birds too severely injured to be returned to the wild are used in educational programs for children. Tours of the facility are available to members by appointment.

Habitats at the property are diverse: lake, wetlands, mixed hardwood/evergreen forests, pine stands, and open fields. Birds recorded at the sanctuary in spring include migrant waterfowl, along with an occasional Common Loon and Osprey. Great Horned and Barred Owls have been observed. Many warblers migrate through the site.

In summer, most northeastern passerines can be observed. Eastern Bluebird breeds, as does Wild Turkey and waterfowl. Bald Eagles nest not far from DVRC.

In fall, raptors migrate on the nearby Kittatinny Flyway. Bald Eagles winter in the area.

The address is Delaware Valley Raptor Center, RD 2, Box 9335, Milford, PA 18337, (717) 296-6025.

Kettle Creek Wildlife Sanctuary

Kettle Creek Wildlife Sanctuary is owned by the Monroe County Conservation District and is located 1.5 miles south of Bartonsville. The 120-acre sanctuary is the home of the Monroe County Environmental Education Center. To reach the sanctuary, take I-80 to Exit 46B, and take SR 611 northwest to the traffic light in Bartonsville. Follow Rimrock Drive for about 0.4 mile and turn right onto North Easton-Belmont Pike. Drive 0.2 mile, and bear right onto Running Valley Road. The sanctuary is 0.7 mile from the intersection.

Habitats at the sanctuary include mature deciduous forest, evergreen forest, a pond, early successional forests, old fields, and mowed fields. There are 1.5 miles of trails; a 0.25-mile wheelchair-accessible trail is nearing completion. Picnics are permitted, but there is no food concession. Free maps are available, but there is no bird checklist for the site. The center does have a resource library, an observation deck, and a backyard wildlife feeding area. The building is open from 8:30 a.m. to 4:30 p.m., Monday to Friday, and 9 a.m. to 4 p.m. on Saturdays.

The environmental education center offers year-round environmental education programs, including bird walks, for all ages. Exhibits include hands-on displays that explain the local environment. A quarterly newsletter is published for members, who also receive discounts on programs and in the gift shop/bookstore.

Naturalists from the environmental education center also provide interpretive tours of The Nature Conservancy's nearby Tannersville Bog (see next listing). Access to the bog is limited; birders must contact the center to arrange for visits.

Because of its location on the Delaware Flyway, the sanctuary is a good place to visit during migration. Breeding birds include Red-tailed Hawk, Pileated Woodpecker, Eastern Bluebird, Blue-winged Warbler, and Prairie Warbler. Winter birds include Red-tailed Hawk, Great Horned Owl, Downy and Red-bellied Woodpeckers, Black-capped Chickadee, Tufted Titmouse, White-breasted Nuthatch, and kinglets. Bald Eagles have been recorded in November.

The address is Monroe County Environmental Education Center, 8050 Running Valley Road, Stroudsburg, PA 18360, (717) 629-3061.

Tannersville Bog

Access to this site is limited. For information about the bog or to schedule a tour, contact the Monroe County Environmental Education Center, 8050 Running Valley Road, Stroudsburg, PA 18360, (717) 629-3061.

Meesing Site

The Meesing Site is a 100-acre tract located in the Delaware State Forest north of Marshall Creek. It is owned by the Pennsylvania Bureau of Forestry and maintained by the Monroe County Conservation District. The site is a large clear cut where a young forest is emerging, a stand of pines, a small swamp, a stream, and a pond. Four miles of trails are open to the public from dawn to dusk.

To reach the site, take I-80 to Exit 52, then take SR 209 north to Marshall's Creek. Turn left at the general store, and bear left at the firehouse. Follow Marshall's Creek Road for about 5.5 miles. The site is on the right as you enter the Delaware State Forest.

The address is Meesing Site, Delaware State Forest, c/o Monroe County Environmental Education Center, 8050 Running Valley Road, Stroudsburg, PA 18360, (717) 629-3061.

SOUTH MOUNTAIN

The South Mountain area is the finger-shaped prong of the Appalachians that is geophysically part of the Ridge and Valley Province, but juts into the Piedmont Region of Pennsylvania. It is located east of I-81 and west of US 15 in Franklin, Adams, and Cumberland counties.

Michaux State Forest

Michaux State Forest is 85,000 acres of mature or post-mature forests. Most of the area was timbered in the late 19th century. Recent harvesting has been irregularly spaced throughout the forest; the result is many areas where the forest is between one and 25 years old. There are a few conifer plantations, including one of the oldest in Pennsylvania, planted in 1902.

Most of the forest is uplands. The few patches of wetlands are widely spaced. There are several municipal reservoirs, ranging in size from a few acres to 150 acres, and many small headwater streams. Free maps are available from the district forest office.

There are three state parks in the Michaux State Forest: Mont Alto, Caledonia, and Pine Grove Furnace. The King's Gap Environmental Education Center is located at the northern edge of the forest.

The address is Michaux State Forest, District Forester, 10099 Lincoln Way East, Fayetteville, PA 17222-9609, (717) 352-2211 or 352-2260.

Mont Alto State Park is a tiny park (24 acres) located in the Michaux State Forest. Located in Franklin County, the park is reached by driving south from Caledonia State Park 7.5 miles on PA 233. Free maps of the park are available at the Caledonia State Park office.

Mont Alto is open daily, year-round from dawn to dusk. Facilities are limited to restrooms and picnic tables and pavilions. **Warning:** Local dirt roads through Michaux State Forest are used by both snowmobiles and cars in winter.

The West Branch of Antietam Creek runs through the park. Birds in Mont Alto are similar to Caledonia State Park.

The address is Mont Alto State Park, c/o Caledonia State Park, 40 Rocky Mountain Road, Fayetteville, PA 17222, (717) 352-2161.

Caledonia State Park is located in Franklin County. The park, one of Pennsylvania's oldest, is 1,230 acres of hardwood forests on Chinquapin Hill, an evergreen forest along Conococheague Creek, and the open grass area of an 18-hole golf course. Caledonia State Park is located on the Blue Ridge, known locally as South Mountain. The park was the site of an iron furnace in the early 19th century. During the battle of Gettysburg, Confederate troops used pastures in the area for field hospitals.

To reach the park, travel 13 miles west of Gettysburg on US 30, or drive 10 miles east of Chambersburg, also on US 30. Stop at the park office for a free map and bird checklist with 117 species and 3 accidentals.

The park is open daily from dawn to dusk and has 185 campsites, an organized-group camping area, a swimming pool, snack bar, picnic areas, and environmental education programs during the summer. Hunting is not permitted in the park, so this is a good place to visit during hunting season. The park also has a summer stock theater, the Totem Pole Playhouse.

There are about 10 miles of hiking trails in Caledonia. The Appalachian Trail passes through the park, and the Whispering Pine Nature Trail is a self-guided interpretive trail.

Caledonia State Park is near a large vulture roost. It is not uncommon to see 50 to 60 Turkey Vultures and smaller numbers of Black Vultures soaring above the park. Breeding birds include Broad-winged Hawk, Eastern Screech-Owl, Barred Owl, Whip-poor-will, Belted Kingfisher, Pileated Woodpecker, Black-capped and Carolina Chickadee, Brown Creeper, Blue-gray Gnatcatcher, Veery, Swainson's Thrush, Wood Thrush, Northern Parula, Yellow Warbler, Chestnut-sided Warbler, Yellow-Rumped Warbler, Black-throated Green Warbler, Pine Warbler, Ovenbird, Louisiana Waterthrush, Common Yellowthroat, Hooded Warbler, Scarlet Tanager, Indigo Bunting, Rufous-sided Towhee, and Bobolink.

Fish Crows have been observed in the park in all seasons. In spring migration, 26 warbler species have been recorded. Both Orchard and Northern Oriole have been recorded in summer.

The address is Caledonia State Park, 40 Rocky Mountain Road, Fayetteville, PA 17222, (717) 352-2161.

Pine Grove Furnace State Park is 696 acres of deciduous forest, two lakes (Laurel Lake is 25 acres, and Fuller Lake is 1.7 acres), and forested wetlands in Cumberland County. The site was an iron furnace from 1764 until the mid-1800s. A self-guided interpretive trail passes through the historic sites in the park. Pine Grove Furnace is surrounded by more than 80,000 acres of oak, pine, and hemlock in the Michaux State Forest.

To reach Pine Grove Furnace, take Exit 11 from I-81 and drive south on SR 233 for 8 miles to the park headquarters where you can pick up a free map.

The park is open seven days a weeks during daylight hours. There are 74 tent/trailer campsites and a youth hostel at the Ironmaster's Mansion. A camp store is operated during the summer months.

The halfway point of the Appalachian Trail is located at Pine Grove Furnace. Other trails located in the park provide access to several habitats: Creek Trail winds along Mountain Creek; Swamp Trail circles around a small forested swamp; and Koppenhaver Trail passes through mature pines and hemlocks. The Cumberland County Hiker-Biker Trail is accessible to wheelchairs.

A visitors' center provides nature and history walks, talks, evening shows, and demonstrations. Exhibits feature animals, geology, local history, and recycling. A breeding bird survey is conducted in the park.

Spring birds observed at Pine Grove Furnace include migrant Bald Eagle sighted at Laurel Lake. American Woodcock are regularly observed. Wood Duck use boxes placed in the park by the Pennsylvania Game Commission. Whip-poor-will can be heard late at night during the summer. In fall, small flocks of migrating waterfowl stop at the park's lakes. Regular visitors to the park's feeders in winter include Pileated Woodpeckers and Red-breasted Nuthatches.

In recent years, Black-crowned Night-Heron have been dispersing from the Huntsdale Fish Hatchery nearby, where they encounter net barriers.

The address is Pine Grove Furnace State Park, RD 2, Box 399B, Gardners, PA 17324, (717) 486-7174.

King's Gap Environmental Education and Training Center is 1,443 acres of mostly mixed deciduous forest, pine plantation, and small pond in Cumberland County. The center is located at the northern end of Michaux State Forest.

To reach King's Gap from I-81, take Exit 11 onto SR 233. Drive south on SR 233. Cross SR 174, a small creek, and then railroad tracks. At the next intersection, turn left onto Pine Road. About 2.5 miles ahead is the entrance to the center. You may want to explore the pine plantation at the entrance before driving to the top of the mountain, where you will see the headquarters, a stone mansion.

The pine plantation includes White Pine, Douglas Fir, and Tamarack. A quarter-mile self-guided trail circles the plantation; this trail is paved and accessible to wheelchairs. Signs are in both script and braille. There are an observation blind and feeding station in the plantation. Look for pine species such as Golden-crowned Kinglet and Pine Warbler.

At a "Y" in the road, veer to the right and park at the pond use area. This area's White Oaks Trail is one-quarter mile and paved, thus accessible to wheelchairs. It also has interpretive signs in script and braille. The Watershed Trail leads from this area to a small pond where you may see Green-backed Heron or Spotted Sandpiper.

Parking is just beyond the mansion. Pick up a free map of the site here. King's Gap allows picnics, but there is no food concession, and there are no picnic tables at the site. There are 15 miles of trails at the center.

King's Gap offers a wide variety of programs for students from preschool to college, teachers, and the general public. A free schedule of programs open to the public is published twice a year.

King's Gap has a bluebird trail, and Eastern Bluebird is easily found year-round. Spring birds at the center include owls and many migrant warblers. Summer breeding species include owls, various woodpeckers (including Pileated), Great Crested Flycatcher, Veery, and Scarlet Tanager.

The address is King's Gap Environmental Education and Training Center, 500 King's Gap Road, Carlisle, PA 17013, (717) 486-5031.

Chapter 6
Piedmont

 The Piedmont, a gently rolling area, extends from western Philadelphia near US 1 to the Ridge and Valley Province, which begins at Blue Mountain. South Mountain, a small area of the Ridge and Valley Province, intrudes into the Piedmont in Adams and Franklin counties. The Piedmont comprises about 10% of Pennsylvania and is narrower here than in the southern states. The elevation of the region ranges from 60 to 1,100 feet. The average annual temperature of the region is 50° Fahrenheit, with a January average of 28° and a July average of 74°. Average extreme temperatures range from a low of 20° in January to a high of 94° in July. The average annual precipitation ranges from 40 to 44 inches, with more precipitation in the eastern section of the region than in the west. Snowfall averages 30 inches per year.

Much of the Piedmont in Pennsylvania is devoted to intensive agriculture, but urbanization is encroaching from the southeast. This is the least forested region of Pennsylvania.

Year-round residents abundant in the Piedmont include Canada Goose, American Kestrel, Mourning Dove, Red-bellied Woodpecker, Downy Woodpecker, Carolina Chickadee, Tufted Titmouse, Northern Mockingbird, Northern Cardinal, House Finch, and House Sparrow. Abundant winter residents are Ring-billed Gull and Dark-eyed Junco.

Abundant breeding birds include Barn Swallow, Blue Jay, Wood Thrush, Red-eyed Vireo, Ovenbird, and Field Sparrow. The American Black Duck is abundant during spring and fall migration, while the Herring Gull is commonly seen in the fall.

Several southern species reach the northern edges of their ranges in this region: Cattle Egret, Carolina Chickadee, and Blue Grosbeak. In addition, the area is good for rarities blown inland after hurricanes or major northeastern storms: Royal Tern, Dovekie, and Common Ground Dove are the most unusual.

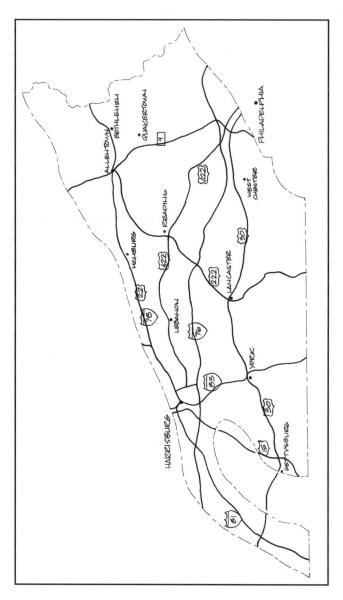

Piedmont

Check fallow fields and meadows in this region for Upland Sandpiper (rare), Savannah and Grasshopper Sparrows, Bobolink, and
Eastern Meadowlark. Dickcissel were seen in this region in 1988 during a severe summer drought.

The rare bird alert for eastern Pennsylvania covers this region; call
(215) 567-2473.

HARRISBURG

Harrisburg is the capital of Pennsylvania and the county seat of
Dauphin County. Its population is 52,376. In addition to state and
county officials and bureaucrats, the city is home to employees of

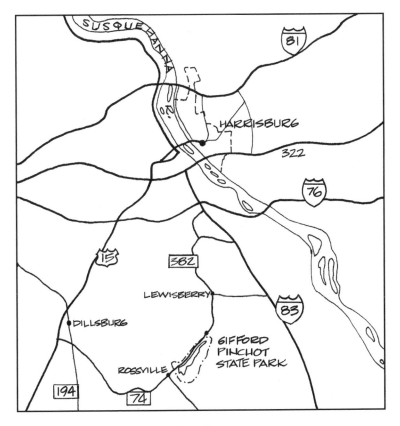

Harrisburg

both service and manufacturing companies. Its location at the crossroads of I-81, I-83, and the Pennsylvania Turnpike makes the hospitality industry important.

The State Museum of Pennsylvania, located near the Capitol Complex, has outstanding displays both of Pennsylvania history and antiques, and natural and earth science. Another museum of interest, especially to children, is the Museum of Scientific Discovery, located in the Strawberry Square Mall directly opposite the state capitol. It features hands-on exhibits. Admission is charged.

The city is a good base for birding trips to the state parks of the Piedmont (Gifford Pinchot, Codorus, and Samuel Lewis) as well as the adjacent Ridge and Valley Province (King's Gap, Pine Grove Furnace, Memorial Lake, Swatara, Little Buffalo, and Colonel Denning).

Wildwood Lake Nature Center

Owned by Dauphin County, Wildwood Lake is 230 acres of wetlands, open water, and upland forest. Access to the site is from Industrial Road. From Harrisburg, take US 22/322 north to Linglestown Road, turn left toward Rockville, and take the first left onto Industrial Road.

Wildwood is an excellent example of an urban wetland. It was originally constructed as a flood control impoundment but has been allowed to revert to a "wild" state.

The park is open daily from dawn to dusk, and picnics are permitted. The East Shore Trail, Tow Path Trail, and Macadam Bike/Hike Trail are accessible to wheelchairs. The park plans to build an observation blind, nature center, and exhibits. Members of Friends of Wildwood Nature Center receive a newsletter and discounts on special events. Public and school programs are offered throughout the year. The park is included in the Harrisburg Christmas Bird Count.

The park has an extensive tract of the endangered American Lotus, and the flower is the subject of a research project conducted at the park.

In spring, Great Egret, American Bittern, and migrating waterfowl and songbirds have been recorded. Canada Goose, Wood Duck, and American Black Duck nest at the park, which is also a loafing area for egrets and herons from a rookery on the Susquehanna River, one-half mile away. Marsh Wren has been recorded.

In winter look for Great Blue Heron, Green-winged and Blue-winged Teal, Common Snipe, Great Horned Owl, Eastern Screech-Owl, Yellow-rumped Warbler, and Swamp Sparrow.

The park's address is Wildwood Lake Nature Center, P.O. Box 1295, Harrisburg, PA 17108, (717) 255-1369.

SUSQUEHANNA RIVER

Almost any area along the Susquehanna is good for migratory waterfowl. A scope is useful for river birding. In winter, check the warm-water area below the Peach Bottom Nuclear Power Plant for Bald Eagles. From York, take SR 74 southeast to LR 2024, also known as Paper Mill Road, about 25 miles. Another good spot, on the eastern shore of the river, for winter eagles is the discharge from the Muddy Run Power Plant. The overlook on the scenic trail at Susquehannock State Park provides a good view of this area. (See listing later in this chapter.)

Both Lancaster and York counties have published brochures, maps, and other information that are useful for planning a trip to the lower Susquehanna. "An Access Guide to the Lower Susquehanna River" is a brochure intended for anglers. It includes a map showing 17 access sites that also would be good for birding. Most have restrooms and picnic areas. Contact the Lancaster County Department of Parks and Recreation, 1050 Rockford Road, Lancaster, PA 17602, (717) 299-8215. The address for York County is York County Board of Parks and Recreation, 400 Mundis Race Road, York, PA 17402, (717) 771-9440.

Safety note: Each of the dams along the lower Susquehanna has warning systems such as flashing lights and warning sirens to alert hikers, anglers, and others along the shore or on the river that water is about to be released. Be aware that these releases cause quickly changing water levels or turbulence in the river. For your safety, take the time to read notices regarding the warning systems in place at sites you visit and follow the instructions given.

Riverfront Park

Riverfront Park extends for 5 miles along the east shore of the Susquehanna River in the city of Harrisburg. It's a good place to view waterfowl, especially during migration. The park is an easy walk from most points downtown, or you can drive to Front Street and try to find a parking place.

West Fairview Boat Launch

West Fairview Boat Launch, at the mouth of Conodoguinet Creek, is owned by the Pennsylvania Fish and Boat Commission. A local birder says that in spring it is "good for about any bird that swims." To reach the launch, located on the west shore of the Susquehanna across from Harrisburg, follow SR 22 across the river and turn north onto US 11/15. After entering the town of West Fairview, take the first right, then two more rights to reach the boat launch.

The area has no facilities besides parking and a short trail along the Conodoguinet Creek. It is included in the Harrisburg Christmas Bird Count. Besides the spring waterfowl seen during migration, Black Tern occasionally are seen. In summer, Yellow-crowned Night-Heron fly over this area, and Hooded Merganser is a rare but confirmed breeder. Shorebirds can be seen during fall migration when the river level is low. In winter look for American Wigeon, Bufflehead, Hooded Merganser, American Coot, and Ring-billed Gull.

The address of the Pennsylvania Fish and Boat Commission is 3542 Walnut Street, Harrisburg, PA 17105-1673, (717) 657-4542.

Washington Boro

Washington Boro, on the east shore of the Susquehanna is a good spot for viewing a major resting area used by thousands of Tundra Swan in late February and early March. They apparently like the shelter provided by wooded islands offshore.

To reach the site, take US 30 to the Columbia exit. Drive south on SR 441, about 5 miles. At the intersection with PA 999, there is a small parking lot on the shore. Be careful to watch for trains on the railroad tracks.

The island to the left is Rookery Island and on the right, Green Island. Formerly nesting places for herons and egrets, these islands are strictly protected from disturbance during the breeding season.

When water levels fluctuate because of Safe Harbor Dam (downstream), mudflats are exposed between the islands. Known as the Conejohela Flats, these are excellent for shorebirds, especially during migration.

SHIPPENSBURG

Shippensburg, population 4,328, is the home of Shippensburg State University. A local hot spot for birding is Mud Level Road, northeast of Shippensburg. To reach Mud Level Road, take SR 696 north about 2 miles and turn right onto LR 4002 (shown on older maps as TR 305). The best birding is about 2 to 3 miles east of this intersection.

The area is mostly flat farmland, with the major crops being corn and alfalfa. Because this is private property, bird from the car only. The area is included in the Newville Christmas Bird Count.

Spring migrants include Upland Sandpiper (rare), American Pipit, and Bobolink. In summer, Northern Harrier, Upland Sandpiper, Barn Owl, Purple Martin, Vesper Sparrow, Savannah Sparrow, and Grasshopper Sparrow all breed. Dickcissel is a possible nesting species; the species became widespread in Pennsylvania in 1988 when a drought caused midwestern birds to move into the East.

Rare fall migrants have included Black-bellied Plover and Lesser Golden-Plover. More common is American Pipit. In winter, Northern Harrier, Rough-legged Hawk, Short-eared Owl, and Snow Bunting have been observed. Rare winter visitors are Snowy Owl (recorded in January 1988 and December 1991), Lapland Longspur, and Common Redpoll (1987).

Year-round, look for Red-tailed Hawk, American Kestrel, Ring-necked Pheasant, Northern Bobwhite, Killdeer, Red-headed Woodpecker, Horned Lark, and Eastern Meadowlark.

YORK

York, population 42,192, served as the capital of the United States from September 30, 1777, to June 27, 1778, while the British occupied Philadelphia. While stationed in York, Congress adopted the Articles of Confederation. Today, York is the county seat of York County and is known for its farmers' markets and factory outlets.

The area around York is intensively farmed; in winter drive down any country road and look for freshly manured fields to find flocks of Horned Lark (common), Lapland Longspur (uncommon), or Snow Bunting (uncommon). On lucky winter days, birders will see a Rough-legged Hawk.

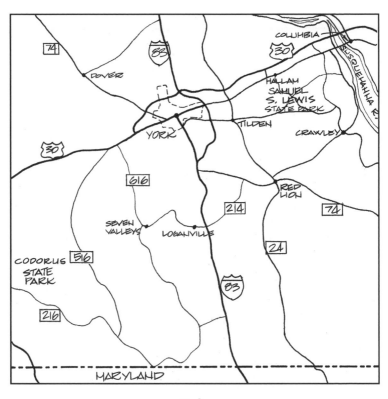

York

Codorus State Park

Located in the southwest corner of York County, Codorus State Park is 3,326 acres of mixed hardwoods, pines, old fields reverting to woodland, marshlands, and mudflats. The park also includes 1,275-acre Lake Marburg.

To reach Codorus, drive south from York on US 30 to a "Y" intersection with SR 116. Go toward the left on SR 116 and continue 11 miles to the intersection with SR 216. Take SR 216 southeast to the park. At the park office, on SR 216, pick up a free map.

The park, open daily from 8 a.m. to dusk, offers family and organized group camping, hunting, fishing, boating, and swimming in a pool. A naturalist provides environmental education programs during the summer months. Check at the park office for a schedule. Picnicking is permitted; there is a food concession near the pool. Codorus has a 5-mile hiking trail system, including a short stretch near the camping area that is accessible to wheelchairs. This section of trail is very good for birding because several habitats come together here: a small marsh, open meadow, and wood lot bordered by a shrubby overgrown field.

Lake Marburg attracts a variety of waterfowl during spring and fall migration. The best areas to view waterfowl are the marina and the Marburg Flats boat launch on Smith Station Road (turn left just past the park office). Although the park does not have a bird checklist, management plan records list Tundra Swan; Mute Swan; Canada Goose; Wood Duck; Green-winged Teal; American Black Duck; Blue-winged Teal; Northern Shoveler; Canvasback; Redhead; Ring-necked Duck; Bufflehead; and Hooded, Common, and Red-breasted Mergansers among the many species recorded at Codorus.

The park, especially the Blackrock Flats and Marburg Flats areas, is good for shorebirds, especially when water levels are low in the lake and wide mudflats are exposed. Look for Solitary, Spotted, Semipalmated, Least, and White-rumped Sandpipers. Rarities recorded at the park include Red-necked Phalarope and the state's first Ross' Gull in October 1991.

Ring-billed Gulls are present year-round and often are joined by Herring Gulls. Franklin's and Bonaparte's Gulls occasionally visit the park. Caspian and Forster's Terns blow in before, during, or after storms.

The Maryann Furnace Trail and Lahoe Trail are good for warbler migration in the spring. Local birders report that they avoid the Bridal Trail and Cross Country Skiing Area in spring, summer, and early fall because of large numbers of ticks.

The park has a bluebird trail with 200 boxes. Tours of the trail can be arranged by contacting Karen Lippy, 432 Penn Street, Hanover, PA 17331, (717) 637-9347.

The park's address is Codorus State Park, 1066 Blooming Grove Road, Hanover, PA 17331-9545, (717) 637-2816.

Long Arm Creek Reservoir

Long Arm Creek Reservoir is a city reservoir for Hanover. It is located along Grand Valley Road about 2 miles south of Hanover. Take Westminster Avenue south from town until it becomes Grand Valley Road. The reservoir is on your right; there are several parking areas where you can stop to check for waterfowl. The lake is bordered on one side by pines (closed to the public) and on the other by grassy fields. Check these fields for Eastern Meadowlark, Savannah Sparrow, and Grasshopper Sparrow. Short-eared Owls have been seen in this area.

Hanover Impounding Reservoir

Hanover Impounding Reservoir is southeast of Long Arm Creek Reservoir. It is a smaller lake but offers good birding, especially for fall shorebirds. To reach this reservoir, back track from Long Arm Creek Reservoir to the first right-hand turn beyond the breast of the dam. The Impounding Reservoir is about 2 miles down Impounding Dam Road, known locally as St. Bartholomew Road.

Gettysburg

Gettysburg, best known for its battlefield, is southwest of York on US 30. The park can be extremely crowded, and a local birder reports

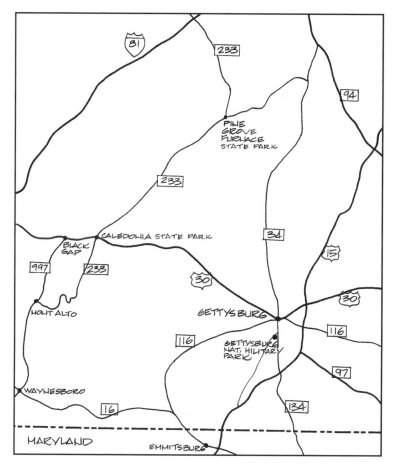

Gettysburg

that park officials discourage nature study on the battlefield. Still, if you want to visit the historic park, do not leave your binoculars behind. There are both Black and Turkey Vultures; hundreds of vultures roost at Devil's Den in winter. Other birds of interest include Red-headed and Pileated Woodpeckers, Great Horned Owl, and Eastern Bluebird.

The address is Gettysburg National Military Park, P.O. Box 1080, Taneytown Road, Gettysburg, PA 17325, (717) 334-1122.

Holtwood & Lake Aldred

Holtwood & Lake Aldred is an 8,000-acre recreation area owned by the Pennsylvania Power & Light Company (PP&L). The area includes 5,000 acres of land on both shores of the 3,000-acre Lake Aldred, which was created by two dams on the Susquehanna River.

A bird checklist with 145 species is free. One outstanding species is the Bald Eagle pair that nests just north of the Holtwood Dam. The area immediately around the nest site is a restricted zone patrolled by the Pennsylvania Game Commission. If you are caught in the zone, you will be fined. However, throughout the nesting season, PP&L offers guided trips to see the eagles. Call the naturalist at (717) 284-2278 to make arrangements. The largest holly tree north of the Mason-Dixon Line is located near the Indian Steps Museum.

Birds recorded at the site include nesting Osprey. Both Turkey and Black Vultures are very common; in fall and winter, roosts with hundreds of birds have been found. Depending on the water level below the spillway, numerous herons and gulls may be seen. In late summer, check for Double-crested Cormorant and White and Glossy Ibis. Sixteen shorebird species have been recorded. Long-eared, Short-eared, and Northern Saw-whet Owls have been observed in winter. There is a Cliff Swallow colony on the east side of the dam, and Northern Rough-winged Swallows nest near the Pequea Boat Ramp.

The Pinnacle Overlook, located at the end of Pinnacle Road near a narrow section of the river is excellent for both spring and fall raptor migrations. Gulls also are common at this area, especially in winter. Check the flocks of Great Black-backed, Herring, and Ring-billed Gulls for rarities such as Laughing, Franklin's, Lesser Black-backed, and Glaucous Gulls. Common, Forster's, Caspian, and Black Terns are uncommon or rare migrants.

The address is Holtwood Land Management Project, 9 New Village Road, Holtwood, PA 17532, (717) 284-2278.

Gifford Pinchot State Park

Located between Harrisburg and York, Gifford Pinchot State Park is 2,339 acres of woods, overgrown fields and Conewago Lake. To reach the park, take I-83 south from Harrisburg to Exit 15. Drive southwest on SR 177 about 6 miles to the park.

The park has 115 miles of hiking trails, 340 campsites, a summer snack bar, and facilities for picnicking. It is open from 8 a.m. to sunset daily. There is an observation blind at the Conewago Day-Use Area, and a nature center features "touch and feel" exhibits and posters. Campground programs are offered in the evening; pick up a schedule at the park office. The park is included in the York Christmas Bird Count. A free map and bird checklist are available. A brochure published by the Bureau of Topographic and Geologic Survey explains the geology of the park.

The park's bird checklist includes records from 1968 to 1990. A total of 212 species have been seen. Some examples are Red-throated Loon, Common Loon, Pied-billed Grebe, Horned Grebe, Red-necked Grebe, American Bittern, Great Blue Heron, Great Egret, Little Blue Heron, Green-backed Heron, Black-crowned Night-

Lesser Scaup

Heron, Tundra Swan, Snow Goose, Brant, Wood Duck, Green-winged Teal, American Black Duck, Northern Pintail, Blue-winged Teal, Northern Shoveler, Gadwall, American Wigeon, Canvasback, Redhead, Ring-necked Duck, Greater Scaup, Lesser Scaup, Old-squaw, Surf Scoter, White-winged Scoter, Common Goldeneye, Buf-flehead, Hooded Merganser, Common Merganser, Red-breasted Merganser, Ruddy Duck, Black Vulture, and Turkey Vulture.

The park is also a good place to look for migrating shorebirds: Semipalmated Plover, Greater Yellowlegs, Lesser Yellowlegs, Solitary Sandpiper, Spotted Sandpiper, Red Knot, Semipalmated Sandpiper, Least Sandpiper, Pectoral Sandpiper, Dunlin, Short-billed Dowitcher, and Common Snipe have been observed. Six vireo and 29 warbler species have been recorded.

The address is Gifford Pinchot State Park, 2200 Rosstown Road, Lewisberry, PA 17339, (717) 432-5011.

Samuel S. Lewis State Park

Samuel S. Lewis State Park is 71 acres of woodlands, open fields, and rocky ledges on Mount Pisgah, an 865-foot "mountain" in York County. To reach the park, take SR 462 northeast from York to SR 624 and turn right (south). A "Pennsylvania Trail of Geology" brochure describes the geology and topography of the area.

The address is Samuel S. Lewis State Park, c/o Gifford Pinchot State Park, 2200 Rosstown Road, Lewisberry, PA 17339, (717) 432-5011.

Rocky Ridge Park

Rocky Ridge is owned by York County and has been a sanctioned Hawk Migration Association of North America Hawk Watch since 1984. This site is the closest northern Appalachian hawk watch to Baltimore and Washington.

The park is located northeast of York. To reach it drive east from York on US 30 to the SR 24 exit. Drive north on SR 24, also known as Mount Zion Road, for about one mile to the park entrance. In the park, follow Deininger Road to a dead-end parking lot for the hawk watch. The hawk watch site is a scrubby area under a high-tension power line.

In addition to the hawk watch, the park has nine trails through a variety of habitats: mature mixed woodlands, low scrubland, and a small creek. Rocky Ridge is open 365 days a year from dawn to dusk. Picnics are permitted. The park staff offers various nature study programs, and hawk watch participants are available for informal instruction in hawk migration and identification. Photocopies of Migratory Raptor Site Registry Datasheets are available from Jerry Dyer (see contact information at the end of this section).

In spring, summer, and fall the park is good for all eastern birds common to dry, upland woods and fields. During fall migration, 17 species of raptors have been observed. Observers believe that the raptors using the Rocky Ridge route are the southern wave of those following the Appalachian "front" centered on Hawk Mountain and Waggoner's Gap.

Raptors observed here are Black Vulture, Turkey Vulture, Osprey, Bald Eagle, Northern Harrier, Sharp-shinned Hawk, Cooper's Hawk, Northern Goshawk, Red-shouldered Hawk, Broad-winged Hawk, Swainson's Hawk (seen once, in 1989), Red-tailed Hawk, Rough-legged Hawk, Golden Eagle, American Kestrel, Merlin, and Peregrine Falcon.

The most common migrating raptors are Broad-winged, Sharp-shinned, and Red-tailed Hawks. Black and Turkey Vultures are common all year in this area.

For more information about the hawk watch, contact the compiler, Jerry Dyer, 445 Quaker Drive, York, PA 17402, (717) 755-5900.

LANCASTER

Lancaster is widely known as the heart of Pennsylvania Dutch County, a misnomer for the region settled by German ("Deutsche") members of the Amish and Mennonite Churches. The population of the city is 55,551, and it is the county seat of Lancaster County.

Agriculture is very important in this region. Many small farms dot the rolling hills. A farmers' market has operated in downtown Lancaster since 1730. Birders may want to stock up on homemade bologna, fresh cheese, and fruits and vegetables for picnics. Or take home a supply of egg noodles, jelly, and Pennsylvania pretzels. In

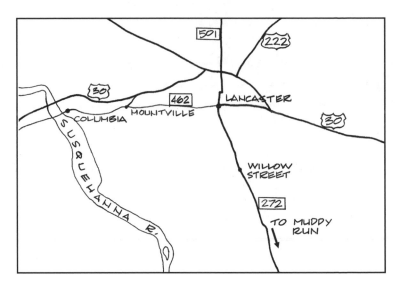

Lancaster

addition to agriculture and its associated businesses, the area has many retail businesses, including factory outlets.

An excellent, in-depth guide to birding in the county is *A Guide to the Birds of Lancaster County, Pennsylvania* published by the Lancaster County Bird Club in 1991.

Muddy Run

Muddy Run, owned by the Philadelphia Electric Company, is a 985-acre pumped-storage hydroelectric plant on the eastern shore of the Susquehanna River. At the site, there are a 100-acre recreation lake and a 500-acre park. Nearly 2,000 acres of old fields, woodlands, and cultivated fields surround the facilities. Muddy Run is well known as a birding spot. Birds are attracted to the variety of habitats, the ice-free river in winter, and the fluctuating water levels in the reservoir.

To reach Muddy Run, drive south from Lancaster on US 222 to Willow Street. US 222 becomes SR 272 in Willow Street. Continue on this road until you come to the village of Buck, where you will turn right (west) onto LR 372 (also known as Holtwood Road). Drive 3.5 miles and turn left (south) onto West Bethesda Church Road. At the next intersection (a "T"), turn left (east) to enter the park.

Pick up a map and bird checklist (267 species recorded at Muddy Run and nearby areas on the Lower Susquehanna) at the park office. Other Philadelphia Electric Company brochures available at the park are "Wildflower and Natural Areas of the Lower Susquehanna River Valley," "Muddy Run Trees, Shrubs, and Vines," "Muddy Run Wildflower Checklist," and a calendar of events. Of special interest to birders are Muddy Run's bird identification classes; the series of six weekly sessions is offered several times a year. Muddy Run offers facilities for camping, picnicking, boat rentals, and fishing.

For many birders, Bald Eagles are the highlight of a trip to Muddy Run. The birds may be seen in the park year-round, especially during the summer. When the water in the reservoir is low, the eagles feed on mudflats and exposed islands. Late afternoon is the best time for finding these conditions.

The park has many nesting boxes for Eastern Bluebirds, and this species and others that use the boxes are abundant. Look for Tree Swallow, Carolina Chickadee, Tufted Titmouse, and House Wren.

In the pine plantation near Muddy Run Cove, both Long-eared and Short-eared Owls have been seen. This area is also good for both Black-capped and Carolina Chickadees, White-breasted and Red-breasted Nuthatches, and Ruby-crowned and Golden-crowned Kinglets in winter.

Check the park's fields for Northern Bobwhite; Willow Flycatcher; Northern Mockingbird; Brown Thrasher; Yellow and Prairie Warblers; Common Yellowthroat; Yellow-breasted Chat; Eastern Meadowlark; and Field, Grasshopper, and Song Sparrows. This park is one of the few places in Pennsylvania where Blue Grosbeaks are found reliably. Check the area around the breast of the dam for this species.

Rarities recorded at Muddy Run in recent years have included Peregrine Falcon, Whimbrel, Red-necked Phalarope, Iceland Gull, Lesser Black-backed Gull, Black Skimmer, Olive-sided Flycatcher, Loggerhead Shrike, and Lapland Longspur.

The park's address is Muddy Run Recreation Park, 172 Bethesda Church Road West, Holtwood, PA 17532, (717) 284-4325.

Loggerhead Shrike

Susquehannock State Park

Susquehannock State Park is 224 acres of mostly wooded land overlooking the Susquehanna River south of Muddy Run. To reach the park, take SR 372 south to Susquehannock Drive and continue south to the park.

The park has facilities for picnicking, four hiking trails, and one horseback riding trail. This is a quiet, beautiful park where hitching posts are provided for the local Amish community. This park is included in the area covered by the "Birds of the Lower Susquehanna" checklist of 267 species available from Philadelphia Electric

Company, Muddy Run Recreation Park, 172 Bethesda Church Road West, Holtwood, PA 17532, (717) 284-4325.

The management plan for the park lists 143 species.

The address is Susquehannock State Park, c/o Gifford Pinchot State Park, 2200 Rosstown Road, Lewisberry, PA 17339, (717) 432-5011.

Middle Creek Waterfowl Management Area

Middle Creek, owned by the Pennsylvania Game Commission, is more than 5,134 acres of upland woods, fields, ponds, a lake, and some wetlands. The area is operated primarily as a propagation site for Canada Goose and other waterfowl, but is a favorite location for birders in search of rarities. For example, Glossy and White Ibis, Barnacle and White-fronted Goose, Fulvous Whistling-Duck, Marbled Godwit, Wilson's and Red-necked Phalarope, American Avocet, Black-necked Stilt, Say's Phoebe, Mountain Bluebird, Prothonotary Warbler, and Dickcissel all have been recorded at Middle Creek. In addition, Bald Eagle may be a year-round resident in this area, which is included in the Lititz Christmas Bird Count.

To reach Middle Creek, which is located just south of Kleinfeltersville on Hopeland Road, take SR 501 from Lebanon north to Brickerville, and turn east (right) onto SR 322. Drive less than a mile and turn left onto Hopeland Road (LR 1026). Just past the village of Hopeland, turn north (left) onto LR 1035 and continue to Middle Creek. All approaches to the area are well-marked with signs.

Stop at the visitors' center to pick up a free map, brochure, bird checklist with 238 species, and directions for a self-guided tour that highlights seven stops including waterfowl habitat, observation point, buckwheat fields, and millet dikes. In the visitors' center are an auditorium where programs are presented and several exhibits about Middle Creek, including habitats and mounted specimens of birds and mammals. The center is open from 8 a.m. to 4 p.m., except on Sundays from noon to 5 p.m.

Middle Creek is open seven days a week. About 750 acres have been set aside for wildlife propagation. Access to these areas is forbidden. Picnicking is permitted only at picnic areas. A short trail to the observation platform on the north side of Middle Creek is wheelchair-accessible. Stop 5 on the self-guided tour features a braille trail.

Camping is not available at Middle Creek, but there are several nearby commercial campgrounds. For information, contact the Pennsylvania Dutch Convention and Visitors Bureau, 501 Greenfield Road, Lancaster, PA 17601, (717) 295-7001.

In early spring, Middle Creek is a staging area for waterfowl, especially Canada Goose and Tundra Swan. In recent years, up to 5,000 Tundra Swan have arrived at Middle Creek in March. Later, landbird migrants and some shorebirds pass through the area. Breeding birds include herons and egrets, Least Bittern, and Bobolink (this is one of few local areas where the species breeds). Savannah, Grasshopper, Vesper, and Swamp Sparrows have been recorded. Migrant shorebirds begin arriving in mid-July; numbers depend on the availability of mudflats. Shorebird migration peaks around Labor Day, with vireos and warblers arriving in mid-September. Look for migrating sparrows in October and waterfowl in November. Short-eared and Long-eared Owls sometimes spend the winter here. Long-eared Owls used to nest at Middle Creek, but seem to have been chased away by too much human activity. Rough-legged Hawks and Northern Saw-whet Owl are occasional winter visitors.

The address is Middle Creek Wildlife Management Area, P.O. Box 110, Kleinfeltersville, PA 17079, (717) 733-1512.

Octoraro Lake

Octoraro Lake is a municipal reservoir on the Octoraro Creek. The creek itself has been designated as a Pennsylvania Scenic River. Much of the area around the lake is private property, so birding is best done from the public parking areas or from the road.

To reach the lake, drive south from Lancaster on US 222 to Quarryville, where you will turn left onto SR 372 (State Street East). Drive east to SR 472 (about a half mile). Turn right onto SR 472 (Kirkwood Pike) and drive about 9 miles to Mount Eden Road. Turn left and drive to the parking area at the north end of the lake.

By midsummer, the areas where the branches of Octoraro Creek enter the lake become mudflats attractive to migrating shorebirds and other species, including uncommon Double-crested Cormorant and rare Glossy Ibis. Shorebirds observed at Octoraro have included Killdeer, Greater Yellowlegs, Lesser Yellowlegs, Semipalmated Sand-

Cliff Swallow

piper, Least Sandpiper and Pectoral Sandpiper. Less common are Black-bellied Plover, Semipalmated Plover, and Short-billed Dowitcher. Rarities have included Lesser Golden-Plover, Red Knot, Baird's Sandpiper, Buff-breasted Sandpiper, and Long-billed Dowitcher. Caspian Tern sometimes rest on the mudflats.

Large numbers of migrating swallows can be seen at the mudflats. In August, look for Purple Martin, Northern Rough-winged Swallow, numerous Bank Swallows, Cliff Swallow, and Barn Swallow. Tree Swallows follow in September.

The lake itself is good for waterfowl in winter. Snow Goose—both blue and white phases—have been seen in mid-March.

Pine plantations around the lake are good for Red-breasted Nuthatch and Golden- and Ruby-crowned Kinglet in winter. Seven species of owls have been recorded in recent years in this area, including Northern Saw-whet Owl.

Check the marshy fields north of the lake for Common Snipe during migration and in winter. These same fields should be checked for Prairie Warbler and Blue Grosbeak in early summer.

Cornwall Fire Tower Hawk Watch

The Cornwall Fire Tower, located on South Mountain near Brickerville, is good for autumn hawk flights. To reach the site, drive north from Lancaster on SR 501 to Brickerville, about 10 miles. In Brickerville, turn left onto US 322 and drive 4.1 miles to an unpaved road on the left. Turn onto this road and drive about one mile to the tower.

The following raptors have been recorded recently at the site: Turkey Vulture, Black Vulture, Osprey, Bald Eagle, Northern Harrier, Sharp-shinned Hawk, Cooper's Hawk, Northern Goshawk, Red-shouldered Hawk, Broad-winged Hawk, Red-tailed Hawk, Golden Eagle, American Kestrel, Merlin, and Peregrine Falcon.

The use of the cabin at the top of the tower is restricted to members of the Lancaster County Bird Club, and only four people at a time are permitted inside. This site has been a hawk watch since 1975.

READING

Reading, population 78,380, is the county seat of Berks County and is known for its many factory outlets. Reading is a good place to base trips to Hawk Mountain Sanctuary (see Chapter 5), Blue Marsh Lake, Lake Ontelaunee, French Creek State Park, and Nolde Forest Environmental Education Center.

Nolde Forest Environmental Education Center

Nolde Forest Environmental Education Center is one of four environmental education centers operated by the Bureau of State Parks. It is located just south of Reading on SR 625 (New Holland Road) near the village of Angelica.

The center is 665 acres of mature oak-beech-maple forest, coniferous plantations, two small ponds, and three small streams. There are 10

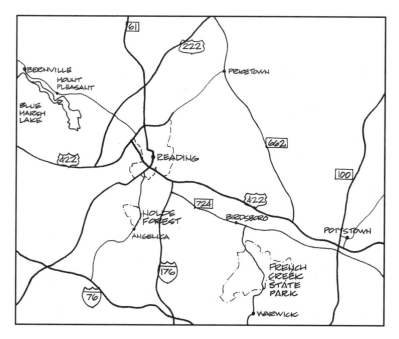

Reading

miles of trails; two short loops are wheelchair-accessible. The grounds are open from sunrise to sunset seven days a week. Programs are offered for preschool through college students, and for the general public. A library is open to the public. A map and bird checklist with 117 species are available.

Check the evergreen stands for Great Horned Owl and Golden-crowned Kinglet, as well as other conifer-loving species. Veery and Wood Thrush are both common. Twenty-five warbler species have been recorded, most during spring and fall migration. Common summer warblers are American Redstart, Ovenbird, and Louisiana Waterthrush. During migration the most common warblers are Yellow-rumped, Black-throated Green, Bay-breasted, and Canada Warblers.

Winter Wren is uncommon in fall and winter, as is Ruby-crowned Kinglet. Both Black-capped and Carolina Chickadees have been observed at Nolde, but Black-capped is more common.

The center's address is Nolde Forest Environmental Education Center, RD 1, Box 392, Reading, PA 19607, (610) 775-1411.

Blue Marsh Lake Recreation Area

Blue Marsh Lake Recreation Area is an Army Corps of Engineers flood-control project in the Delaware River watershed. The lake was created when Tulpekocken Creek was dammed. This Berks County site is 6,800 acres; about one-quarter of the site is wooded, primarily with oaks. The area around the 1,150-acre lake is intensively farmed.

To reach Blue Marsh from I-78, take the Strausstown exit to SR 183. Drive south 8 miles. The lake will be on your right. Look for brown and white direction signs to the main access points.

There is a visitors' center where you can pick up a free checklist of 219 species and 5 accidentals. A wildlife management area is leased to the Pennsylvania Game Commission, and there are hiking trails (two interpretive), picnicking facilities, and a swimming beach.

Blue Marsh is especially good for migrating waterfowl. Osprey can be seen here in the early spring. A Sandhill Crane was observed here in August 1992.

The address is Blue Marsh Lake Project, US Army Corps of Engineers, Philadelphia District, RD 1, Box 1239, Leesport, PA 19533, (610) 376-6337 or 6338.

ALLENTOWN/BETHLEHEM/EASTON

Allentown (population 105,090) is the county seat of Lehigh County. Bethlehem (52,561) is its Siamese twin. Nearby Easton (26,276) is the county seat of Northampton County. From its earliest settlement by Europeans, the area has focused on industry and agriculture.

Pool Wildlife Sanctuary

Pool Wildlife Sanctuary is 72 acres of riparian, old fields, new- and middle-growth forests with several ponds and a wildflower meadow in Lehigh County. To reach the sanctuary, take SR 309 to Route 29 (Cedar Crest Boulevard). Turn left onto River Bend Road, then right onto Orchid Place. Follow signs to the sanctuary, which is owned by

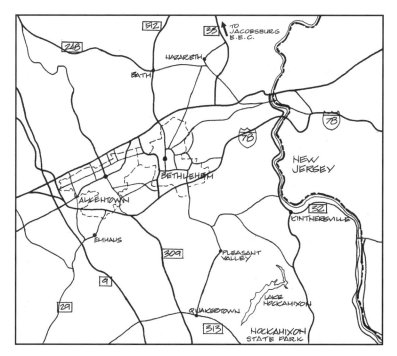

Allentown/Bethlehem/Easton

the Wildlands Conservancy. Free maps are available at the sanctuary. A bird checklist of 118 species costs $0.50.

The sanctuary is open Monday to Friday from 8 a.m. to 4 p.m. and Sunday from 2 p.m. to 4 p.m. Trails are open seven days a week from dawn to dusk. Picnics are allowed, but food is not available at the site. There are five trails; the Backyard and Pheasant Run Trails are wheelchair-accessible.

The Trexler Environmental Education Center offers programs for schools, groups, and families. Exhibits feature nature, land preservation, and ecological concepts. Memberships are available. Members receive a quarterly newsletter, discounted program fees, and free admission to the sanctuary.

Birds at the sanctuary are typical for the habitats. The best times to visit are during spring and fall migration.

The address is Pool Wildlife Sanctuary, 601 Orchid Place, Emmaus, PA 18049, (610) 965-4397.

Minsi Lake and Bear Swamp

Minsi Lake and Bear Swamp are county parks in Northampton County. Both are located on Johnsonville Road near Bangor. Minsi Lake is owned by the Pennsylvania Fish and Boat Commission and administered by the county. To reach the parks, drive north from Easton on SR 33 to SR 512. Take SR 512 east to Bangor, and turn left onto Johnsonville Road. Follow the signs to the parks. Free brochures with maps are available.

Minsi Lake is a 117-acre park that is good for waterfowl. Bear Swamp is best known for wetlands wildflower species, but is good for birds as well. A free checklist includes 193 species. There are 7 miles of trails in the parks, including a self-guided nature trail with an elevated boardwalk through the swamp and an observation deck. Guided nature walks are available for groups. Contact the park office to make arrangements. Hunting and fishing are permitted in the parks. Bear Swamp has large archery complex. Be careful!

The address is County of Northampton, Division of Parks and Recreation, RD 4, Nazareth, PA 18064-9211, (610) 746-1975.

Mariton Wildlife Preserve

Mariton Wildlife Preserve is 200 acres of meadows, Tuliptree/oak forest, and rhododendron thickets near Riegelsville, Northampton County. The preserve is owned by the Mariton Wilderness Trust.

To reach the preserve, drive south from Easton on SR 611 to Spring Hill Road in Riegelsville. Drive about a half mile, turn right (west) onto Sunnyside Road. Drive about a half mile and turn left (south) at the preserve sign.

There is no admission charge, but visitors are asked to become members of the Friends of Mariton for $5 per year. The preserve is open daily during daylight hours. Facilities include a nature center with natural history displays, including bird nests, skulls, and geologic specimens. Programs are offered, including nature walks.

The preserve overlooks the Delaware River and has good to excellent warbler migration in the spring and fair raptor migration in the fall. In spring, look for Wild Turkey; Osprey; Belted Kingfisher; Hermit Thrush; Northern Parula; Black-throated Green, Black-and-white, Black-throated Blue, Cerulean, Magnolia, Yellow-rumped (common), Chestnut-sided, and Blackburnian Warblers; American Redstart; Pine, Prairie, Worm-eating, Hooded, and Kentucky Warblers; Ovenbird (common); Scarlet Tanager (common); and Rose-breasted Grosbeak (common).

In summer, Wood Thrush, Veery, Indigo Bunting, and Blue-winged Warbler are common. Less common residents include Broad-winged Hawk, Eastern Bluebird, Great Crested Flycatcher, Hooded Warbler, Cerulean Warbler, Kentucky Warbler, and Common Yellowthroat.

In fall, look for migrating raptors and woodpeckers, including Yellow-bellied Sapsucker. Winter residents include Great Horned Owl, Eastern Screech-Owl, Ruffed Grouse, and an occasional Red-breasted Nuthatch.

The address is Mariton Wildlife Preserve, 240 Sunnyside Road, Easton, PA 18042, (610) 749-0515.

Jacobsburg Environmental Education Center

Jacobsburg Environmental Education Center is 1,167 acres of upland forest, cultivated fields, old fields in various stages of succession, emergent and forested wetlands, virgin hemlocks, two small ponds, and two streams on Blue Mountain in Northampton County. The center offers educational and interpretive programs year-round. Historic sites in the center include an 18th century industrial community.

To reach the center, take SR 33 north to the Belfast exit, about 12 miles from Easton. Follow the signs to the center. Be sure to pick up a map; parts of the center are open to hunting. Jacobsburg is open daily from 8 a.m. to sunset.

Facilities include a visitors' center. There is a 10-mile mountain-bike trail, several miles of hiking trails, and a horseback-riding trail. Henry's Woods Nature Trail is a self-guided interpretive trail.

Birds listed on the center's checklist of 145 species include Northern Harrier (rare breeder), Long-eared Owl (rare, fall through spring), both Black-billed and Yellow-billed Cuckoos, Belted Kingfisher (common), migrant Yellow-bellied Sapsucker, Willow Flycatcher (rare breeder), Northern Rough-winged Swallow (uncommon breeder), Brown Creeper (year-round), Blue-gray Gnatcatcher, 35 species of warbler, and 21 species of finches and sparrows.

The address is Jacobsburg Environmental Education Center, 835 Jacobsburg Road, Wind Gap, PA 18901, (610) 759-7616.

DOYLESTOWN

Doylestown, population 8,575, was settled in 1735 and has been the county seat of Bucks County since 1812. Bucks County was one of four original counties created by William Penn in 1682. Today the area is known for its historic structures, including covered bridges, antique shops, art galleries, wineries, and the nation's oldest summer theater, The Bucks County Playhouse. Birders who have small children may want to visit Sesame Place near Langhorne so the kiddies can add Big Bird to their life lists.

Nockamixon State Park

Located 5 miles east of Quakertown and 9 miles northwest of Doylestown, Nockamixon is a 5,283-acre park that includes forest, fields, and Nockamixon Lake. The main entrance to the park is on SR 563. To reach it, drive north from Doylestown on SR 611. Just past the village of Harrow, turn left onto SR 563. Continue along the west shore of the lake to the park office, where you may get a free park map and bird checklist of 195 species and 5 accidentals. A brochure published by the Pennsylvania Bureau of Topographic and Geologic Survey explains the topography and geology of the park, including Sentinel Rock, an erosional pinnacle located about 1,000 feet downstream from the breast of Nockamixon Dam.

Nockamixon is open daily from 8 a.m. to sunset. The park has no campground, but it does have 10 modern, three-bedroom cabins for rent. Reservations are a must. Call the park office for information. Other facilities at the park include a food concession, marina, boat rental concession, picnic tables, swimming pool, and the Weisel Youth Hostel, operated by the Bucks County Department of Parks and Recreation. Environmental education programs for children are scheduled.

Habitats in the park include old fields, hardwood forest, marsh, and a 1,450-acre lake. There are young plantations of Larch and White Pine. Lake Nockamixon has attracted many waterfowl; the following have been recorded: Tundra Swan, Mute Swan, Snow Goose, Canada Goose, Wood Duck, Green-winged Teal, American Black Duck, Mallard, Northern Pintail, Blue-winged Teal, Gadwall, American Wigeon, Canvasback, Redhead, Ring-necked Duck, Lesser Scaup, Oldsquaw, Common Goldeneye, Bufflehead, Hooded Merganser, Common Merganser, Red-breasted Merganser, and Ruddy Duck.

The park is also good for the following birds of prey: Turkey Vulture, Osprey, Bald Eagle (rare fall migrant), Northern Harrier, Sharp-shinned Hawk, Cooper's Hawk, Northern Goshawk, Red-shouldered Hawk, Broad-winged Hawk, Red-tailed Hawk, Rough-legged Hawk (occasional in winter), Golden Eagle (rare fall migrant), and American Kestrel.

Shorebirds seen at the Nockamixon include Killdeer, Greater Yellowlegs, Lesser Yellowlegs, Solitary Sandpiper, Spotted Sandpiper,

Spotted Sandpiper

Least Sandpiper, Pectoral Sandpiper, Common Snipe, and American Woodcock. The following gulls and terns have been recorded: Bonaparte's Gull, Ring-billed Gull, Herring Gull, Great Black-backed Gull, and Common Tern. None are common, but this park would be a good place to check after a storm.

Long-eared Owl has been recorded in all seasons. Check pine plantations carefully, especially in winter.

Thrushes recorded at the park include Eastern Bluebird, Veery, Gray-cheeked Thrush (rare spring and fall migrant), Swainson's Thrush (uncommon spring and fall migrant), and Hermit Thrush (common spring and fall migrant). Wood Thrush is common in spring, summer, and fall.

Twenty-seven warbler species have been recorded at the park; most are migrants. Winter sparrows include American Tree Sparrow, Field Sparrow, Fox Sparrow, Song Sparrow, Swamp Sparrow, White-throated Sparrow, and White-crowned Sparrow.

The park's address is Nockamixon State Park, 1542 Mountain View Drive, Quakertown, PA 18951, (215) 538-2151. For information about the youth hostel call (215) 536-8749.

Peace Valley Park

Owned by Bucks County, Peace Valley Park is 1,500 acres of woods, meadows, scrub, wetlands, pine forest, ponds, streams, and 365-acre Lake Galena (shown on some maps as Peace Valley Reservoir).

To reach Peace Valley, take SR 313 west from Doylestown to about a mile beyond Fountainville. At the traffic light at the intersection with New Galena Road, turn left, and drive 0.75 mile to Chapman Road. Turn left again. The park is ahead on the left.

The park is open year-round from dawn to dusk. Admission is charged. A map and bird checklist are free. The checklist is based on 15 years of bird records. The park is included in the Central Bucks County Christmas Bird Count.

The Solar Building, which demonstrates passive solar technology, houses changing exhibits that feature a variety of environmental and wildlife topics. Dioramas, taxidermy specimens, and a beehive are examples. Members of Friends of Peace Valley Nature Center receive a quarterly newsletter and discount at the gift shop.

Peace Valley has nine miles of trails and two observation blinds—one near the Solar Building and the other on the opposite side of Lake Galena. A birding information station in the hallway of the nature center provides current information.

Birding is best during spring and fall migration, but is good all year. Birds recorded at the park include migratory waterfowl: Tundra Swan, Mute Swan, Greater White-fronted Goose (in winter), Snow Goose, Brant, Canada Goose (all year), Barnacle Goose (accidental), Wood Duck (all year), Green-winged Teal, American Black Duck, Mallard (all year), Northern Pintail, Blue-winged Teal, Northern Shoveler, Gadwall, American Wigeon, Canvasback, Redhead, Ring-necked Duck, Greater Scaup, Lesser Scaup, Oldsquaw, Black Scoter, Surf Scoter (accidental), White-winged Scoter (accidental), Common Goldeneye, Bufflehead, Hooded Merganser, Common Merganser, Red-breasted Merganser, and Ruddy Duck. Gulls and terns recorded at the park include Laughing Gull (accidental), Bonaparte's Gull, Ring-billed Gull (all year), Herring Gull, Great Black-backed Gull (winter to early spring), Caspian Tern and Common Tern (in migration), Forster's Tern, Least Tern (accidental), and Black Tern.

Both Yellow-billed and Black-billed Cuckoos nest. Six vireo and 35 warbler species have been observed at Peace Valley. In addition, both Brewster's and Lawrence's Warbler have been recorded. Rose-breasted and Blue Grosbeaks nest in the park, as do Orchard and Northern Oriole.

Sparrows such as Chipping Sparrow, Field Sparrow, Vesper Sparrow (accidental), Savannah Sparrow, Grasshopper Sparrow, Song Sparrow, Lincoln's Sparrow, and Swamp Sparrow have been observed.

Check the area around the Chapman Bridge for American Bittern in late April and early May.

The address is Peace Valley Nature Center, 170 Chapman Road, Doylestown, PA 18901, (215) 345-7860 or 345-5988.

Tyler State Park

Located near Newtown, Tyler State Park is 1,700 acres of woods, open fields, low wooded wetlands, meandering Neshaminy Creek, hedgerows, and thickets. To reach the park, take I-95 to the Newtown-Yardley exit, and go west on the SR 332 to the park (about a half mile past Newtown), which is on the right.

Tyler is open daily from 8 a.m. to sunset. The park has 24 miles of trails; one is a self-guided nature trail. About 10.5 miles of paved bicycle trail are accessible to wheelchairs. The park has an environmental education program during the summer; check at the park office for a schedule of events. While there, pick up a free map and bird checklist of 185 species.

Tyler has had a bluebird trail for more than 10 years, so expect to see Tree Swallows and Eastern Bluebirds. Other breeding birds include Acadian Flycatcher (near the streams), Louisiana Waterthrush, and Kentucky Warbler (both recorded as nesting along Porter Run), and numerous Bobolink near the youth hostel. Grasshopper Sparrow last nested in 1986. Check with park staff for its status.

During migration 33 warbler species have been observed. In winter, Horned Lark is an uncommon visitor to the open fields, and Common Redpoll, Pine Siskin, Evening Grosbeak, and Fox Sparrow also are uncommon. Swamp Sparrow is uncommon but can be seen year-round.

The park's address is Tyler State Park, 101 Swamp Road, Newtown, PA 18940-1151, (215) 968-2021.

Churchville Nature Center

This small, county-owned nature center about 25 miles northeast of Philadelphia has 55 acres of young and mature mixed hardwood forest, some meadows, a pond, and a reservoir shown on some maps as Springfield Lake. To reach the Churchville Nature Center, take SR 532 north from Philadelphia to Holland. In Holland, take Churchville Lane to the park.

Churchville Nature Center is open Tuesday and Sunday from noon to 5 p.m. and Wednesday to Saturday from 10 a.m. to 5 p.m. Picnicking is allowed, but there is no food concession. There are several trails; the orange trail near the farmhouse has an observation blind. The yellow trail is wheelchair-accessible. Free trail maps are available, but the park does not have a bird checklist. It is included in the Southern Bucks County Christmas Bird Count. Programs and exhibits feature nature and environmental education. Memberships are available; members receive a quarterly newsletter and discounts in the center's bookstore and gift shop and on trips sponsored by the center.

Birds that are seen year-round at the park include Great Blue Heron, Cooper's Hawk, Great Horned Owl, Red-bellied Woodpecker, Yellow-bellied Sapsucker, and Northern Flicker.

Many waterfowl migrate through the center in spring. Wood Duck nest. Osprey migrate through; a nesting platform has been constructed, but none has spent the summer here. Scarlet Tanager and Northern Oriole are common. The center is a good place for a variety of warblers in spring—mostly migrants. Yellow Warbler and Common Yellowthroat breed.

In summer, look for Double-crested Cormorant, Great Egret, and American Coot on the reservoir. Green-backed Herons and an occasional Black-crowned Night-Heron are seen at the pond. Wood Thrush, Brown Thrasher, and Rufous-sided Towhee can be seen in forested areas of the park. Prothonotary Warbler is rare, but has been recorded.

Fall migrants include Osprey and, rarely, Bald Eagle. The reservoir is good for waterfowl in fall. Loons, grebes, and mergansers sometimes pass through. In winter, the Snowy Owl is occasional, and waterfowl can be found; look for Canvasback, Ring-necked Duck, and Common Merganser. Several years ago, a Barnacle Goose and Oldsquaw were observed here. The park staff reports a decline in winter species such as kinglets and Red-breasted Nuthatch.

The address is Churchville Nature Center, 501 Churchville Lane, Churchville, PA 18966, (215) 357-4005.

Delaware Canal State Park

Delaware Canal State Park is a 60-mile long park on the Pennsylvania shore of the Delaware River extending from Bristol, Bucks County, to Easton, Northampton County. The total area is about 1,000 acres. There are numerous access points to the park. Mule-drawn barges leaving New Hope take visitors on 4.5-mile rides; these operate from Memorial Day to Labor Day. Food is readily available in adjacent towns; picnicking is permitted.

The National Heritage Trail is parallel to the Delaware Canal, which is parallel to the river. Habitats include the river, farms, cliffs, islands, wetlands, and forests.

Although the park emphasizes historic features, this is an excellent place for birding during migration when numerous warblers and other species migrate along the Delaware Flyway.

The address is Delaware Canal State Park, RD 1, Box 615A, Upper Black Eddy, PA 18972, (610) 982-5560.

Bowman's Hill Wildflower Preserve

Located in the northern section of Washington Crossing Historic Park, Bowman's Hill Wildflower Preserve is about 40 miles northeast of Philadelphia. The reserve has 80 acres of mixed mesophytic woodlands, meadows, and constructed sphagnum bog, serpentine and shale barrens, and limestone habitats. The preserve is administered by the Pennsylvania Historical and Museum Commission and the Washington Crossing Park Commission near the site where George Washington and his troops crossed the Delaware River on Christmas night 1776 to surprise Hessian troops garrisoned in Trenton, New Jersey. Washington's Crossing is re-enacted every Christmas Day. Admission to the park and the Memorial Building, which displays a copy of the famous Emanuel Leutze painting, "Washington Crossing the Delaware" is free; however, a small fee is charged for admission to the Bowman's Hill Tower and several of the historic buildings.

To reach Bowman's Hill, drive south from New Hope about 2.5 miles on SR 32, also known as River Road. The grounds are open from 8:30 a.m. to sunset daily; the headquarters building is open from 9 a.m. to 5 p.m. daily and from noon to 5 p.m. on Sundays. A map of the preserve is available for a small fee; a bird list with 151 species is free. The preserve publishes a newsletter, *Twinleaf Newsletter*, for members of the Bowman's Hill Wildflower Preserve Association. Members receive additional benefits.

The preserve has 26 trails, varying in length from 150 feet to 2,000 feet. The excellent preserve map lists the flowers on each trail by both common and scientific name and provides information about when the flowers bloom. The Woods Edge Walk is accessible to wheelchairs. Picnicking is permitted in designated picnic areas, but not in the preserve itself. Programs are offered frequently; most feature plants and wildflowers, but Saturday Morning Bird Walks are featured in April and May.

Of interest to birders are the Platt Museum of Birds, Nests, and Eggs in the headquarters and the Sinkler Observation Area, a bird feeding station directly behind the building.

In spring, it is possible to see 16 warbler species in one day: Blue-winged Warbler; Northern Parula; Yellow, Chestnut-sided, Magnolia, Black-throated Blue, Black-throated Green, Blackburnian, Prairie, Blackpoll, Cerulean, and Black-and-white Warblers; American Redstart; Kentucky, Wilson's, and Canada Warblers.

Summer residents include Wood Duck, Ruby-throated Hummingbird, Pileated Woodpecker, Veery, Wood Thrush, Scarlet Tanager, Rose-breasted Grosbeak, and Northern Oriole.

Fall migrants include Yellow-bellied Sapsucker, hawks (especially Red-tailed and Sharp-shinned), and Turkey and Black Vultures. Winter visitors include Carolina Wren, White-throated Sparrow, and Pine Siskin.

The preserve's address is Bowman's Hill Wildflower Preserve, Washington Crossing Historic Park, P.O. Box 103, Washington Crossing, PA 18977, (215) 862-2924.

NORRISTOWN

Norristown, population 30,754, is the county seat of Montgomery County.

Gwynedd Wildlife Preserve

Gwynedd Wildlife Preserve is 215 acres of ponds, wetlands, open meadows, hedgerows, deciduous forests, and coniferous plantations. To reach Gwynedd, take US 202 from Norristown north to a traffic light at the intersection of US 202 and Morris Road. Continue north on US 202 for 0.3 mile and turn left onto Township Line Road. At 0.3 mile, turn right (the first right) onto Swedesford Road. The preserve is 0.5 mile ahead; there is a sign. Park by the maintenance building. A brochure with map is available at the preserve.

The preserve is owned by the Natural Lands Trust and is open 7 days a week during daylight hours. Food is not available, and picnics are not permitted. There are 2.5 miles of trails. Memberships are available. Members receive a quarterly newsletter and invitations to special programs and field trips.

A total of 136 species of birds has been recorded here. The area is fairly productive for migrant songbirds in spring. Look for Osprey, American Woodcock, Palm and Prairie Warblers, and Bobolink. Raptor flights have been observed in the fall. In summer look for the following nesting species: Killdeer, Wood Duck, Red-tailed Hawk, American Kestrel, Eastern Meadowlark, Eastern Bluebird, and Northern Oriole. Winter birds include Northern Harrier, Great Horned Owl, Belted Kingfisher, Winter Wren, and several sparrow species: White-throated, Field, Swamp, American Tree, Fox, and Song.

The preserve's address is Gwynedd Wildlife Preserve, 640 South Swedesford Road, Ambler, PA 19002, (215) 699-6751.

Fort Washington State Park

Located about 5 miles northwest of Philadelphia, Fort Washington State park is 493 acres divided into four units: Flourtown Day-Use Area, Militia Hill Day-Use Area, Fort Hill Area, and Sandy Run Area. Wissahickon Creek runs through the Flourtown Area and forms the eastern boundary of the Militia Hill Area. The Green Ribbon Trail runs parallel to the creek on land owned by Montgomery County.

To reach Fort Washington, take the Pennsylvania Turnpike to Exit 26. Drive west on Pennsylvania Avenue to the third traffic light, at the intersection of Pennsylvania Avenue and Bethlehem Pike. Turn left. The park office is 0.6 mile ahead on the right. This is the Fort Hill Area. Pick up a park map here.

Fort Washington State Park is the site of the Militia Hill Hawk Watch (see next listing). The park also has a bluebird trail.

The park's address is Fort Washington State Park, 500 Bethlehem Park, Fort Washington, PA 19034, (215) 646-2942.

Militia Hill Hawk Watch has been an organized hawk watch since 1988. To reach the hawk watch from the Fort Washington State Park office, continue on Bethlehem Pike to SR 73 (Skippack Pike) where you will take a sharp right onto SR 73. Drive one block and turn left onto Militia Hill Road. Drive 100 yards to the entrance to the Militia Hill Day-Use Area on the left. Park at the first parking area. There are picnic tables and restrooms at this site. One of the notable features of this hawk watch is that it is wheelchair-accessible. The hawk watch site is an easy 50 yards from the parking area.

Volunteers staff the hawk watch from September to November, 7 days a week, from 9 a.m. to 5 p.m. in September and 10 a.m. to 4 p.m. in October and November. For more information or to schedule a group, call Marylea Klauder, (215) 884-2558.

Militia Hill is 330 feet above sea level and was an important military site in 1777 when the British forced the American troops out of Germantown. It is now one of the few natural areas in a sea of suburban landscape.

Raptors recorded here include Black Vulture, Turkey Vulture, Osprey, Bald Eagle, Northern Harrier, Sharp-shinned Hawk, Cooper's Hawk, Northern Goshawk, Red-shouldered Hawk, Broad-winged Hawk, Red-tailed Hawk, Rough-legged Hawk, Golden Eagle, American Kestrel, Merlin, and Peregrine Falcon. Numbers of birds recorded have ranged from a low of 3,857 during the first year records were kept (1988) to a high of 12,289 in 1990. Broad-winged Hawks are the most numerous raptors seen at this site.

Pennypack Wilderness

Pennypack Wilderness is 418 acres of old-growth and second-growth forests, meadows, agricultural fields, freshwater marsh, and perennial streams in Montgomery County. The area is owned by the Pennypack Watershed Association and is located near Bryn Athyn borough. To reach the area, take Exit 27 from the Pennsylvania Turnpike and drive south on SR 611. At the third traffic light, turn left (east) onto Fitzwatertown Road. Stay on this road through the intersection of Fitzwatertown and York Road. The road name of Fitzwatertown Road then changes to Terwood. Proceed past Upper Moreland High School and through the intersection with Davisville Road. Continue to a stop sign at the top of a long rise at Edge Hill Road, turn left (north) and proceed to the parking lot 0.3 mile ahead on the right (east). Stop at the visitors' center for a free map and bird check-list of 151 species.

Pennypack Wilderness is open daily, Monday to Saturday 9 a.m. to 5 p.m., and Sunday 1 p.m. to 5 p.m. Although food is not available, picnics are permitted in the picnic grove. There is an observation blind at the headquarters building, and there are 10 trails totalling 7.5 miles. The 500-foot trail from the parking lot to the observation blind is wheelchair-accessible.

Programs offered include guided nature walks, an organized volunteer program, a photo group, bird walks, creek cleanups, and others. Exhibits at the visitors' center include natural history of the Pennypack Wilderness and many mounted specimens. Memberships are available; members receive a quarterly newsletter, notice of coming events, and reduced rates on birdseed, purchases, and programs.

The wilderness is included in the Audubon Christmas Bird Count and conducts a Breeding Bird Survey. An annual spring bird count has been conducted in early to mid-May since 1974.

Spring migrants include 26 warbler species. Some rarities such as Pied-billed Grebe, Long-eared Owl, Northern Saw-whet Owl, and Rusty Blackbird have been observed.

Breeding birds include Eastern Wood-Pewee, Acadian Flycatcher, Eastern Phoebe, Great Crested Flycatcher, Eastern Kingbird, and Barn, Rough-winged, and Tree Swallows. This is a good place to compare Black-capped and Carolina Chickadees; both are year-round residents. Breeding vireos include Red-eyed, Warbling, and White-eyed Vireos. Warblers that breed here are American Redstart, Black-and-white Warbler, Common Yellowthroat, Ovenbird, Yellow Warbler, and Yellow-rumped Warbler. Both Northern and Orchard Orioles also breed.

Winter birds that have been observed include Great Blue Heron, Brown Creeper, Winter Wren, and Evening Grosbeak.

The address is Pennypack Wilderness, 2955 Edge Hill Road, Huntingdon Valley, PA 19006-5099, (215) 657-0830.

Valley Forge National Historical Park

Valley Forge is a 3,300-acre historic site owned by the National Park Service in Chester County. Located 3 miles north of Turnpike

Exit 24, the park is devoted to historic interpretation and can be very crowded. There are fields and forests worth checking, and the trailhead for the Horseshoe Trail is located at the park. One notable bird is the Worm-eating Warbler, often found near the covered bridge.

Given a choice between Valley Forge and Mill Grove, I'll take nearby Mill Grove (see next listing).

The address is Valley Forge National Historic Park, P.O. Box 122, Route 23 and North Gulph Road, Valley Forge, PA, (610) 783-1077.

Audubon Wildlife Sanctuary (Mill Grove)

Audubon Wildlife Sanctuary (Mill Grove) is a good place for both birding and history. To reach the site, take Exit 24 from the Pennsylvania Turnpike (I-276) to SR 202 south. At the Betzwood Bridge exit, bear right up the exit ramp onto County Line Expressway. Immediately after crossing the bridge over the Schuylkill River, bear right on the exit for SR 363 North (Trooper Road). At the end of the exit ramp, turn right (east), and immediately get into the left lane. Turn left (north) at the first stop light on Audubon Road. The sanctuary is directly ahead.

Known to birders as "Mill Grove," the 175-acre site was the residence of John James Audubon from 1803 to 1806. Although he lived at Mill Grove for only a little more than two years, those two years were important. At Mill Grove, John James Audubon courted his wife, Lucy Blackwell, by taking her for walks around the property. And it was at Mill Grove that he banded Eastern Phoebe nestlings in 1804. When the birds returned in 1805, they were still wearing the silver threads he had placed on their legs.

Since 1951, Mill Grove has been maintained as a park by Montgomery County. The mansion's rooms are furnished with period furniture and exhibits about the life and works of Audubon. The grounds are managed as a bird sanctuary, with feeding stations, nesting boxes, and plantings attractive to birds. More than 175 species of birds and 400 species of flowering plants have been identified here.

Mill Grove is open Tuesday to Saturday from 10 a.m. to 4 p.m. and Sundays from 1 p.m. to 4 p.m.; the grounds are open at 7 a.m. The sanctuary is closed on Mondays. Reservations are requested for groups.

The address is Audubon Wildlife Sanctuary, P.O. Box 25, Audubon, PA 19047, (610) 666-5593.

Morris Arboretum

Owned by the University of Pennsylvania, the Morris Arboretum is 92 acres of gardens in Philadelphia County. To reach the arboretum, take the Pennsylvania Turnpike (I-276) to Exit 25. Drive east on Germantown Avenue toward the city limits of Philadelphia (about 4.5 miles). Turn left onto Northwestern Avenue, and continue until you see the entrance on the right. Stop at the visitors' center for a free map and to pay a small admission fee. The Arboretum is open Monday to Friday, 10 a.m. to 4 p.m., and Saturday and Sunday, 10 a.m. to 5 p.m. Picnicking is not permitted.

Habitats at the Arboretum include meadows, urban woodlands, and streams. More than 6,000 trees and shrubs from around the world are displayed at the Arboretum. In addition, research is conducted here on urban forestry, ecologically sound pest management, and medical use of plants.

Birds recorded at this site include most suburban birds. In spring look for migrating warblers. Wood Duck, Red-bellied Woodpecker, and Eastern Bluebird can be seen in spring. Summer birds include American Kestrel, Belted Kingfisher, Rough-winged Swallow, Carolina Wren, Wood Thrush, Eastern Meadowlark, and Northern Oriole. In fall both warblers and hawks migrate through. American Woodcock has been recorded in winter. Occasionally seen are Cattle Egret, Cooper's Hawk, Northern Bobwhite, Spotted Sandpiper, Yellow-billed Cuckoo, Great Crested Flycatcher, Indigo Bunting, and Orchard Oriole.

The address is Morris Arboretum of the University of Pennsylvania, 9414 Meadowbrook Avenue, Philadelphia, PA 19118, (215) 247-5777.

WEST CHESTER

West Chester, population 18,041, is the county seat of Chester County. The area is historically important; settlement dates to the late 17th century, and several Revolutionary War Battlefields are located nearby. West Chester State University is located here. Marsh Creek, Ridley Creek, and White Clay Creek State Parks are all nearby.

Ridley Creek State Park

Located about 10 miles west of Philadelphia, Ridley Creek State Park is 2,606 acres of woods, meadows, streams, and wetlands. To reach the park, travel west from Newtown Square on SR 3 for 3.3 miles to the park entrance.

Ridley Creek, open daily from 8 a.m. to sunset, has facilities for picnicking but does not have a food concession. The paved trail at the visitors' center is accessible to wheelchairs. The park is included in the Glenolden Christmas Bird Count. Within the park is the Colonial Pennsylvania Plantation, a living museum of a 1776 farm. There is a fee for admission to this area, which is open only during the summer.

Ridley Creek has one of the best bird checklists of any facility in Pennsylvania. It's an annotated list of 194 species, and it highlights 14 trails and other areas. Stop at the park office for a free copy.

The Bridal Path Trail is especially good for birding, wildflowers, trees, and ferns. In spring, look for migrating warblers and vireos. In late spring and summer, the following birds breed in the area near the trail: Red-tailed Hawk, Red-bellied Woodpecker, Downy Woodpecker, Hairy Woodpecker, Northern Flicker, Eastern Wood-Pewee, Great Crested Flycatcher, Eastern Kingbird, Blue Jay, American Crow, Carolina Chickadee, Tufted Titmouse, White-breasted Nuthatch, Carolina Wren, House Wren, Blue-gray Gnatcatcher, Veery, Wood Thrush, American Robin, Gray Catbird, Mockingbird, Brown Thrasher, White-eyed Vireo, Yellow-throated Vireo, Red-eyed Vireo, Blue-winged Warbler, Yellow Warbler, Chestnut-sided Warbler, Prairie Warbler, American Redstart, Ovenbird, Louisiana Waterthrush, Kentucky Warbler, Common Yellowthroat, Yellow-breasted Chat, Scarlet Tanager, Northern Cardinal, Indigo Bunting, Rufous-sided Towhee, Field Sparrow, Song Sparrow, Red-winged Blackbird, Common Grackle, Brown-headed Cowbird, Northern Oriole, and American Goldfinch.

The marsh in front of the plantation is a breeding area for Willow Flycatcher and Swamp Sparrow. Virginia Rail also has been found in the marsh. Check the large sycamores along the creek for Yellow-throated and Warbling Vireos and Orchard Oriole.

Barn Swallows nest in the park's barn. Kentucky Warblers nest on the hillside near the entrance to the bicycle trail. This area is also good for migrating thrushes and warblers in May. Check the ravine near the park mailbox for Louisiana Waterthrush in summer.

The Lower Sycamore Mills Road area is good for spring migrants and the following nesting species: Ruby-throated Hummingbird, Blue-gray Gnatcatcher, Yellow-throated Vireo, Yellow-throated Warbler (occasional), Cerulean Warbler, and American Redstart. Downstream from the parking area is good for Broad-winged Hawk, Yellow-billed Cuckoo, and Swamp Sparrow.

The fields near Picnic Area No. 17 are excellent for American Woodcock, White-eyed Vireo, Blue-winged Warbler, Prairie Warbler, and Yellow-breasted Chat.

In winter, the feeders at the park office attract the usual southeastern Pennsylvania feeder birds: Downy Woodpecker, Carolina Chickadee, Tufted Titmouse, White-breasted Nuthatch, Carolina Wren, House Finch, American Goldfinch, and occasionally Red-breasted Nuthatch, Pine Siskin, and Evening Grosbeak.

The pond is a good place to check for Wood Duck, Mallards, and Solitary Sandpiper in spring. The open fields are good for migrating hawks in the fall.

The park's address is Ridley Creek State Park, Sycamore Mills Road, Media, PA 19063-4398,(610) 566-4800.

Tyler Arboretum

Tyler Arboretum is a 700-acre tract of woods, streams, wetlands, and fields located in Lima, about 10 miles west of Philadelphia and adjacent to Ridley Creek State Park. From the park, take Barren Road to Painter Road and drive one mile to the arboretum parking lot. Stop at the education center for a free map and bird checklist for which there is a small fee. The bird checklist includes 154 species and 25 accidentals.

Tyler Arboretum is privately owned, and admission is charged. The grounds are open daily from 8 a.m. to 5 p.m. The arboretum does not allow picnicking. It does schedule frequent programs for both adults and children. Fees are charged for some programs, but discounts are given to members. Members also receive free admission to the arboretum, a quarterly newsletter, and discounts at the gift shop. Some programs are open only to members.

The site has 10 miles of trails, and many of the trails are wheelchair-accessible. There is a nature center with a variety of nature exhibits. The arboretum is included in the Glenolden Christmas Bird Count.

The site is best known for its plant collections, including an herb garden, a butterfly garden, rhododendron collection, and a variety of trees. Of special interest to birders is the bird habitat garden.

Birds recorded on the grounds include 32 warbler species, of which the following are nesters: Blue-winged Warbler, Northern Parula, Chestnut-sided Warbler, Pine Warbler, Cerulean Warbler, Black-and-white Warbler, American Redstart, Worm-eating Warbler, Ovenbird, Louisiana Waterthrush, Kentucky Warbler, Common Yellowthroat, Hooded Warbler, and Yellow-breasted Chat.

Northern Bobwhite is a rare breeding species. Both Black-billed and Yellow-billed Cuckoo also breed, with Yellow-billed being more common. Northern Saw-Whet Owl is a rare winter visitor. Red-bellied Woodpecker is common year-round. Golden-crowned and Ruby-

Northern Saw-whet Owl

crowned Kinglets are common migrants and sometimes spend the winter. Veery is abundant in spring and summer, as is Wood Thrush. Gray-cheeked, Swainson's, and Hermit Thrush may be seen during migration. Rose-breasted Grosbeak is a common migrant and rare nesting species. Swamp Sparrow has been recorded in all seasons. Both Orchard and Northern Oriole nest in the arboretum.

The address is Tyler Arboretum, 515 Painter Road, Lima, PA 19037, (610) 566-9133.

Marsh Creek State Park

Marsh Creek State Park is 1,705 acres of woodlands, wetlands, and fields in Chester County. The park also has a 535-acre lake.

To reach the park, take Exit 23 from the Pennsylvania Turnpike (I-76) and take SR 100 north to the park's access road. Pick up a free map at the park office.

Facilities include boat rentals, picnic tables, and two hiking trails. A portion of the park is open to hunting; check at the office for details.

During spring migration, Common Loon; Red-necked, Horned, and Pied-billed Grebes; Tundra Swan; Snow Goose; Wood Duck; Green-winged Teal; American Black Duck; Northern Pintail; Blue-winged Teal; Northern Shoveler; Gadwall; American Wigeon; Canvasback; Redhead; Ring-necked Duck; Greater Scaup; Lesser Scaup; Oldsquaw; Black Scoter; White-winged Scoter; Common Goldeneye; Bufflehead; Hooded Merganser; Common Merganser; Red-breasted Merganser; and Ruddy Duck have been recorded. A Eurasian Wigeon was recorded here in February 1992.

Gulls and terns recorded here include Bonaparte's Gull, Caspian Tern, and Forster's Tern.

Marsh Creek is a good location for Grasshopper Sparrow in summer.

In late fall and winter, check fields for American Pipit, Snow Bunting, and Rusty Blackbird.

The address is Marsh Creek State Park, 675 Park Road, Downingtown, PA 19335, (610) 458-8515.

French Creek State Park

French Creek State Park is 7,339 acres of mostly wooded habitat and 108-acre Lake Hopewell in Berks County. To reach the park, take SR 724 east of Reading to Monocacy and turn right onto LR 2083, which goes through the park. Stop at the park office for a free map. A "Pennsylvania Trail of Geology" brochure also is available; it explains the geology of the park and adjacent Hopewell Furnace National Historical Site.

Facilities at the park include 209 modern campsites, a food concession in summer months, and more than 30 miles of trails. Interpretive programs are offered from April to December; check the schedule at the park office.

The park naturalist reports that Osprey always appear at French Creek on the day the Fish Commission stocks the lake in the spring and stay until anglers take over the park on the first day of trout season. He advises birders to follow the fish truck!

Other birds seen during spring migration include Common Loon, Pied-billed Grebe, and Hooded and Common Merganser. Green-backed Heron can be seen in summer, and Pileated Woodpecker is common year-round.

In 1993, Black Vultures nested under one of the park's camp buildings. Turkey Vultures nest in the quarry. The quarry itself is off-limits because of its hazards, but the presence of both species in this park makes it a good place to compare them.

The address is French Creek State Park, 834 Park Road, Elverson, PA 19520, (610) 582-9680.

White Clay Creek Preserve

White Clay Creek State Park is 1,253 acres managed jointly by Pennsylvania and Delaware. The Pennsylvania section of the park is located in Chester County and can be reached by taking US 1 south to SR 41. Continue on SR 41 to the intersection with SR 896. Turn left, and proceed to the park.

The park is located in floodplain wetlands. A "Pennsylvania/Delaware Trail of Geology" brochure explains the geologic features of the area.

Facilities include five hiking trails, a 5.5-mile horseback-riding trail, and picnicking facilities.

Birds at the park are similar to those found at Ridley Creek State Park, but this park is closer to the upper Chesapeake Bay so look (listen!) for Fish Crow.

The address is White Clay Creek Preserve, P.O. Box 172, Landenberg, PA 19350, (610) 255-5415. Or White Clay Creek Preserve, 425 Wedgewood Road, Newark, DE 19711, (302) 731-1310.

Chapter 7
Atlantic Coastal Plain

 The Atlantic Coastal Plain in Pennsylvania is a very narrow strip of land, extending from the Delaware River to US Route 1. The region makes up less than 1% of the Commonwealth. This tiny sliver of Pennsylvania is its most urban area, and only a few remnants of natural habitat exist. The elevation of the region ranges from sea level to 60 feet. The average annual temperature of the region is 52° Fahrenheit, with a January average of 28° and a July average of 74°. The average annual precipitation is 42 inches, with 30 inches of snow on average. Summers in this region of Pennsylvania are the state's longest and hottest. Prevailing winds are weak and from the southwest. High humidity, weak winds, and an abundance of pavement and buildings combine to make the summer heat oppressive.

If you read descriptions of the area written by William Penn 300 years ago, it's difficult to believe he was describing the same area that today includes refineries, shipyards, and commercial centers. Nevertheless, there are local birding hot spots, and some of these are very hot. The region's position on the Atlantic Flyway makes migration an exciting semiannual event. Perhaps it's a combination of a concentration of excellent birders together with a paucity of natural habitats that makes this region the home of many unique records. For example, breeding Black-necked Stilt have been recorded at the Philadelphia Sewage Treatment Ponds.

To be sure, birders will enjoy visiting one of several fine city parks—Pennypack and Fairmount, especially—and one state park—Neshaminy—and even a national wildlife refuge at Tinicum. And birders may also enjoy educational trips to the Philadelphia Zoo or one of the city's museums. Although essentially all of the region has been drained, paved, or otherwise urbanized, a side effect of this urbanization is that visitors will be able to visit several birding locations by using public transportation.

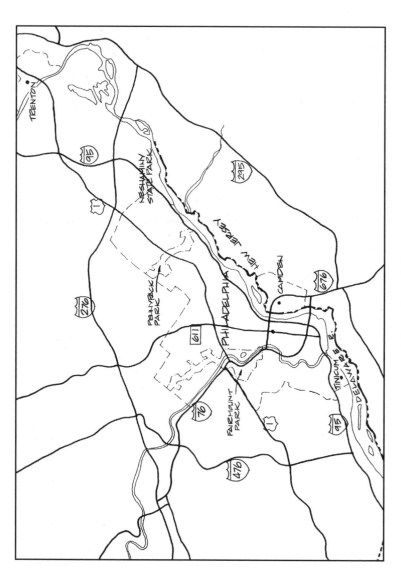

Atlantic Coastal Plain

Abundant year-round residents of the Atlantic Coastal Plain include Canada Goose, Ring-billed Gull, Rock Dove, Mourning Dove, Tufted Titmouse, Northern Mockingbird, Northern Cardinal, House Finch, and House Sparrow. Abundant winter residents are Herring Gull, Great Black-backed Gull, and Dark-eyed Junco.

Abundant nesters are Barn Swallow and Blue Jay. Other breeding birds include American Bittern; Least Bittern; Great Egret; Snowy Egret; Green-backed Heron; Black-crowned Night-Heron; Canada Goose; Wood Duck; American Black Duck; Mallard; Blue-winged Teal; Northern Shoveler; Northern Harrier; Sharp-shinned, Broad-winged, and Red-tailed Hawks; American Kestrel; Peregrine Falcon; Ring-necked Pheasant; Northern Bobwhite; Virginia Rail; Sora; Common Moorhen; Killdeer; Black-necked Stilt; Spotted Sandpiper; American Woodcock; Mourning Dove; Black-billed and Yellow-billed Cuckoos; Barn Owl; Eastern Screech-Owl; Great Horned Owl; Short-eared Owl; Common Nighthawk; Chimney Swift; Ruby-throated Hummingbird; Belted Kingfisher; Red-bellied, Downy, and Hairy Woodpeckers; Northern Flicker; Pileated Woodpecker; Eastern Wood-Pewee; Acadian Flycatcher; Willow Flycatcher; Eastern Phoebe; Great Crested Flycatcher; Eastern Kingbird; Horned Lark; Purple Martin; Tree, Northern Rough-winged, Bank, and Barn Swallows; Blue Jay; American Crow; Fish Crow; Carolina Chickadee; Tufted Titmouse; White-breasted Nuthatch; Carolina, House, and Sedge Wren; Blue-gray Gnatcatcher; Eastern Bluebird; Veery; Wood Thrush; American Robin; Gray Catbird; Northern Mockingbird; Brown Thrasher; Cedar Waxwing; White-eyed, Yellow-throated, Warbling, and Red-eyed Vireos; Blue-winged Warbler; Northern Parula; Yellow, Chestnut-sided, Cerulean, and Black-and-white Warblers; American Redstart; Prothonotary and Worm-eating Warblers; Ovenbird; Louisiana Waterthrush; Kentucky Warbler; Common Yellowthroat; Hooded Warbler; Yellow-breasted Chat; Scarlet Tanager; Northern Cardinal; Rose-breasted Grosbeak; Blue Grosbeak; Indigo Bunting; Rufous-sided Towhee; Chipping, Field, Savannah, Grasshopper, Song, and Swamp Sparrow; Bobolink; Red-winged Blackbird; Eastern Meadowlark; Common Grackle; Brown-headed Cowbird; Orchard Oriole; Northern Oriole; Purple and House Finches; and American Goldfinch.

Least Bittern

PHILADELPHIA

With a population of 1,585,577, Philadelphia is the largest city in Pennsylvania. It is also one of the loveliest cities in the world, especially in May when it seems azaleas bloom everywhere.

Philadelphia is best known for its history; walking tours of Independence National Historical Park, Elfreth's Alley, and Society Hill are popular. Today the City of Brotherly Love is a center for business, industry, and shipping. Although the region is completely urban, there are oases of nature to be found: Fairmount Park, Pennypack Park, and the Schuylkill River.

To report a rare bird alert, call the Academy of Natural Science at (215) 299-1181.

The Peregrine Fund first released young Peregrine Falcons in Philadelphia in 1981. In subsequent years, Peregrine Falcons have bred on the following bridges over the Delaware River: Girard Point, Walt Whitman, Commodore Barry, Betsy Ross, and possibly the Ben Franklin and Tacony-Palmyra. The turnpike bridge between Pennsylvania and New Jersey also has been used by a breeding pair. Bridge birding is hazardous for birders, just as bridge breeding is hazardous for the birds. A safer place to try for Peregrine is in the vicinity of Rittenhouse Square, where the species has been observed. Check the local rare bird alert for recent activity, (215) 567-2473.

Fairmount Park

Fairmount Park is the largest city park in the world; its 8,900 acres along the Schuylkill River and Wissahickon Creek include several small creeks, ponds, woods, and cleared flatlands. History lovers will be interested in tours of the park's historic mansions and in the Fairmount Waterworks, designed in 1812 to provide potable water for the residents of Philadelphia. In fact, the park has something for everyone: the Philadelphia Museum of Art, Rodin Museum, a horticultural center, and the Philadelphia Zoo are all located in the park.

There are many access points for a tour of the park, but in spring, summer, and fall an enjoyable way to tour the park is by replicas of Victorian trolleys. For one fare, riders can ride all day with as many

Peregrine Falcon

stops as they like. Ticket holders receive discounts for admission to the park's historic mansions, museums, and the zoo. The trolley tours begin and end at the Convention and Visitors' Bureau at 16th and J. F. Kennedy Boulevard. Tickets also can be purchased on the trolleys.

If you are driving to the park, take City Line Avenue to Belmont Avenue, which goes through Fairmount Park. Another approach is on the Benjamin Franklin Parkway from downtown to the Art Museum.

The park is open daily from 6 a.m. to 1 a.m. and is closed by curfew the remaining hours. There are 75 miles of bridle paths and hiking trails, and 25 miles of bikeways. Some trails are paved and accessible to wheelchairs. Picnics are allowed, and food is readily available.

Birds in the park include notable warbler and other songbird migrations during the spring. Many hawks winter in the park: Red-tailed, Red-shouldered, and Sharp-shinned Hawks have been observed, as have Great Horned Owls. Black-crowned Night-herons may breed. Double-crested Cormorants are often seen on the river.

The address is Fairmount Park Commission, Memorial Hall, Philadelphia, PA 19131; (215) 686-1776, park information; (215) 879-4044, trolley information.

The Philadelphia Zoo is 42 acres within Fairmount Park. To reach the zoo, take Exit 36 from I-76 (the Schuylkill Expressway) and follow the signs to Girard Avenue and the zoo. The No. 15 trolley and the No. 38 and No. 76 buses also serve the zoo. The zoo is open daily, except for Thanksgiving, Christmas Eve, Christmas, New Year's Eve, and New Year's Day. Admission is charged; memberships are available. Members receive free admission and two free quarterly publications. Maps of the facility are free with admission.

The trails through the zoo are wheelchair-accessible. One trail of interest is Penn's Woodland Trail, which reconstructs the forests of the 1600s. There are food concessions and a bookstore and gift shop.

The zoo—the oldest in the United States—has a collection of more than 600 birds. Research at the zoo focuses on conservation of endangered species. The zoo participates in Species Survival Plans for 21 species. Of interest to birders are programs to preserve the Guam Rail and the Micronesian Kingfisher.

The address is Philadelphia Zoo, 3400 West Girard Avenue, Philadelphia, PA 19104-1196, (215) 243-1100.

The Academy of Natural Sciences is located at 19th Street and Ben Franklin Parkway. Founded in 1812, the Academy features dinosaur and geologic exhibits as well as exhibits of Egyptian mummies, and many animals, including birds. There is a special hands-on children's area. The academy is wheelchair-accessible. Admission is charged.

The address is The Academy of Natural Sciences, 19th and Benjamin Franklin Parkway, Philadelphia, PA 19103, (215) 299-1000.

Pennypack Park

Pennypack Park, in northeast Philadelphia, is mostly wooded. Pennypack Creek meanders through the park; there are open areas such as ball fields and playgrounds. The park has a nature center. One vantage point of interest is where Pennypack Creek enters the Delaware River. Great Cormorant and Double-crested Cormorant have been observed here.

US 1 goes through Pennypack Park. There are numerous parking areas. Call (215) 671-0440 for more information.

Taylor Arboretum

The Taylor Arboretum is 30 acres of upland and floodplain meadows, woodlands, and pond owned by the Taylor Trust and managed by the Natural Lands Trust. Ridley Creek borders the site. The arboretum is open to the public from 9 a.m. to 4 p.m. daily, except for major holidays. It is an excellent place to study wildflowers and trees.

To reach the arboretum, take I-476 to Exit 1 and merge onto McDade Boulevard West. Continue to the fourth traffic light if you have approached from the north; from the south you will go through five traffic lights. There is no street sign, but the light is at Chestnut Street. Look for a sign for SR 320N; the Campus Medical Center is on the far right. Turn right. Continue past one stop sign and two traffic lights, downhill and around a bend to Ridley Drive. Turn left onto Ridley Drive. The arboretum is ahead on the left.

The Taylor Arboretum does not allow picnicking on the grounds. There are several trails through the site; they are grass or mulch and are not wheelchair-accessible. An education and research center is open by appointment and has classrooms and limited displays. Tours and educational programs can be scheduled by groups. Memberships in the Natural Lands Trust are available; members receive a quarterly magazine and invitations to special events at trust preserves.

Visit the arboretum in mid-May when azaleas and wildflowers are blooming and the following birds have been recorded: Carolina Wren; Wood Thrush; Blue-winged, Yellow-rumped, Black-throated Green, Bay-breasted, Blackpoll, and Black-and-white Warblers; American Redstart; Ovenbird; and Canada Warbler.

In summer, Green-backed Heron, Little Blue Heron, and Belted Kingfisher have been recorded. A Little Blue Heron spent the winter of 1991–92 at the Arboretum.

The address is Taylor Arboretum, 10 Ridley Drive, Wallingford, PA 19086, (610) 876-2649.

JOHN HEINZ NATIONAL WILDLIFE REFUGE AT TINICUM

The John Heinz National Wildlife Refuge at Tinicum recently was renamed to honor Pennsylvania's Senator John Heinz, who was tragically killed in a helicopter crash in 1991. Known to birders as "Tinicum," the refuge is 900 acres of tidal freshwater marsh and other habitats near the Philadelphia airport. Although Tinicum's marsh is the largest tidal wetland remaining in Pennsylvania, it is just a fraction of the original 5,700 acres found by the first European settlers in 1643. Tinicum is owned by the U.S. Fish and Wildlife Service.

To reach the refuge, drive south from Philadelphia on I-95 to the Bartram Avenue Exit. At the end of the exit ramp, go straight through the traffic light. You are on Bartram Avenue. At 84th Street, turn right. At the second traffic light, turn left on Lindbergh Boulevard. The refuge entrance is the first right off Lindbergh Boulevard. Park at the visitors' center, where you can pick up a free bird checklist, map, brochure, and calendar of guided walks featuring topics such as birds, trees, and flowers.

The refuge is open daily from 8 a.m. to sunset. The visitors' center is open daily from 9 a.m. to 4 p.m. Picnicking is not permitted in the refuge. Camping is not allowed. There is a canoe launch near the visitors' center. Hunting is not permitted in the refuge. This is a good birding spot in the fall when hunters take over State Game Lands and many areas of state parks. In addition to special walks and programs, guided walks are offered every Saturday and Sunday at 9 a.m. Tinicum is included in the Glenolden Christmas Bird Count.

Handicapped birders are permitted, between 9 a.m and 4 p.m. only, to drive through part of the refuge. The main trail is flat, and it is possible, but difficult, to use a wheelchair on it. An observation blind on the main trail overlooks the Darby Creek tidal mudflats.

In addition to the 200 acres of freshwater tidal marsh, Tinicum has ponds, streams, old field, and lowland forest. About 288 bird species have been recorded in or near the refuge; more than 85 species have bred. Tinicum is a good place for flowers, 800 species, and butterflies, 50 species.

The refuge's location on the Atlantic Flyway and the fact that it is surrounded by heavily urbanized land make it an important resting and feeding stop during both spring and fall migration, especially for waterfowl, shorebirds, and warblers (more than 30 species have been recorded). The birds at Tinicum are very vulnerable during their visits. Nearby refineries, pipelines, a major airport, and shipping lanes all present hazards. An oil spill or refinery accident at the wrong time could be catastrophic to migrating birds.

One of the best times to visit Tinicum is during the first two weeks of May, when warbler migration is at its peak. The following species have been recorded: Blue-winged, Golden-winged, Tennessee, Orange-crowned, and Nashville Warblers; Northern Parula; Yellow, Chestnut-sided, Magnolia, Cape May, Black-throated Blue, Yellow-rumped, Black-throated Green, Blackburnian, Pine, Prairie, Palm, Bay-breasted, Blackpoll, Cerulean, and Black-and-white Warblers; American Redstart; Prothonotary and Worm-eating Warblers; Ovenbird; Northern and Louisiana Waterthrushes; Kentucky, Connecticut, and Mourning Warblers; Common Yellowthroat; Hooded, Wilson's, and Canada Warblers; and Yellow-breasted Chat. All of these warblers also have been recorded in the fall. Only four of these species have bred in the refuge: Yellow Warbler, American Redstart, Common Yellowthroat, and Yellow-breasted Chat.

Also in May, birders have recorded shorebirds such as Black-bellied Plover, Semipalmated Plover, Greater and Lesser Yellowlegs, Solitary Sandpiper, Spotted Sandpiper, Semipalmated Sandpiper, Least Sandpiper, Pectoral Sandpiper, Dunlin, Short-billed Dowitcher, Long-billed Dowitcher, Common Snipe, and American Woodcock.

Rarities include Lesser Golden-Plover, Piping Plover, Willet, Upland Sandpiper, Ruddy Turnstone, Red Knot, Sanderling, and Curlew Sandpiper.

Other notable spring migrants include waterfowl from mid-March to May. Look for Wood Duck, Green-winged Teal, American Black Duck, Northern Pintail, Blue-winged Teal, Northern Shoveler, Gadwall, Eurasian Wigeon (rare), American Wigeon, Canvasback, Redhead (rare), Greater Scaup, Lesser Scaup, Oldsquaw (rare), White-winged Scoter (rare), Common Goldeneye (rare), Bufflehead, Hooded Merganser, Red-breasted Merganser, and Ruddy Duck. Northbound hawks, herons, egrets, and sparrows pass through the refuge in April.

The refuge mudflats are good for late summer shorebirds (more than 30 species have been recorded). Also in late summer, look for wandering herons, Marsh Wren (common), Warbling Vireo (occasional), and Swamp Sparrow (common).

Fall migrants include Pied-billed Grebe, raptors (15 species have been recorded), shorebirds (34 species), Forster's Tern, Bobolink, and Rusty Blackbird.

In winter, look for Northern Harrier and Rough-legged Hawk (rare). Short-eared Owls also have been recorded here in winter.

The refuge's mailing address is John Heinz National Wildlife Refuge at Tinicum, Scott Plaza II, Suite 104, Philadelphia PA 19113, (610) 521-0662. The visitors' center is located at 86th Street and Lindbergh Boulevard, Philadelphia PA 19153, (215) 365-3118.

Philadelphia Sewage Ponds/Old Fort Mifflin

Local birders refer to this area as "behind the airport." From I-95, take the Island Avenue Exit and follow signs south to Fort Mifflin, an historic site that dates to 1772. At the Fort Mifflin sign, bear left to reach the sewage treatment ponds and landfill area. This site is good for both spring and fall shorebird migrations. The sewage treatment ponds are the only confirmed breeding location for Black-necked Stilt in Pennsylvania.

If you bear right at the Fort Mifflin sign, you can check the fields for Rough-legged Hawk and Short-eared Owl in winter.

NESHAMINY STATE PARK

Neshaminy State Park is 330 acres bordering the Delaware River and Neshaminy Creek in Bucks County. To reach the park, take I-95 to Exit 23, and then take US 13, also known as Bristol Pike, to the park. Stop at the office for a free map.

The park's management plan lists 107 bird species. Unfortunately, the park does not have a bird checklist. Because the park is an oasis of green in a sea of urban and suburban landscape and because of its position on the Delaware Flyway, it is worth checking at any time, but especially during migration. Share your records.

The address is Neshaminy State Park, 263 Dunks Ferry Road, Bensalem, PA 19020, (215) 639-4538.

Silver Lake Nature Center

Silver Lake Nature Center is 255 acres of freshwater marsh, an unglaciated bog, coastal plain forest, wet meadow, fields, lawn, and a small lake located in Silver Lake Park. The park is owned by Bucks County.

To reach Silver Lake from Philadelphia, take I-95 to Exit 26 at Bristol. Turn right onto SR 413 and continue to US 13. Turn left. At the second traffic light, take a jug handle right turn around the Golden Eagle Diner. The nature center is 0.75 mile from the intersection of US 13 and Bath Road. Free maps of the park are available at the nature center.

The grounds are open daily from sunrise to sunset. The nature center building is open Tuesdays through Saturdays from 10 a.m. to 5 p.m., and Sundays from noon to 5 p.m. Picnics are allowed, but food is not sold at the center. Three miles of trails go through varied habitats; none is wheelchair-accessible.

The center has hands-on exhibits that explain the park's habitats and ecological concepts. The center publishes a seasonal newsletter, *Swallowtales,* for members, who also receive a discount in the park's gift/bookshop.

Field trips are scheduled. The center is included in the Southern Bucks County Christmas Bird Count. For bird information, call

Robert Mercer at (215) 785-1177. Mr. Mercer reports that 160 species have been observed here, and that the best time for birders is during spring and fall migration. Bird species are generally woodland species found in urban areas.

The address is Silver Lake Nature Center, 1306 Bath Road, Bristol, PA 19007, (215) 785-1177.

Appendix 1
A Checklist of Pennsylvania Birds

 This checklist is based on the official list of birds in Pennsylvania produced by the Pennsylvania Ornithological Records Committee (PORC), published in *Pennsylvania Birds* (Kwater), and annotated in Santner et al., *Annotated List of the Birds of Pennsylvania*. This list includes 418 species, of which two are extinct, two are extirpated, and 40 are hypothetical. Of course, new birds continue to be added to the state list; these additions are published in *Pennsylvania Birds*. I have included several recent additions to the list, such as the Pacific Loon. Two species, Chukar and Ringed Turtle-Dove, have been recorded in Pennsylvania only as escapes. Two species, Clark's and Western Grebe, are listed together because there is only one record, and that was before the American Ornithological Union (AOU) split.

The PORC requests information on accidentals, hypothetical, certain other designated rarities, and new records. Please send as many details as possible, including time, location, weather and light conditions, number of observers, photographs, recordings, etc. for all species with (A), (H), or (D) to Barbara Haas, Secretary, Pennsylvania Ornithological Records Committee, 2469 Hammertown Road, Narvon, PA 17555-9726, (717) 445-9609.

Breeding status is as documented in the recently published *Atlas of Breeding Birds in Pennsylvania* based on seven years of field work by more than 2,000 volunteers. I have included both "probable" and "confirmed" records.

The checklist names and sequence follow the *Checklist of North American Birds*, Sixth Edition, 1983, American Ornithologists' Union, as amended through the Thirty-eighth Supplement, 1991.

The following symbols are used:

(X) Extinct
(E) Extirpated
(A) Accidental (fewer than 10 records in Pennsylvania)
(H) Hypothetical
(D) PORC requests details of future records
°Currently breeds in Pennsylvania (nesting documented during atlas project, 1983–89).
°°Historically bred in Pennsylvania.

AVES: Birds

GAVIIFORMES: Loons

GAVIIDAE: Loons

> Red-throated Loon
> *Gavia stellata*
> Pacific Loon (A)
> *Gavia pacifica*
> Common Loon°°
> *Gavia immer*

PODICIPEDIFORMES: Grebes

PODICIPEDIDAE: Grebes

> Pied-billed Grebe°
> *Podilymbus podiceps*
> Horned Grebe
> *Podiceps auritus*
> Red-necked Grebe
> *Podiceps grisegena*
> Eared Grebe (D)
> *Podiceps nigricollis*

> Western/Clark's Grebe (H)
> *Aechmophorus* sp.

PROCELLARIIFORMES: Tube-nosed Swimmers

PROCELLARIIDAE: Petrels and Shearwaters

> Northern Fulmar (A)
> *Fulmaris glacialis*
> Black-capped Petrel (A)
> *Pterodroma hasitata*
> Kermadec Petrel (H)
> *Pterodoma neglecta*
> Greater Shearwater (H)
> *Puffinus gravis*
> Audubon's Shearwater (H)
> *Puffinus lherminieri*

HYDROBATIDAE: Storm-Petrels

> Wilson's Storm-Petrel (H)
> *Oceanites oceanicus*

Leach's Storm-Petrel (D)
Oceanites leucorhoa
Band-rumped Storm-
Petrel (H)
Oceanodroma castro

**PELECANIFORMES:
Totipalmate Swimmers**

PHAETHONTIDAE:
Tropicbirds

White-tailed Tropicbird (H)
Phaethon lepturus

SULIDAE: Boobies and Gannets

Northern Gannet (A)
Morus bassanus

PELECANIDAE: Pelicans

American White Pelican (D)
*Pelecanus
erythrorhynchos*
Brown Pelican (A)
Pelecanus occidentalis

PHALACROCORACIDAE:
Cormorants

Great Cormorant (D)
Phalacrocorax carbo
Double-crested Cormorant
Phalacrocorax auritus

FREGATIDAE: Frigatebirds

Magnificent Frigatebird (A)
Fregata magnificens

**CICONIIFORMES: Herons,
Ibises, and Storks**

ARDEIDAE: Bitterns and
Herons

American Bittern°
Botaurus lentiginosus
Least Bittern°
Ixobrychus exilis
Great Blue Heron°
Ardea herodias
Great Egret°
Casmerodius albus
Snowy Egret°
Egretta thula
Little Blue Heron
Egretta caerulea
Tricolored Heron
Egretta tricolor
Reddish Egret (H)
Egretta rufescens
Cattle Egret°
Bubulcus ibis
Green-backed Heron°
Butorides striatus
Black-crowned Night-Heron°
Nycticorax nycticorax
Yellow-crowned
Night-Heron°
Nyctanassa violacea

THRESKIORNITHIDAE:
Ibises and Spoonbills

White Ibis (D)
Eudocimus albus
Glossy Ibis°° (D)
Plegadis falcinellus

Roseate Spoonbill (A)
Ajaia ajaja

CICONIIDAE: Storks

Wood Stork (D)
Mycteria americana

PHOENICOPTERIFORMES: Flamingos

PHOENICOPTERIDAE: Flamingos

Greater Flamingo (H)
Phoenicopterus ruber

ANSERIFORMES: Swans, Geese, and Ducks

ANATIDAE: Swans, Geese, and Ducks

Fulvous Whistling-Duck (H)
Dendrocygna bicolor
Tundra Swan
Cygnus columbianus
Trumpeter Swan (H)
Cygnus buccinator
Mute Swan°
Cygnus olor
Greater White-fronted Goose
Anser albifrons
Snow Goose
Chen caerulescens
Ross' Goose (A)
Chen rossii
Brant
Branta bernicla
Barnacle Goose (H)
Branta leucopsis

Canada Goose°
Branta canadensis
Wood Duck°
Aix sponsa
Green-winged Teal°
Anas crecca
American Black Duck°
Anas rubripes
Mallard°
Anas platyrhynchos
Northern Pintail°°
Anas acuta
Blue-winged Teal°
Anas discors
Cinnamon Teal (A)
Anas cyanoptera
Northern Shoveler°
Anas clypeata
Gadwall°°
Anas strepera
Eurasian Wigeon (D)
Anas penelope
American Wigeon°
Anas americana
Canvasback
Aythya valisineria
Redhead°°
Aythya americana
Ring-necked Duck°°
Aythya collaris
Tufted Duck (A)
Aythya fuligula
Greater Scaup
Aythya marila
Lesser Scaup
Aythya affinis
Common Eider (H)
Somateria mollissima

King Eider (D)
   Somateria spectabilis
Harlequin Duck (D)
   Histrionicus histrionicus
Oldsquaw
   Clangula hyemalis
Black Scoter
   Melanitta nigra
Surf Scoter
   Melanitta perspicillata
White-winged Scoter
   Melanitta fusca
Common Goldeneye
   Bucephala clangula
Barrow's Goldeneye
   Bucephala islandica
Bufflehead
   Bucephala albeola
Hooded Merganser*
   Lophodytes cucullatus
Common Merganser*
   Mergus merganser
Red-breasted Merganser
   Mergus serrator
Ruddy Duck**
   Oxyura jamaicensis
Masked Duck (A)
   Oxyura dominica

FALCONIFORMES: Diurnal Birds of Prey

CATHARTIDAE: American Vultures

Black Vulture*
   Coragyps atratus
Turkey Vulture*
   Cathartes aura

ACCIPITRIDAE: Kites, Eagles, and Hawks

Osprey*
   Pandion haliaetus
American Swallow-tailed Kite (D)
   Elanoides forficatus
Mississippi Kite (D)
   Ictinia mississippiensis
Bald Eagle*
   Haliaeetus leucocephalus
Northern Harrier*
   Circus cyaneus
Sharp-shinned Hawk*
   Accipiter striatus
Cooper's Hawk*
   Accipiter cooperii
Northern Goshawk*
   Accipiter gentilis
Red-shouldered Hawk*
   Buteo lineatus
Broad-winged Hawk*
   Buteo platypterus
Swainson's Hawk (D)
   Buteo swainsoni
Red-tailed Hawk*
   Buteo jamaicensis
Rough-legged Hawk
   Buteo lagopus
Golden Eagle
   Aquila chrysaetos

FALCONIDAE: Caracaras and Falcons

American Kestrel*
   Falco sparverius
Merlin
   Falco columbarius

Peregrine Falcon°
  Falco peregrinus
Gyrfalcon (D)
  Falco rusticolus

**GALLIFORMES:
Gallinaceous Birds**

PHASIANIDAE: Partridges,
Turkey, and Quail

Chukar (H)
  Alectoris chukar
Ring-necked Pheasant°
  Phasianus colchicus
Ruffed Grouse°
  Bonasa umbellus
Greater Prairie-Chicken°° (E)
  Tympanuchus cupido
Wild Turkey°
  Meleagris gallopavo
Northern Bobwhite°
  Colinus virginianus

**GRUIFORMES: Cranes and
Rails**

RALLIDAE: Rails, Gallinules,
and Coots

Yellow Rail (D)
  *Coturnicops
   noveboracensis*
Black Rail° (D)
  Laterallus jamaicensis
Clapper Rail (A)
  Rallus longirostris
King Rail° (D)
  Rallus elegans

Virginia Rail°
  Rallus limicola
Sora°
  Porzana carolina
Spotted Rail (A)
  Pardirallus maculatus
Purple Gallinule (D)
  Porphyrula martinica
Common Moorhen°
  Gallinula chloropus
American Coot°
  Fulica americana

GRUIDAE: Cranes

Sandhill Crane (D)
  Grus canadensis
Whooping Crane (H)
  Grus americana

**CHARADRIIFORMES:
Shorebirds and Gulls**

CHARADRIIDAE: Plovers

Black-bellied Plover
  Pluvialis squatarola
Lesser Golden-Plover
  Pluvialis dominica
Snowy Plover (A)
  Charadrius alexandrinus
Wilson's Plover (D)
  Charadrius wilsonia
Semipalmated Plover
  Charadrius semipalmatus
Piping Plover°° (D)
  Charadrius melodus
Killdeer°
  Charadrius vociferus

HAEMATPODIDAE: Oyster-catchers

American Oystercatcher (H)
Haematopus palliatus

RECURVIROSTRIDAE: Stilts and Avocets

Black-necked Stilt° (D)
Himantopus mexicanus
American Avocet (D)
Recurvirostra americana

SCOLOPACIDAE: Sandpipers and Phalaropes

Greater Yellowlegs
Tringa melanoleuca
Lesser Yellowlegs
Tringa flavipes
Spotted Redshank (H)
Tringa erythropus
Solitary Sandpiper
Tringa solitaria
Willet (D)
Catoptrophorus semipalmatus
Spotted Sandpiper°
Actitis macularia
Upland Sandpiper°
Bartramia longicauda
Eskimo Curlew (H)
Numenius borealis
Whimbrel (D)
Numenius phaeopus
Long-billed Curlew (H)
Numenius americanus
Black-tailed Godwit (A)
Limosa limosa

Hudsonian Godwit (D)
Limosa haemastica
Marbled Godwit (D)
Limosa fedoa
Ruddy Turnstone
Arenaria interpres
Surfbird (A)
Aphriza virgata
Red Knot
Calidris canutus
Sanderling
Calidris alba
Semipalmated Sandpiper
Calidris pusilla
Western Sandpiper
Calidris mauri
Least Sandpiper
Calidris minutilla
White-rumped Sandpiper
Calidris fuscicollis
Baird's Sandpiper
Calidris bairdii
Pectoral Sandpiper
Calidris melanotos
Purple Sandpiper (D)
Calidris maritima
Dunlin
Calidris alpina
Curlew Sandpiper (H)
Calidris ferruginea
Stilt Sandpiper
Calidris himantopus
Buff-breasted Sandpiper (D)
Tryngites subruficollis
Ruff (D)
Philomachus pugnax
Short-billed Dowitcher
Limnodromus griseus

Long-billed Dowitcher (D)
  Limnodromus
  scolopaceus
Common Snipe°
  Gallinago gallinago
Eurasian Woodcock (H)
  Scolopax rusticola
American Woodcock°
  Scolopax minor
Wilson's Phalarope
  Phalaropus tricolor
Red-necked Phalarope (D)
  Phalaropus lobatus
Red Phalarope (D)
  Phalaropus fulicaria

LARIDAE: Gulls, Terns, and
Skimmers

Pomarine Jaeger (D)
  Stercorarius pomarinus
Parasitic Jaeger (D)
  Stercorarius parasiticus
Laughing Gull (D)
  Larus atricilla
Franklin's Gull(D)
  Larus pipixcan
Little Gull (D)
  Larus minutus
Common Black-headed
  Gull (A)
  Larus ridibundus
Bonaparte's Gull
  Larus philadelphia
Mew Gull (A)
  Larus canus
Ring-billed Gull
  Larus delawarensis

Herring Gull
  Larus argentatus
Thayer's Gull
  Larus thayeri
Iceland Gull
  Larus glaucoides
Lesser Black-backed Gull
  Larus fuscus
Glaucous Gull
  Larus hyperboreus
Great Black-backed Gull
  Larus marinus
Black-legged Kittiwake (D)
  Rissa tridactyla
Ross' Gull (A)
  Rhodostethia rosea
Sabine's Gull (D)
  Xema sabini
Gull-billed Tern (H)
  Sterna nilotica
Caspian Tern
  Sterna caspia
Royal Tern (A)
  Sterna maxima
Roseate Tern (A)
  Sterna dougallii
Common Tern°°
  Sterna hirundo
Arctic Tern (A)
  Sterna paradisaea
Forster's Tern
  Sterna forsteri
Least Tern°° (D)
  Sterna antillarum
Sooty Tern (A)
  Sterna fuscata

Black Tern°
Chlidonias niger
Black Skimmer (D)
Rynchops niger

ALCIDAE: Auks, Murres, and Puffins

Dovekie (D)
Alle alle
Thick-billed Murre (D)
Uria lomvia
Razorbill (H)
Alca torda
Black Guillemot (H)
Cepphus grylle
Ancient Murrelet (A)
Synthliboramphus antiquus
Atlantic Puffin (H)
Fratercula arctica

COLUMBIFORMES: Pigeons and Doves

COLUMBIDAE: Pigeons and Doves

Rock Dove°
Columba livia
Band-tailed Pigeon (H)
Columba fasciata
Ringed Turtle-Dove (H)
Streptopelia risoria
Mourning Dove°
Zenaida macroura
Passenger Pigeon°° (X)
Ectopistes migratorius
Common Ground-Dove (A)

Columbina passerina

PSITTACIFORMES: Parrots

PSITTACIDAE: Parakeets

Carolina Parakeet (X)
Conuropsis carolinensis

CUCULIFORMES: Cuckoos

CUCULIDAE: Cuckoos and Anis

Black-billed Cuckoo°
Coccyzus erythropthalmus
Yellow-billed Cuckoo°
Coccyzus americanus
Smooth-billed Ani (H)
Crotophaga ani

STRIGIFORMES: Owls

TYTONIDAE: Barn-Owls

Barn Owl°
Tyto alba

STRIGIDAE: Typical owls

Eastern Screech-Owl°
Otus asio
Great Horned Owl°
Bubo virginianus
Snowy Owl
Nyctea scandiaca
Northern Hawk Owl (A)
Surnia ulula
Barred Owl°
Strix varia
Great Gray Owl (A)
Strix nebulosa

Long-eared Owl°
  Asio otus
Short-eared Owl°
  Asio flammeus
Boreal Owl (A)
  Aegolius funereus
Northern Saw-whet Owl°
  Aegolius acadicus

CAPRIMULGIFORMES: Goatsuckers

CAPRIMULGIDAE: Goatsuckers

Common Nighthawk°
  Chordeiles minor
Chuck-will's-widow° (D)
  Caprimulgus carolinensis
Whip-poor-will°
  Caprimulgus vociferus

APODIFORMES: Swifts and Hummingbirds

APODIDAE: Swifts

Chimney Swift°
  Chaetura pelagica

TROCHILIDAE: Hummingbirds

Ruby-throated Hummingbird°
  Archilochus colubris

Rufous Hummingbird (A)
  Selasphorus rufus

CORACIIFORMES: Kingfishers

ALCEDINIDAE: Kingfishers

Belted Kingfisher°
  Ceryle alcyon

PICIFORMES: Woodpeckers

PICIDAE: Woodpeckers

Red-headed Woodpecker°
  Melanerpes erythrocephalus
Red-bellied Woodpecker°
  Melanerpes carolinus
Yellow-bellied Sapsucker°
  Sphyrapicus varius
Downy Woodpecker°
  Picoides pubescens
Hairy Woodpecker°
  Picoides villosus
Red-cockaded Woodpecker (H)
  Picoides borealis
Three-toed Woodpecker (H)
  Picoides tridactylus
Black-backed Woodpecker (D)
  Picoides arcticus
Northern Flicker°
  Colaptes auratus
Pileated Woodpecker°
  Dryocopus pileatus

PASSERIFORMES: Passerine Birds

TYRANNIDAE: Tyrant Flycatchers

Olive-sided Flycatcher°
Contopus borealis
Eastern Wood-Pewee°
Contopus virens
Yellow-bellied Flycatcher°
Empidonax flaviventris
Acadian Flycatcher°
Empidonax virescens
Alder Flycatcher°
Empidonax alnorum
Willow Flycatcher°
Empidonax trailii
Least Flycatcher°
Empidonax minimus
Hammond's Flycatcher (H)
Empidonax hammondii
Dusky Flycatcher (H)
Empidonax oberholseri
Pacific-slope Flycatcher (A)
Empidonax difficilis
Eastern Phoebe°
Sayornis phoebe
Say's Phoebe (A)
Sayornis saya
Vermillion Flycatcher (A)
Pyrocephalus rubinus
Great Crested Flycatcher°
Myiarchus crinitus
Western Kingbird (D)
Tyrannus verticalis

Eastern Kingbird°
Tyrannus tyrannus
Scissor-tailed Flycatcher (D)
Tyrannus forficatus
Fork-tailed Flycatcher (H)
Tyrannus savana

ALAUDIDAE: Larks

Horned Lark°
Eremophila alpestris

HIRUNDINIDAE: Swallows

Purple Martin°
Progne subis
Tree Swallow°
Tachycineta bicolor
Northern Rough-winged Swallow°
Stelgidopteryx serripennis
Bank Swallow°
Riparia riparia
Cliff Swallow°
Hirundo pyrrhonota
Barn Swallow°
Hirundo rustica

CORVIDAE: Jays and Crows

Blue Jay°
Cyanocitta cristata
Eurasian Jackdaw° (A)
Corvus monedula
American Crow°
Corvus brachyrhynchos
Fish Crow°
Corvus ossifragus

Common Raven*
Corvus corax

PARIDAE: Titmice

Black-capped Chickadee*
Parus atricapillus
Carolina Chickadee*
Parus carolinesis
Boreal Chickadee (D)
Parus hudsonicus
Tufted Titmouse*
Parus bicolor

SITTIDAE: Nuthatches

Red-breasted Nuthatch*
Sitta canadensis
White-breasted Nuthatch*
Sitta carolinensis
Brown-headed Nuthatch (A)
Sitta pusilla

CERTHIIDAE: Creepers

Brown Creeper*
Certhia americana

TROGLODYTIDAE: Wrens

Carolina Wren*
*Thryothorus
ludovicianus*
Bewick's Wren** (D)
Thryomanes bewickii
House Wren*
Troglodytes aedon
Winter Wren*
Troglodytes troglodytes
Sedge Wren* (D)
Cistothorus platensis

Marsh Wren*
Cistothorus palustris

MUSCICAPIDAE: Muscapids

Golden-crowned Kinglet*
Regulus satrapa
Ruby-crowned Kinglet
Regulus calendula
Blue-gray Gnatcatcher*
Polioptila caerulea
Northern Wheatear (H)
Oenanthe oenanthe
Eastern Bluebird*
Sialia sialis
Mountain Bluebird (A)
Sialia currucoides
Townsend's Solitaire (A)
Myadestes townsendi
Veery*
Catharus fuscescens
Gray-cheeked Thrush
Catharus minimus
Swainson's Thrush*
Catharus ustulatus
Hermit Thrush*
Catharus guttatus
Wood Thrush*
Hylocichla mustelina
American Robin*
Turdus migratorius
Varied Thrush (D)
Ixoreus naevius

MIMIDAE: Mockingbirds and
Thrashers

Gray Catbird*
Dumetella carolinensis

Northern Mockingbird*
Minus polyglottos
Brown Thrasher*
Toxostoma rufum

MOTACILLIDAE: Pipits

American Pipit
Anthus rubescens
Sprague's Pipit (H)
Anthus spragueii

BOMBYCILLIDAE: Waxwings

Bohemian Waxwing (A)
Bombycilla garrulus
Cedar Waxwing*
Bombycilla cedrorum

LANIIDAE: Shrikes

Northern Shrike
Lanius excubitor
Loggerhead Shrike* (D)
Lanius ludovicianus

STURNIDAE: Starlings

European Starling*
Sturnus vulgaris

VIREONIDAE: Vireos

White-eyed Vireo*
Vireo griseus
Bell's Vireo (H)
Vireo bellii
Solitary Vireo*
Vireo solitarius
Yellow-throated Vireo*
Vireo flavifrons

Warbling Vireo*
Vireo gilvus
Philadelphia Vireo
Vireo philadelphicus
Red-eyed Vireo*
Vireo olivaceus

EMBERIZIDAE: Emberizids

Blue-winged Warbler*
Vermivora pinus
Golden-winged Warbler*
Vermivora chrysoptera
Tennessee Warbler
Vermivora peregrina
Orange-crowned Warbler
Vermivora celata
Nashville Warbler*
Vermivora ruficapilla
Northern Parula*
Parula americana
Yellow Warbler*
Dendroica petechia
Chestnut-sided Warbler*
Dendroica pensylvanica
Magnolia Warbler*
Dendroica magnolia
Cape May Warbler
Dendroica tigrina
Black-throated Blue Warbler*
Dendroica caerulescens
Yellow-rumped Warbler*
Dendroica coronata
Black-throated Gray
Warbler (A)
Dendroica nigrescens
Townsend's Warbler (A)
Dendroica townsendi

Black-throated Green
  Warbler*
  Dendroica virens
Blackburnian Warbler*
  Dendroica fusca
Yellow-throated Warbler*
  Dendroica dominica
Pine Warbler*
  Dendroica pinus
Kirtland's Warbler (A)
  Dendroica kirtlandii
Prairie Warbler*
  Dendroica discolor
Palm Warbler
  Dendroica palmarum
Bay-breasted Warbler
  Dendroica castanea
Blackpoll Warbler
  Dendroica striata
Cerulean Warbler*
  Dendroica cerulea
Black-and-white Warbler*
  Mniotilta varia
American Redstart*
  Setophaga ruticilla
Prothonotary Warbler*
  Protonotaria citrea
Worm-eating Warbler*
  Helmitheros vermivorus
Swainson's Warbler* (D)
  Limnothlypis swainsonii
Ovenbird*
  Seiurus aurocapillus
Northern Waterthrush*
  Seiurus noveboracensis
Louisiana Waterthrush*
  Seiurus motacilla

Kentucky Warbler*
  Oporornis formosus
Connecticut Warbler
  Oporornis agilis
Mourning Warbler*
  Oporornis philadelphia
Common Yellowthroat*
  Geothlypis trichas
Hooded Warbler*
  Wilsonia citrina
Wilson's Warbler
  Wilsonia pusilla
Canada Warbler*
  Wilsonia canadensis
Yellow-breasted Chat*
  Icteria virens
Summer Tanager* (D)
  Piranga rubra
Scarlet Tanager*
  Piranga olivacea
Western Tanager (D)
  Piranga ludoviciana
Northern Cardinal*
  Cardinalis cardinalis
Rose-breasted Grosbeak*
  Pheucticus ludovicianus
Black-headed Grosbeak (D)
  *Pheucticus
  melanocephalus*
Blue Grosbeak*
  Guiraca caerula
Lazuli Bunting (A)
  Passerina amoena
Indigo Bunting*
  Passerina cyanea
Painted Bunting (A)
  Passerina ciris

Dickcissel*
Spiza americana
Green-tailed Towhee (A)
Pipilo chlorurus
Rufous-sided Towhee*
Pipilo erythrophthalmus
Bachman's Sparrow** (A)
Aimophila aestivalis
American Tree Sparrow
Spizella arborea
Chipping Sparrow*
Spizella passerina
Clay-colored Sparrow* (D)
Spizella pallida
Field Sparrow*
Spizella pusilla
Vesper Sparrow*
Pooecetes gramineus
Lark Sparrow** (D)
Chondestes grammacus
Lark Bunting (D)
Calamospiza melanocorys
Savannah Sparrow*
Passerculus sandwichensis
Grasshopper Sparrow*
Ammodramus savannarum
Henslow's Sparrow*
Ammodramus henslowii
LeConte's Sparrow (A)
Ammodramus leconteii
Sharp-tailed Sparrow (D)
Ammodramus caudacutus
Seaside Sparrow (A)
Ammodramus maritimus
Fox Sparrow
Passerella iliaca

Song Sparrow*
Melospiza melodia
Lincoln's Sparrow
Melospiza lincolnii
Swamp Sparrow*
Melospiza georgiana
White-throated Sparrow*
Zonotrichia albicollis
Golden-crowned
Sparrow (H)
Zonotrichia atricapilla
White-crowned Sparrow
Zonotrichia leuchophrys
Harris' Sparrow (D)
Zonotrichia guerula
Dark-eyed Junco*
Junco hyemalis
Lapland Longspur
Calcarius lapponicus
Snow Bunting
Plectrophenax nivalis
Bobolink*
Dolichonyx oryzivorus
Red-winged Blackbird*
Agelaius phoeniceus
Eastern Meadowlark*
Sturnella magna
Western Meadowlark* (D)
Sturnella neglecta
Yellow-headed
Blackbird (D)
Xanthocephalus xanthocephalus
Rusty Blackbird
Euphagus carolinus
Brewer's Blackbird (D)
Euphagus cyanocephalus

Boat-tailed Grackle (H)
Quiscalus major
Common Grackle°
Quiscalus quiscula
Brown-headed Cowbird°
Molothrus ater
Orchard Oriole°
Icterus spurius
Northern Oriole°
Icterus galbula

FRINGILLIDAE: Cardueline Finches

Brambling (A)
Fringilla montifringilla
Pine Grosbeak
Pinicola enucleator
Purple Finch°
Carpodacus purpureus
House Finch°
Carpodacus mexicanus
Red Crossbill°°
Loxia curvirostra

White-winged Crossbill
Loxia leucoptera
Common Redpoll
Carduelis flammea
Hoary Redpoll (H)
Carduelis hornemanni
Pine Siskin°
Carduelis pinus
Lesser Goldfinch (H)
Carduelis psaltria
American Goldfinch°
Carduelis tristis
Evening Grosbeak
Coccothraustes vespertinus

PASSERIDAE: Old World Sparrows

House Sparrow°
Passer domesticus

Appendix 2
Pennsylvania Bird Organizations

Statewide

Audubon Council of Pennsylvania, 1104 Fernwood Ave., Suite 300, Camp Hill, PA 17011. Meetings spring and fall, special Issues Day annually; field trips in conjunction with fall meeting; 25,000 members. Projects: environmental activism, wetlands workshops, environmental education, co-sponsored breeding birds atlas project, Partners in Flight activities.

Pennsylvania Society for Ornithology, c/o Hawk Mountain Sanctuary, RD 2, Box 191, Kempton, PA 19529. Newsletter, *PSO Newsletter*, published quarterly; journal, *Pennsylvania Birds,* published quarterly; meetings annually; field trips in conjunction with annual meeting. Projects: Special Areas Projects to census birds in parks, state game lands, and state forest natural areas; co-sponsor of breeding birds atlas project, Partners in Flight activities.

Allentown/Bethlehem/Easton

Lehigh Valley Audubon Society, P.O. Box 290, Emmaus, PA 18049. Newsletter, *Osprey*; meetings monthly; field trips monthly; 1,400 members. Projects: environmental education, land preservation, and conservation of wildlife; Wild Creek-Little Gap Christmas Bird Count.

Altoona

Juniata Valley Audubon Society, P.O. Box 2378, Altoona, PA 16603. Newsletter, *The Gnatcatcher*, published monthly, September to June; meetings monthly; field trips monthly; 350 members. Projects: Culp

Christmas Bird Count, two Special Areas Projects, speakers' bureau, annual conservation award, environmental education. For bird information call Dave Kyler, (814) 643-6030.

Bloomsburg

North Branch Bird Club, c/o Alan Gregory, P.O. Box 571, Conyngham, PA 18219-0571. Newsletter, *The North Branch*, published quarterly; meetings bimonthly; field trips, 1-2 per quarter; 55 members. Projects: Bloomsburg Christmas Bird Count; six Special Areas Projects. For bird information call Alan Gregory, (717) 788-1425 (day) or (717) 455-3636 (evening).

Butler

Bartramian Audubon Society. Projects: Butler Christmas Bird Count. Contact Audubon Council of Pennsylvania for more information.

Chambersburg

Conococheague Audubon Society, P.O. Box 210, Scotland, PA 17254. Newsletter, *Naturally*, published monthly; meetings monthly; field trips as scheduled; 400 members. Projects: Chambersburg Christmas Bird Count.

Dallas

Greater Wyoming Valley Audubon Society, P.O. Box 535, Dallas, PA 18612. Newsletter, *Valley Views*, published bimonthly; meetings monthly September to May, except December; field trips monthly; 500 members. Projects: Dallas Area and Southeast Bradford Christmas Bird Count, Tubs Trail project, sanctuary project. For bird information call the bird hot line, (717) 825-BIRD.

Erie

Presque Isle Audubon Society, P.O. Box 1783, Erie, PA 16507. Newsletter, *Tern of Events*, published monthly; meetings monthly, field trips several times per month; 850 members. Projects: Erie Christmas Bird Count, conservation, environmental education.

Gettysburg

South Mountain Audubon Society, P.O. Box 3671, Gettysburg, PA 17325. Newsletter, *South Mountain Airs*, published monthly; meetings monthly September to May; field trips monthly; 335 members. Projects: Gettysburg Christmas Bird Count, annual bird seed sale.

Harrisburg

Appalachian Audubon Society, P.O. Box 15123, Harrisburg, PA 17105-5123. Newsletter, *Kingfisher Courier*, published monthly; meetings monthly September to May, except December; field trips as scheduled; 1,600 members. Projects: Harrisburg Christmas Bird Count, wetlands watch, environmental education, conservation activism.

Honesdale

Northeast Pennsylvania Audubon Society, P.O. Box 711, Honesdale, PA 18431. Newsletter, *Econotes*, published 11 times per year; meetings monthly, April through October; field trips monthly; 700 members. Projects: nature center (wetlands), White Mills Christmas Bird Count, annual craft fair, environmental scholarships, conservation programs. For bird information call Joe and Voni Strasser, (717) 226-8847 or 226-1460.

Indiana

Todd Bird Club, c/o R. V. Higbee, RD 2, Box 166, Indiana, PA 15701. Newsletter, *Todd Bird Club Newsletter*, published quarterly; meetings monthly except June, July, and August; field trips every Tuesday and Saturday during migration; 78 members; Indiana Christmas

Bird Count. Projects: North American Migration Count, Special Areas Project for Yellow Creek State Park. For bird information call Margaret or Roger Higbee, (412) 354-3493; Gloria Lamer, (412) 349-1159; Georgette Syster (412) 349-6293; or Nancy Karp (412) 543-4307.

Johnstown

Allegheny Plateau Audubon Society, 1003 Eisenhower Boulevard, Johnstown, PA 15904. Newsletter, *Chickadee Chatter*; meetings monthly; field trips as scheduled; 350 members; Johnstown Christmas Bird Count. Projects: environmental education, wetlands restoration project, Allegheny Front Hawk Watch.

Kempton

Hawk Mountain Sanctuary Association, Route 2, Kempton, PA 19529. Newsletter, *Hawk Mountain News*, published biannually; lecture series during fall migration; special workshops; operates world's first sanctuary for migrating raptors; conducts research on raptors and other birds and wildlife; environmental education and internships; international cooperative projects; conservation policy.

Lewisburg

Seven Mountains Audubon Society, P.O. Box 389, Lewisburg, PA 17837. Newsletter published monthly. Meetings monthly, field trips monthly.

New Hope

Bucks County Audubon Society, 6324 Upper York Road, New Hope, PA 18938. Newsletter, *Harbinger*, published bimonthly; meetings monthly; field trips weekly; 2,000 members; 3 Christmas Bird Counts. Projects: local and long-distance field trips, historic tree registry, environmental education. Operates Honey Hollow Environmental Education Center. For bird information call BCAS office, (215) 297-5880.

Palmyra

Quittapahilla Audubon Society, P.O. Box 123, Palmyra, PA 17078. Newsletter, *Quittapahilla Audubon Society Newsletter*, published bimonthly; meetings and field trips scheduled monthly, 350 members. Projects: annual bird seed sale, birdathon, environmental education, conservation.

Paoli

Valley Forge Audubon Society, P.O. Box 866, Paoli, PA 19301. Newsletter, *The Conservator*, published monthly; meetings monthly; field trips several times a month; weekly walks on Thursdays; 3,300 members; Christmas Bird Count. Projects: bird seed sale, environmental education, conservation activism. For information about field trips, call Shethra Rigg, (215) 265-1184.

Pittsburgh

Audubon Society of Western Pennsylvania, 614 Dorseyville Road, Pittsburgh, PA 15232. Newsletter, *ASWP Bulletin*; meetings monthly; field trips as scheduled; 4,500 members; Pittsburgh Christmas Bird Count. Projects: environmental education. Operates Beechwood Farms Nature Center. For bird information call the bird hot line, (412) 963-6104.

Western Pennsylvania Conservancy (WPC), 316 Fourth Avenue, Pittsburgh, PA 15222. Newsletter, *Conserve*, published quarterly. Also publishes outing guides to conservancy and public lands. The WPC has been very active in recent years in acquiring land in the Allegheny River and French Creek watersheds. For more information call (412) 288-2777.

Rural Valley

Cowanshannock Creek Watershed Association, P.O. Box 307, Rural Valley, PA 16249. Newsletter published quarterly. Projects: Great Shamokin Path—Cowanshannock Branch; distributes bluebird, Wood

Duck, and bat boxes; environmental scholarships; streamside habitat protection.

Wellsboro

Tiadaghton Audubon Society, P.O. Box 605, Wellsboro, PA 16901. Newsletter, *The Raven*, published quarterly; meetings monthly; field trips four times per year; 250 members. Projects: Mansfield Christmas Bird Count, landfill control, special protection for Pine Creek, scenic river promotion, airport environmental assessment. For bird information call Bob Ross, (717) 724-3322 (day) or (717) 376-5394 (evening).

Williamsport

Lycoming Audubon Society, P.O. Box 4053, Williamsport, PA 17701-0653. Newsletter, *Lycoming Audubon Society Newsletter*, published 8 times per year; meetings monthly, field trips as scheduled; 450 members. Projects: Williamsport Christmas Bird Count, environmental education, members assist with Peregrine Falcon reintroduction project.

Wyncote

Wyncote Audubon Society, 1212 Edgehill Road, Abington, PA 19001, (215) 887-6603. Newsletter, *Naturally*, published monthly; meetings monthly; field trips monthly; 1,300 members. Projects: Wyncote Christmas Bird Count, environmental education, Briar Bush Nature Center, conservation activism.

York

York Audubon Society, P.O. Box 2432, York, PA 17405. Newsletter, *Bluebird Bulletin*, published monthly; meetings monthly, field trips as scheduled; 700 members. Project: York Christmas Bird Count.

Appendix 3
Scientific Bird Collections in Pennsylvania

 The following is a list of museums, colleges, and other organizations that have study skins, skeletons preserved in fluid, mounted birds, and egg set collections. These collections are maintained primarily for research by biologists or for study by students enrolled in ornithology courses; however, they are useful to birders interested in identification and variations within species. If you would like access to a collection, contact the appropriate person in advance. The collections are listed in alphabetical order by city.

Clarion

Biology Department, Clarion University, Clarion PA 16214. 600 skins (most of the passerines are freeze-dried), 6 skeletons, 35 mounted birds, 15 egg sets. Collection available to interested persons by prearrangement. Clarion County best represented. Contact Dr. Peter Dalby, Curator of Vertebrates, (814) 226-2164 or 226-2273.

Edinboro

Edinboro University of Pennsylvania, Department of Biology, Edniboro, PA 16444. 725 skins, 8 skeletons, 25 skulls, 125 mounted birds, 50 extended wings of Pennsylvania waterfowl and a few other species, 1 or several eggs of approximately 100 species (none in sets), nests of 40 Pennsylvania breeding species. Collection available to interested persons by prearrangement. Pennsylvania best represented. Contact Dr. Donald B. Snyder, (814) 732-2561.

Huntingdon

Juniata College Vertebrate Zoology Museum, Biology Department, Huntingdon, PA 16652. 216 skins, 3 skeletons, 16 mounted birds, several fecal pellet samples. Collection available to interested persons by prearrangement. Cannot be removed from museum. Central Pennsylvania best represented. Contact Chuck Yohn, Director, (814) 643-4310, ext. 575.

Lancaster

North Museum of Natural History and Science, Franklin and Marshall College, P.O. Box 3003, Lancaster, PA 17604. 772 skins, several skeletons, 1,290 mounted birds, 2,280 egg sets. Collection available to interested persons by prearrangement. Use restricted by staff availability to access materials and monitor use. Central Pennsylvania best represented. Some tropical specimens. Much of the mounted collection is in visible storage. Contact Bob Gingerich, Director, (717) 291-3943.

Slippery Rock

Biology Department, 123 Vincent Science Hall, Slippery Rock University, Slippery Rock, PA 16057. 540 skins, 64 mounted birds. Collection available to interested persons by prearrangement. Pennsylvania best represented. Contact Dr. Genevieve Tvrdik (412) 738-2485.

Appendix 4
Selected References

American Ornithologists' Union, *Check-list of North American Birds,* Sixth edition. Washington, 1983.

Bonta, Marcia, *Outbound Journeys in Pennsylvania.* University Park, PA: The Pennsylvania State University Press, 1987.

Bull, John and Farrand, John, Jr., *The Audubon Society Field Guide to North American Birds, Eastern Region.* New York: Alfred A. Knopf, Inc., 1977.

Brauning, Daniel B., Editor, *Atlas of Breeding Birds in Pennsylvania.* Pittsburgh: University of Pittsburgh Press, 1992.

Broun, Maurice, *Hawks Aloft: The Story of Hawk Mountain.* New York: Dodd, Mead Co., 1948.

Cuff, D.J., et al., Editors, *The Atlas of Pennsylvania.* Philadelphia, Temple University Press, 1989.

DiFlaviana, Kathleen, Editor, *The Pennsylvania Manual,* Vol. 110. Harrisburg, PA: Department of General Services, Commonwealth of Pennsylvania, 1991.

Farrand, John, Jr., Editor, *The Audubon Society Master Guide to Birding.* New York: Alfred A. Knopf, Inc., 1983.

Grimm, William C., *Birds of the Pymatuning Region.* Harrisburg, PA: Pennsylvania Game Commission, 1952.

Harding, John J., Editor, *Marsh, Meadow, Mountain: Natural Places of the Delaware Valley.* Philadelphia: Temple University Press, 1986.

Harding, John J. and Harding, Justin J., *Birding the Delaware Valley Region.* Philadelphia: Temple University Press, 1980.

Harwood, Michael, *The View from Hawk Mountain.* New York: Charles Scribner's Sons, 1973.

Heintzelman, Donald S. *A Guide to Hawk Watching in North America*. University Park, PA: The Pennsylvania State University Press, 1988.

Leberman, Robert C., *The Birds of the Ligonier Valley*, Special Publication No. 3, Pittsburgh: Carnegie Museum of Natural History, 1976.

Leberman, Robert C., *A Field List of the Birds of Western Pennsylvania and Adjacent Regions*, Special Publication No. 13. Pittsburgh: Carnegie Museum of Natural History, 1988.

Morrin, Harold B., Chairman, *A Guide to the Birds of Lancaster County, Pennsylvania*. Lancaster County Bird Club, 1991.

National Geographic Society, *Field Guide to the Birds of North America*, Second edition. Washington: National Geographic Society, 1987.

Oplinger, Carl S. and Halma, Robert, *The Poconos: An Illustrated Natural History Guide*. New Brunswick, NJ: Rutgers University Press, 1988.

Peterson, Roger Tory, *A Field Guide to the Birds*, Fourth edition. Boston: Houghton Mifflin Co., 1980.

Pettingill, Olin Sewall, Jr., *A Guide to Bird Finding East of the Mississippi*. New York: Oxford University Press, 1977.

Poole, Earl L. *Pennsylvania Birds: An Annotated List*. Narbeth, PA: Livingston Publishing Co. for Delaware Valley Ornithological Club, 1964.

Piehler, Kirk G. "Habitat Relationships of Three Grassland Sparrow Species on Reclaimed Surface Mines in Pennsylvania." Master's thesis, West Virginia University, 1987.

Robbins, Chandler, et al., *Birds of North America: A Guide to Field Identification*, Revised edition. New York: Golden Press, 1983.

Santner, Steven J., et al., *Annotated List of the Birds of Pennsylvania*. Pennsylvania Biological Survey Contribution Number 4, Ornithological Technical Committee, 1992.

Schweinsberg, Allen R., *Birds of the Central Susquehanna Valley*. 1988.

Shepps, Vincent C., *Pennsylvania and the Ice Age*. Pennsylvania Geological Survey, 1962.

Soderlund, Jean R., Editor, *William Penn and the Founding of Pennsylvania: 1680-1684*. Philadelphia: University of Pennsylvania Press, 1983.

Stull, Jean, et al., *Birds of Erie County, Pennsylvania*. Elgin, PA: Allegheny Press, 1985.

Todd, W. E. Clyde, *Birds of Western Pennsylvania*. Pittsburgh: University of Pittsburgh Press, 1940.

Warren, B. H., *Birds of Pennsylvania*. Harrisburg: Commonwealth of Pennsylvania, Board of Agriculture, 1890.

Index of Birds

This index is of English names only. The last page for each species refers to the page in Appendix 1, *A Checklist of Pennsylvania Birds*, where scientific order, family, genus, and species names are listed. Illustrations are listed in bold.

Ani, Smooth-billed, 236
Avocet, American, 156, 187, 234

Bittern, American, 59, 88, 95, 115, 145, 161, 172, 181, 217, 230
Big Bird, 196
Bittern, Least, 13, 18, 125, 188, 217, **218,** 230
Blackbird, Brewer's, 242
Blackbird, Red-winged, 5, 35, 93, 151, 209, 217, 242
Blackbird, Rusty, 40, 69, 70, 88, 94, 109, 161, 206, 212, 225, 242
Blackbird, Yellow-headed, 242
Bluebird, Eastern, 6, 13, 28, 35, 43, 61, 67, 81, 86, 88, 95, 101, 122, 125, 129, 136, 140, 146, 153, 163, 164, 168, 179, 185, 195, 198, 200, 204, 208, 217, 239
Bluebird, Mountain, 187, 239
Bobolink, 28, 41, 58, 60, 61, 68, 82, 166, 171, 175, 188, 200, 204, 217, 225, 242
Bobwhite, Northern, 109, 175, 185, 208, 211, 217, 233
Brambling, 243
Brant, 115, 182, 199, 231

Bufflehead, 13, 34, 39, 48, 59, 62, 80, 88, 93, 106, 107, 115, 120, 125, 143, 148, 156, 161, 174, 177, 182, 197, 199, 212, 225, 232
Bunting, Indigo, 5, 56, 68, 80, 150, 166, 195, 208, 209, 217, 241
Bunting, Lark, 242
Bunting, Lazuli, 241
Bunting, Painted, 241
Bunting, Snow, 41, 60, 62, 70, 118, 125, 129, 161, 175, 176, 212, 242

Canvasback, 13, 30, 88, 107, 115, 120, 177, 182, 197, 199, 201, 212, 225, 231
Cardinal, Northern, 6, 12, 23, 68, 96, 101, 118, 169, 209, 217, 241
Catbird, Gray, 5, 18, 67, 209, 217, 239
Chat, Yellow-breasted, 39, 50, 68, 103, 108, 152, 161, 185, 209, 210, 211, 217, 224, 241
Chickadee, Black-capped, 6, 12, 23, 47, 56, 67, **118,** 164, 166, 185, 191, 206, 239
Chickadee, Boreal, 239
Chickadee, Carolina, 96, 105, 166, 169, 185, 191, 206, 209, 210, 217, 239
Chuck-will's-widow, 237
Chukar, 228, 233
Coot, American, 13, 23, 34, 70, 72, 107, 174, 201, 233
Cormorant, Great, 222, 230

Cormorant, Double-crested, 32, 59, 61, 69, 70, 116, 120, 140, 156, 180, 188, 201, 221, 222, 230

Cowbird, Brown-headed, 5, 6, 57, 209, 217, 243

Crane, Sandhill, 192, 233

Crane, Whooping, 233

Creeper, Brown, 6, 41, 64, 67, 77, 115, 128, 143, 146, 150, 152, 156, 166, 196, 206, 239

Crossbill, Red, 41, 64, 70, 84, 129, 143, 161, 243

Crossbill, White-winged, 41, 70, 72, 84, 161, 243

Crow, American, 5, 6, 56, 209, 217, 238

Crow, Fish, 167, 214, 217, 238

Cuckoo, Black-billed, 34, 37, 40, 61, 67, 105, 156, 195, 199, 211, 217, 236

Cuckoo, Yellow-billed, 37, 40, 56, 61, 67, **105,** 156, 195, 199, 208, 210, 211, 217, 236

Curlew, Eskimo, 234

Curlew, Long-billed, 234

Dickcissel, 61, 171, 175, 187, 242

Dove, Common Ground, 169

Dove, Mourning, 6, 12, 23, 96, 118, 169, 217, 236

Dove, Rock, 6, 12, 23, 96, 118, 217, 236

Dovekie, 169, 236

Dowitcher, Short-billed, 24, 32, 120, 127, 182, 189, 224, 234

Dowitcher, Long-billed, 189, 224, 235

Duck, American Black, 6, 30, 34, 39, 67, 89, 93, 107, 115, 118, 161, 169, 172, 177, 182, 197, 199, 212, 217, 225, 231

Duck, Harlequin, 232

Duck, Masked, 232

Duck, Ring-necked, 13, 30, 34, 59, 107, 115, 120, 125, 128, 153, 156, 177, 182, 197, 199, 201, 212, 231

Duck, Ruddy, 26, 39, 48, 115, 120, 125, 140, 182, 197, 199, 212, 225, 232

Duck, Tufted, 107, 231

Duck, Wood, 13, 24, 28, 34, 40, 43, 47, 59, 62, 67, 72, 77, 83, 88, 89, 93, 95, 101, 107, 115, 116, 120, 128, 129, 146, 149, 161, 167, 172, 177, 182, 197, 199, 201, 203, 204, 208, 210, 212, 217, 225

Dunlin, 13, 32, 34, 121, 182, 224, 231, 234

Eagle, Bald, 19, 26, 27, 28, 34, 44, 55, 61, 69, 76, 81, 82, 83, 93, 111, 112, 115, 125, 127, 130, 135, 136, 137, 140, 146, 153, 157, 161, 162, 163, 164, 167, 173, 180, 183, 185, 187, 190, 197, 201, 205, 232

Eagle, Golden, 119, 130, 136, 157, 183, 190, 197, 205, 232

Egret, American 172

Egret, Cattle, 169, 208, 230

Egret, Great, 28, 106, 116, 161, 172, 181, 201, 217, 230

Egret, Reddish, 230

Egret, Snowy, 18, 161, 217, 230

Eider, Common, 231

Eider, King, 232

Falcon, Peregrine, 19, 101, 119, 139, 157, 183, 185, 190, 205, 217, 219, **220,** 233

Finch, House, 6, 12, 68, 96, 118, 169, 210, 217, 243

Finch, Purple, 44, 68, 217, 243

Flamingo, Greater, 231

Flicker, Northern, 5, 6, 56, 138, 201, 209, 217, 237

Flycatcher, Acadian, 35, 49, 59, 67, 70, 105, 106, 107, 135, 145, 149, 156, 200, 206, 217, 238

Flycatcher, Alder, 49, 56, 70, 92, 94, 145, 238

Flycatcher, Dusky, 238

Flycatcher, Fork-tailed, 238
Flycatcher, Great Crested, 18, 35, 40, 49, 56, 67, 70, 77, 83, 106, 129, 144, 151, 156, 168, 195, 206, 208, 209, 217, 238
Flycatcher, Hammond's, 238
Flycatcher, Least, 13, 35, 49, 56, 59, 67, 70, 81, 83, 89, 105, 107, 145, 149, 238
Flycatcher, Olive-sided, 49, 70, 145, 185, 238
Flycatcher, Pacific-slope, 238
Flycatcher, Scissor-tailed, 238
Flycatcher, Vermillion, 238
Flycatcher, Willow, 13, 18, 35, 49, 59, 70, 92, 105, 116, 145, 149, 185, 196, 209, 217, 238
Flycatcher, Yellow-bellied, 49, 63, 70, 84, 238
Frigatebird, Magnificent, 230
Fulmar, Northern, 229

Gadwall, 30, 59, 70, 88, 107, 115, 120, 182, 197, 199, 212, 225, 231
Gallinule, Purple, 115, 233
Gannet, Northern, 230
Gnatcatcher, Blue-gray, 18, 67, 80, 125, 128, 136, 146, 156, 166, 196, 209, 210, 217, 239
Godwit, Black-tailed, 234
Godwit, Hudsonian, 115, 234
Godwit, Marbled, 18, 187, 234
Goldeneye, Barrow's, 18, 232
Goldeneye, Common, 13, 39, 70, 102, 106, 107, 115, 161, 162, 182, 197, 199, 212, 225, 232
Golden-Plover, Lesser, 26, 32, 175, 189, 225, 233
Goldfinch, American, 6, 68, 93, 209, 210, 217, 243
Goldfinch, Lesser, 243
Goose, Barnacle, 187, 199, 201, 231
Goose, Canada, 6, 12, 23, 24, 27, 34, 47, 62, 67, 88, 89, 93, 96, 107, 115,

118, 125, 136, 169, 172, 177, 187, 188, 197, 199, 217, 231
Goose, Greater White-fronted, 24, 140, 187, 199, 231
Goose, Ross', 231
Goose, Snow, 24, 39, 69, 70, 107, 115, 146, 161, 182, 189, 197, 199, 212, 231
Goshawk, Northern, 31, 67, 70, 72, 119, 122, 157, **158,** 183, 190, 197, 205, 232
Grackle, Boat-tailed, 243
Grackle, Common, 6, 209, 217, 243
Grebe, Eared, 31, 229
Grebe, Horned, 13, 25, 31, 47, 107, 109, 120, 125, 128, 145, 148, 156, 181, 212, 229
Grebe, Pied-billed, 31, 59, 61, 80, 95, 106, 107, 109, 120, 125, 128, 136, 145, 150, 156, 161, 181, 206, 212, 213, 225, 229
Grebe, Red-necked, 31, 109, 120, 140, 181, 212, 229
Grebe, Western/Clark's, 228, 229
Grosbeak, Black-headed, 241
Grosbeak, Blue, 169, 185, 190, 199, 217, 241
Grosbeak, Evening, 15, 41, 44, 60, 64, 70, 72, 76, 109, 129, 143, 145, 146, 161, 200, 206, 210, 243
Grosbeak, Pine, 64, 70, 88, 92, 129, 145, 146, 161, 243
Grosbeak, Rose-breasted, 15, 35, 37, 40, 43, 56, 68, 70, 77, 102, 129, 150, 152, 157, 195, 199, 203, 212, 217, 241
Ground-Dove, Common, 169, 236
Grouse, Ruffed, 47, 59, 67, 71, 75, 93, 112, 136, 138, 195, 233
Guillemot, Black, 236
Gull, Bonaparte's, 13, 14, 59, 61, 106, 107, 121, 178, 198, 199, 212, 235
Gull, Common Black-headed, 235
Gull, Franklin's, 14, 115, 178, 180, 235

Gull, Glaucous, 13, 14, 180, 235
Gull, Great Black-backed, 14, 180, 198, 199, 217, 235
Gull, Herring, 13, 14, 107, 169, 178, 198, 199, 217, 235
Gull, Iceland, 13, 14, 185, 235
Gull, Laughing, 14, 180, 199, 235
Gull, Lesser Black-backed, 14, 180, 185, 235
Gull, Little, 13, 14, 235
Gull, Mew, 235
Gull, Ring-billed, 12, 13, 14, 59, 93, 96, 107, 118, 121, 169, 174, 178, 180, 198, 199, 217, 235
Gull, Ross', 177, 235
Gull, Sabine's, 142, 235
Gull, Thayer's, 14, 235
Gyrfalcon, 154, 233

Harrier, Northern, 28, 31, 55, 60, 72, 119, 150, 157, 175, 183, 190, 195, 197, 204, 205, 217, 225, 232
Hawk, Broad-winged, 31, 34, 40, 67, 75, 80, 103, 119, 128, 129, 143, 155, 157, 158, 166, 183, 190, 195, 197, 205, 210, 217, 232
Hawk, Cooper's, 6, 31, 40, 47, 67, 89, 93, 119, 122, 133, 143, 146, 157, 183, 190, 197, 201, 205, 208, 232
Hawk, Red-shouldered, 13, 31, 34, 40, 67, 72, 119, 122, 128, 138, 145, 157, 183, 190, 197, 205, 221, 232
Hawk, Red-tailed, 6, 31, 47, 67, 86, 102, 118, 119, 128, 136, 138, 155, 157, 158, 164, 175, 183, 190, 197, 203, 204, 205, 209, 217, 221, 232
Hawk, Rough-legged, 24, 25, 60, 119, 146, 157, 162, 175, 176, 183, 188, 197, 205, 225, 232
Hawk, Sharp-shinned, 6, 13, 31, 40, 67, 89, 118, 119, 143, 155, 157, 158, 183, 190, 197, 203, 205, 217, 221, 232
Hawk, Swainson's, 154, 183, 232

Heron, Great Blue, 6, 28, 32, 34, 42, 67, 73, 82, 86, 88, 93, 102, 103, 105, 106, 111, 122, 132, 136, 143, 146, 161, 173, 181, 201, 206, 230
Heron, Green-backed, 15, 18, 32, 34, 42, 67, 82, 88, 103, 106, 129, 146, 161, 168, 181, 201, 213, 217, 223, 230
Heron, Little Blue, 8, 181, 223, 230
Heron, Tricolored, 230
Hummingbird, Ruby-throated, 13, 67, 75, 93, 143, 203, 210, 217, 237
Hummingbird, Rufous, 237

Ibis, Glossy, 140, 180, 187, 188, 230
Ibis, White, 180, 187, 230

Jackdaw, Eurasian, 140, 238
Jaeger, Parasitic, 235
Jaeger, Pomarine, 235
Jay, Blue, 6, 23, 47, 56, 98, 102, 118, 169, 209, 217, 238
Junco, Dark-eyed, 6, 43, 47, 57, 58, 65, 68, 79, 92, 96, 118, 129, 143, 169, 217, 242

Kestrel, American, 6, **12,** 23, 28, 67, 95, 96, 101, 119, 125, 136, 140, 157, 169, 175, 183, 190, 197, 204, 205, 208, 217, 232
Killdeer, 5, 32, 67, 88, 93, 118, 175, 188, 197, 204, 217, 233
Kingbird, Eastern, 49, 61, 67, 70, 206, 209, 217, 238
Kingbird, Western, 238
Kingfisher, Belted, 6, 13, 67, 72, 82, 93, 102, 103, 112, 129, 136, 143, 146, 151, 166, 195, 204, 208, 217, 223, 237
Kinglet, Golden-crowned, 6, 15, 17, 41, 143, 161, 164, 168, 185, 189, 191, 192, 211, 239
Kinglet, Ruby-crowned, 6, 17, 41, 143, 161, 164, 185, 189, 191, 211, 239
Kite, American Swallow-tailed, 232

Kite, Mississippi, 19, 232
Kittiwake, Black-legged, 14, 235
Knot, Red, 13, 24, 115, 182, 189, 225, 234

Lark, Horned, 13, 40, 60, 82, 93, 115, 118, 124, 129, 161, 175, 176, 200, 217, 238
Longspur, Lapland, 31, 41, 60, 62, 70, 118, 161, 175, 176, 185, 242
Loon, Common, 13, 47, 48, 59, 61, 69, 77, 80, 106, 107, 109, 120, 125, 128, 140, 145, 148, 156, 163, 181, 212, 213, 229
Loon, Pacific, 228, 229
Loon, Red-throated, 181, 229

Mallard, 5, 6, 27, 34, 67, 93, 101, 107, 115, 116, 197, 199, 210, 217, 231
Martin, Purple, 13, 67, 149, 175, 189, 217, 238
Meadowlark, Eastern, 28, 35, 60, 61, 68, 82, 152, 171, 175, 178, 185, 204, 208, 217, 242
Meadowlark, Western, 242
Merganser, Common, 13, 23, 39, 43, 47, 48, 59, 67, 70, 72, 77, 80, 83, 88, 89, 107, 115, 125, 143, 146, 161, 162, 177, 182, 197, 199, 201, 212, 213, 232
Merganser, Hooded, 24, 26, 34, **35,** 62, 67, 70, 107, 115, 125, 128, 146, 161, 174, 177, 182, 197, 199, 212, 213, 225, 232
Merganser, Red-breasted, 13, 26, 39, 59, 62, 70, 107, 115, 120, 156, 177, 197, 199, 212, 225
Merlin, 119, 146, 147, 157, 182, 183, 190, 205, 232
Mockingbird, Northern, 6, 101, 118, 169, 185, 209, 217, 240
Moorhen, Common, 13, 17, 18, 59, 70, 88, 115, 217, 233
Murre, Thick-billed, 236
Murrelet, Ancient, 236

Night-Heron, Black-crowned, **42,** 89, 116, 122, 146, 167, 181, 201, 217, 221, 230
Night-Heron, Yellow-crowned, 3, 18, 156, 174, 230
Nighthawk, Common, 44, 67, 102, 123, 217, 237
Nuthatch, Brown-headed, 239
Nuthatch, Red-breasted, 6, 15, 40, **64,** 67, 77, 81, 143, 146, 151, 152, 156, 162, 167, 185, 189, 195, 201, 210, 239
Nuthatch, White-breasted, 6, 67, 143, 151, 152, 164, 185, 209, 210, 217, 239

Oldsquaw, 13, 59, 107, 115, 120, 156, 182, 197, 199, 201, 212, 225, 232
Oriole, Northern, 68, 82, 105, 132, 136, 149, 167, 199, 201, 203, 204, 206, 208, 209, 212, 217, 243
Oriole, Orchard, 105, 106, 149, 167, 199, 206, 208, 209, 212, 217, 243
Osprey, 28, 32, 44, 47, 61, 69, 72, 76, 80, 81, 82, 83, 86, 88, 105, 106, 111, 119, 125, 128, 132, 137, 140, 143, 146, 153, 157, 163, 180, 183, 190, 195, 197, 201, 204, 205, 213, 232
Ovenbird, **23,** 32, 47, 50, 56, 68, 79, 81, 88, 98, 108, 118, 128, 135, 157, 161, 166, 169, 191, 195, 206, 209, 211, 217, 223, 224, 241
Owl, Barn, 175, 217, 236
Owl, Barred, 13, 35, 40, 44, 62, 63, 67, 83, 89, 93, 95, 129, 130, 136, 138, 143, 144, 145, 151, 163, 166, 236
Owl, Boreal, 237
Owl, Great Gray, 65, 236
Owl, Great Horned, 6, 18, 44, 47, 62, 67, 91, 93, 101, 102, 136, 150, 151, 163, 164, 173, 179, 191, 195, 201, 204, 217, 221, 236
Owl, Long-eared, 18, 115, 180, 185, 188, 195, 198, 206, 237

Owl, Northern Hawk, 236
Owl, Northern Saw-whet, 13, 18, 67, 70, 89, 180, 188, 190, 206, **211,** 237
Owl, Short-eared, 36, 55, 60, 61, 175, 178, 180, 185, 188, 217, 225, 237
Owl, Snowy, 18, 82, 84, 175, 201, 236
Oystercatcher, American, 234

Parakeet, Carolina, 236
Parula, Northern, 49, 58, 64, 84, 108, 159, 161, 166, 195, 203, 211, 217, 224, 240
Pelican, American White, 112, 230
Pelican, Brown, 18, 230
Petrel, Black-capped, 229
Petrel, Kermadec, 229
Phalarope, Red, 235
Phalarope, Red-necked, 140, 177, 185, 187, 235
Phalarope, Wilson's, 24, 70, 187, 235
Pheasant, Ring-necked, 175, 217, 233
Phoebe, Eastern, 49, 70, 82, 138, 143, 206, 207, 217, 238
Phoebe, Say's, 187, 238
Pigeon, Band-tailed, 236
Pigeon, Passenger, 236
Pintail, Northern, 30, 39, 70, 71, 107, 115, 182, 197, 199, 212, 225, 231
Pipit, American, 70, 115, 149, 175, 212, 240
Pipit, Sprague's, 240
Plover, Black-bellied, 26, 32, 140, 175, 189, 224, 233
Plover, Piping, 18, 225, 233
Plover, Semipalmated, 26, 32, 59, 182, 189, 224, 233
Plover, Snowy, 233
Plover, Wilson's, 233
Prairie-Chicken, Greater, 233
Puffin, Atlantic, 236

Rail, Black, 233
Rail, Clapper, 233
Rail, King, 59, 70, 233
Rail, Spotted, 233

Rail, Virginia, 13, 18, **29,** 59, 70, 115, 116, 120, 125, 209, 217, 233
Rail, Yellow, 233
Raven, Common, 55,67, 77, 81, 128, 143, 156, 239
Razorbill, 236
Redhead, 13, 30, 59, 70, 107, 115, 153, 177, 182, 197, 199, 212, 225, 231
Redpoll, Common, 41, 70, 109, 129, 143, 145, 157, 161, 175, 200, 243
Redpoll, Hoary, 70, 243
Redshank, Spotted, 234
Redstart, American, 13, 32, 35, 40, 50, 68, 77, 79, 81, 88, 108, 121, 129, 135, 151, 157, 161, 191, 195, 203, 206, 209, 210, 211, 217, 223, 224, 241
Robin, American, 5, 6, 101, 209, 217, 239
Ruff, 32, 234

Sanderling, 32, 140, 225, 234
Sandpiper, Baird's, 32, 189, 234
Sandpiper, Buff-breasted, 13, 24, 26, 32, 189, 234
Sandpiper, Curlew, 225, 234
Sandpiper, Least, 24, 32, 59, 70, 127, 177, 182, 189, 198, 224, 234
Sandpiper, Pectoral, 24, 32, 127, 182, 189, 198, 224, 234
Sandpiper, Purple, 234
Sandpiper, Semipalmated, 24, 32, 59, 177, 182, 188, 224, 234
Sandpiper, Solitary, 24, 34, 59, 127, 128, 177, 182, 197, 210, 224, 234
Sandpiper, Spotted, 13, 18, 34, 59, 67, 103, 106, 120, 128, 136, 150, 156, 168, 177, 182, **197,** 208, 217, 224, 234
Sandpiper, Stilt, 32, 234
Sandpiper, Upland, 61, 70, 171, 175, 225, 234
Sandpiper, Western, 127, 234
Sandpiper, White-rumped, 13, 32, 177, 234

Sapsucker, Yellow-bellied, 35, 41, 67, 76, 91, **92,** 128, 143, 149, 195, 196, 201, 203, 237

Scaup, Greater, 26, 31, 107, 115, 128, 148, 182, 199, 212, 225, 231

Scaup, Lesser, 31, 39, 59, 107, 115, 120, 125, 128, 148, **181,** 182, 197, 199, 212, 225, 231

Scoter, Black, 115, 199, 212, 232

Scoter, Surf, 115, 182, 199, 232

Scoter, White-winged, 77, 115, 156, 182, 199, 212, 225, 232

Screech-Owl, Eastern, 6, 18, 44, 47, 62, 67, 75, 93, 101, 102, 107, 125, 136, 138, 146, 150, 166, 173, 195, 217, 236

Shearwater, Audubon's, 229

Shearwater, Greater, 229

Shoveler, Northern, 26, 30, 107, 115, 177, 182, 199, 212, 217, 225, 231

Shrike, Loggerhead, 115, 185, **186,** 240

Shrike, Northern, 18, 24, 73, 115, 240

Siskin, Pine, 15, 44, 64, 68, 72, 76, 109, 129, 143, 145, 146, 157, 200, 203, 210, 243

Skimmer, Black, 185, 236

Snipe, Common, 61, 89, **90,** 95, 115, 124, 173, 182, 190, 198, 224, 235

Solitaire, Townsend's, 239

Sora, 3, 18, 34, 59, 70, 115, 120, 125, 217, 233

Sparrow, American Tree, 6, 15, 51, 60, 115, 118, 125, 143, 151, 161, 198, 204, 242

Sparrow, Bachman's, 242

Sparrow, Chipping, 5, 51, 57, 115, 138, 143, 151, 199, 217, 242

Sparrow, Clay-colored, 13, 70, 115, 242

Sparrow, Field, 23, 39, 47, 51, 57, 60, 68, 93, 98, 115, 118, 169, 185, 198, 199, 204, 209, 217, 242

Sparrow, Fox, 51, 64, 72, 115, 143, 161, 162, 198, 200, 204, 242

Sparrow, Golden-crowned, 242

Sparrow, Grasshopper, 31, 39, 41, 51, 58, 60, 61, 68, 70, 149, 171, 175, 178, 185, 188, 199, 200, 212, 217, 242

Sparrow, Harris', 70, 242

Sparrow, Henslow's, 13, 31, 35, 41, 51, 60, 61, 70, 242

Sparrow, House, 5, 6, 12, 47, 96, 118, 169, 217, 243

Sparrow, Lark, 70, 242

Sparrow, LeConte's, 242

Sparrow, Lincoln's, 40, 51, 70, 115, 199, 242

Sparrow, Savannah, 13, 18, 35, 39, 41, 51, 58, 60, 61, 68, 70, 115, 149, 171, 175, 178, 188, 199, 217, 242

Sparrow, Seaside, 242

Sparrow, Sharp-tailed, 70, 242

Sparrow, Song, 6, 51, 101, 115, 143, 185, 198, 199, 204, 209, 217, 242

Sparrow, Swamp, 13, 18, 35, 40, 68, 70, 83, 94, 115, 116, 125, 173, 188, 199, 200, 204, 209, 210, 212, 217, 225, 242

Sparrow, Vesper, 13, 41, 51, 60, 61, 68, 70, 115, 149, 175, 188, 199, 242

Sparrow, White-crowned, 51, 115, 198, 242

Sparrow, White-throated, 6, 15, 17, 51, 60, 68, 77, 79, **85,** 115, 129, 143, 198, 203, 204, 242

Spoonbill, Roseate, 231

Starling, European, 5, 6, 240

Stilt, Black-necked, 187, 215, 217, 234

Stork, Wood, 231

Storm-Petrel, Band-rumped, 230

Storm-Petrel, Leach's, 230

Storm-Petrel, Wilson's, 229

Surfbird, 234

Swallow, Bank, 13, 19, 35, 67, 82, 189, 217, 238

Swallow, Barn, 23, 47, 67, 88, 98, 106, 118, 138, 169, 189, 206, 209, 217, 238

Swallow, Cliff, 28, 32, 39, 59, 67, 82, 143, 149, 180, **189,** 238

Swallow, Northern Rough-winged, 67, 106, 180, 189, 196, 206, 208, 217, 238

Swallow, Tree, 5, 67, 74, 88, 94, 106, 125, 140, 185, 200, 206, 217, 238

Swan, Mute, 161, 177, 197, 199, 231

Swan, Trumpeter, 231

Swan, Tundra, 23, 26, 39, 59, 61, 69, 80, 107, 115, 120, 125, 156, 174, 177, 182, 188, 197, 199, 212, 231

Swift, Chimney, 5, 67, 217, 237

Tanager, Scarlet, 35, 37, 56, 68, 70, 80, 129, 135, 136, 151, 157, 166, 168, 195, 201, 203, 209, 217, 241

Tanager, Summer, 18, 70, 96, 105, 241

Tanager, Western, 241

Teal, Blue-winged, 26, 34, 39, 59, 72, 93, 107, 115, 120, 128, 173, 177, 182, 197, 199, 212, 217, 225, 231

Teal, Cinnamon, 231

Teal, Green-winged, 30, 34, 39, 59, 93, 107, 115, 173, 177, 182, 197, 199, 212, 225, 231

Tern, Arctic, 235

Tern, Black, 13, 18, 24, 28, 121, 174, 180, 199, 236

Tern, Caspian, 121, 178, 189, 199, 212, 235

Tern, Common, 18, 107, 121, 180, 198, 199, 235

Tern, Forster's, 61, 121, 178, 180, 199, 212, 225, 235

Tern, Gull-billed, 235

Tern, Least, 199, 235

Tern, Roseate, 235

Tern, Royal, 169, 235

Tern, Sooty, 235

Thrasher, Brown, 35, 67, 109, 151, 185, 201, 209, 217, 240

Thrush, Gray-cheeked, 108, 115, 198, 212, 239

Thrush, Hermit, 56, 58, 64, 67, 81, 92, **95,** 108, 109, 115, 144, 195, 198, 212, 239

Thrush, Swainson's, 3, 18, 56, 67, 69, 108, 109, 115, 128, 149, 166, 198, 212, 239

Thrush, Varied, 239

Thrush, Wood, 23, 35, 47, 67, 88, 89, 93, 95, 98, 108, 109, 115, 118, 135, 143, 166, 169, 191, 195, 198, 201, 203, 208, 209, 212, 217, 223, 239

Titmouse, Tufted, 6, 23, 67, 96, 118, 143, 164, 169, 185, 209, 210, 217, 239

Towhee, Green-tailed, 242

Towhee, Rufous-sided, 35, 56, 68, 102, **103,** 106, 143, 152, 166, 201, 209, 217, 242

Tropicbird, White-tailed, 230

Turkey, Wild, 7, 43, 47, 58, 67, 71, 72, 75, 80, 91, 93, 112, 136, 159, 163, 195, 233

Turnstone, Ruddy, 32, 140, 225, 234

Turtle-Dove, Ringed, 228

Veery, 35, 67, 77, 81, 89, 108, 109, 115, 135, 143, 149, 166, 168, 191, 195, 198, 203, 209, 212, 217, 239

Vireo, Bell's, 240

Vireo, Philadelphia, 49, 88, 115, 240

Vireo, Red-eyed, 13, 23, 47, 49, 56, 67, 89, 98, 115, 118, 135, 169, 206, 217, 240

Vireo, Solitary, 35, 49, 56, 64, 67, 88, 89, 115, 240

Vireo, Warbling, 13, 18, 35, 49, 67, 89, 115, 206, 209, 217, 225, 240

Vireo, White-eyed, 39, 43, 49, 115, 206, 209, 210, 217, 240

Vireo, Yellow-throated, 35, 49, 67, 88, 89, 95, 115, 157, 209, 210, 217, 240

Vulture, Black, 3, 127, 156, 157, 166, 179, 180, 182, 183, 190, 203, 205, 213, 232

Vulture, Turkey, 67, 98, 118, 127, 138, 143, 156, 157, 166, 179, 180, 182, 183, 190, 197, 203, 205, 213, 232

Warbler, Bay-breasted, 18, 32, 40, 50, 108, 143, 191, 223, 224, 241

Warbler, Black-and-white, 13, 32, 40, 43, 50, 68, 77, 79, 80, 81, 88, 108, 121, 135, 138, 143, 149, 157, 161, 195, 203, 206, 211, 217, 223, 224, 241

Warbler, Blackburnian, 18, 32, 35, 40, 43, 49, 56, 64, 68, 75, 77, **78,** 79, 81, 84, 88, 92, 108, 135, 143, 144, 145, 161, 195, 203, 224, 241

Warbler, Blackpoll, 50, 108, 203, 223, 224, 241

Warbler, Black-throated Blue, 18, 32, 43, 49, **50,** 64, 68, 75, 78, 81, 82, 84, 88, 95, 108, 121, 128, 135, 152, 161, 195, 203, 224, 240

Warbler, Black-throated Gray, 240

Warbler, Black-throated Green, 13, 18, 32, 35, 40, 43, 47, 49, 52, 56, 68, 77, 79, 84, 88, 95, 108, 121, 129, 135, 143, 144, 161, 166, 191, 195, 203, 223, 224, 241

Warbler, Blue-winged, 13, 15, 32, 35, 40, 49, 67, 95, 108, 161, 164, 195, 203, 210, 211, 217, 223, 224, 240

Warbler, Brewster's, 161, 199

Warbler, Canada, 3, 13, 35, 47, 50, 56, 64, 68, 77, 79, 84, 88, 92, 94, 108, 133, 135, 151, 161, 191, 203, 223, 224, 241

Warbler, Cape May, 40, 49, 88, 108, 224, 240

Warbler, Cerulean, 13, 50, 58, 68, 88, 96, 108, 121, 161, 195, 203, 210, 211, 217, 224, 241

Warbler, Chestnut-sided, 13, 18, 32, 35, 40, 49, 52, 68, 75, 78, 81, 84, 88, 108, 121, 129, 161, 166, 195, 203, 209, 211, 217, 224, 240

Warbler, Connecticut, 50, 108, 224, 241

Warbler, Golden-winged, 49, 108, 121, 125, 129, 161, 224, 240

Warbler, Hooded, 13, 15, 32, 35, 40, 43, 50, 58, 68, 82, 108, **121,** 135, 146, 161, 166, 195, 211, 217, 224, 241

Warbler, Kentucky, 32, 40, 50, 58, 108, 161, 195, 200, 203, 209, 211, 217, 224, 241

Warbler, Kirtland's, 241

Warbler, Lawrence's, 161, 199

Warbler, Magnolia, 17, 32, 49, 52, **53,** 68, 75, 77, 78, 81, 108, 161, 195, 203, 224, 240

Warbler, Mourning, 13, 50, 68, 81, 108, 224, 241

Warbler, Nashville, 32, 40, 49, 67, 108, 121, 161, 224, 240

Warbler, Orange-crowned, 41, 49, 108, 224, 240

Warbler, Palm, 18, 50, 204, 224, 241

Warbler, Pine, 32, 50, 64, 68, 77, 121, 128, 146, 149, 161, 166, 168, 195, 211, 224, 241

Warbler, Prairie, 39, 40, 50, 64, 68, 96, 103, 108, 121, 129, 161, 164, 185, 190, 195, 203, 204, 209, 210, 224, 241

Warbler, Prothonotary, 13, 18, 83, 108, 161, 187, 201, 217, 224, 241

Warbler, Swainson's, 3, 18, 47, 50, 51, 115, 241

Warbler, Tennessee, 18, 40, 49, 108, 224, 240

Warbler, Townsend's, 240

Warbler, Wilson's, 32, 50, 108, 121, 203, 224, 241

Warbler, Worm-eating, 50, 68, 108, 135, 157, 161, 195, 211, 217, 224, 241

Warbler, Yellow, 5, 18, 32, 40, 49, 67, 81, 82, 88, 94, 108, 116, 121, 146,

149, 161, 166, 185, 201, 203, 206, 217, 224, 240

Warbler, Yellow-rumped, 6, 17, 32, 40, 49, 68, 75, 78, 84, 88, 108, 121, 128, 143, 166, 173, 191, 195, 206, 223, 224, 240

Warbler, Yellow-throated, 41, 50, 64, 108, 210, 241

Waterthrush, Louisiana, 13, 31, 35, 50, 68, 88, 121, 129, 150, 151, 157, 161, 166, 191, 200, 209, 210, 211, 217, 224, 241

Waterthrush, Northern, 31, 35, 50, 68, 79, 84, 88, 92, 108, 128, 136, 150, 161, 224, 241

Waxwing, Bohemian, 19, 240

Waxwing, Cedar, 6, 19, 43, 56, 67, 73, 93, 125, 143, 144, 151, 217, 240

Wheatear, Northern, 239

Whimbrel, 13, 185, 234

Whip-poor-wil, 43, 134, 144, 149, 152, 166, 167, 237

Whistling-Duck, Fulvous, 187, 231

Wigeon, American, 26, 30, 34, 59, 70, 88, 107, 115, 120, 125, 146, 174, 182, 197, 199, 212, 225, 231

Wigeon, Eurasian, 212, 225, 231

Willet, 13, 70, 225, 234

Woodcock, American, 13, 18, 34, 40, 67, 71, 89, 93, 95, 116, **129,** 130, 143, 145, 150, 167, 198, 204, 208, 210, 217, 224, 235

Woodcock, Eurasian, 235

Woodpecker, Black-backed, 237

Woodpecker, Downy, 5, 6, 56, 138, 164, 169, 209, 210, 217, 237

Woodpecker, Hairy, 6, 209, 217, 237

Woodpecker, Pileated, 6, 35, 37, 40, 67, 75, 81, 88, 93, 102, 112, 129, 136, 138, 143, 146, 151, 164, 166, 167, 168, 179, 203, 213, 217, 237

Woodpecker, Red-bellied, 6, 25, 96, 102, 125, 152, 156, 164, 169, 201, 208, 209, 211, 217, 237

Woodpecker, Red-cockaded, 237

Woodpecker, Red-headed, 35, 96, 151, 175, 179, 237

Woodpecker, Three-toed, 237

Wood-Pewee, Eastern, 23, 47, 49, 67, 70, 98, 107, 118, 152, 156, 206, 209, 217, 238

Wren, Bewick's, 239

Wren, Carolina, 6, 67, 96, 203, 208, 209, 210, 217, 223, 239

Wren, House, 5, 93, 185, 209, 217, 239

Wren, Marsh, 13, 17, 18, 31, 70, 115, 125, 145, 172, 225, 239

Wren, Sedge, **38,** 39, 70, 217, 239

Wren, Winter, 58, 64, 67, 69, 92, 125, 135, 191, 204, 206, 239

Yellowlegs, Greater, 24, 26, 32, 34, 59, 70, 72, 120, 182, 188, 197, 224, 234

Yellowlegs, Lesser, 24, 32, 34, 70, 127, 182, 188, 224, 234

Yellowthroat, Common, 5, 32, 50, 56, 68, 81, 88, 94, 108, 121, 143, 157, 161, 166, 185, 195, 201, 206, 209, 211, 217, 224, 241

Index of Locations

Academy of Natural Sciences, 221–222
Allegheny National Forest, 65–70
Allegheny Plateau, 45-95
Allegheny River Canoe Trips, 42–43
Allentown/Bethlehem/Easton, 192–196
Altoona, 122-125
Armstrong Trail, 112
Asbury Woods Nature Center, 14–15
Atlantic Coastal Plain, 215–227
Audubon Wildlife Sanctuary (Mill Grove), 207–208

Bald Eagle State Park, 135–136
Bear Meadows Natural Area, 133
Beaver Creek Wetlands/Wildlife Project, 62
Bedford, 119–122
Beechwood Farms Nature Reserve, 102–104
Beltzville State Park, 148–149
Bendigo State Park, 72
Big Pocono State Park, 94
Big Spring State Park, 153
Black Moshannon State Park, 74–75
Blue Knob State Park, 58–59
Blue Marsh Lake Recreation Area, 192
Blue Spruce County Park, 116
Bog and Boulder Trail, 56–57
Bowman's Hill Wildflower Preserve, 202–203
Browning Beaver Meadows, 95
Brucker Great Blue Heron Sanctuary, 32
Buchanan State Forest, 155–159

Buchanan's Birthplace State Park, 157
Bucktail State Park, 80–81

Caledonia State Park, 166–167
Canoe Creek State Park, 124–125
Carbon County Environmental Education Center, 146
Carnegie, The, 98
Chapman State Park, 71
Charles F. Lewis State Forest Natural Area, 57
Cherry Springs State Park, 79
Churchville Nature Center, 200–201
Clarion, 60–62
Codorus State Park, 177–178
Col. Denning State Park, 151–152
Colton Point State Park, 82
Cook Forest State Park, 63–65
Cornplanter State Forest, 70–71
Cornwall Fire Tower Hawk Watch, 190
Cowan's Gap State Park, 156–157
Crooked Creek Lake, 110–112

David M. Roderick Wildlife Reserve (SGL 314), 19–20
Delaware Canal State Park, 201–202
Delaware Valley Raptor Center, 162–163
Delaware Water Gap National Recreation Area, 159–165
Denton Hill State Park, 79
Detweiler's Run Natural Area, 134–135
Dorflinger-Suydam Wildlife Sanctuary, 88–89

Doylestown, 196–203
Dunlo Strip Mine Reclamation
    Area, 54–55

Eastern Glaciated Plateau (See
    Poconos, The)
Edinboro, 24
Elk State Park, 72
Elliott, S.B., State Park, 74
Erie, 14-15
Erie National Wildlife Refuge, 33–35
Erie Zoo, 15

Fairmount Park, 219–221
Fort Necessity National
    Battlefield, 110
Fort Roberdeau, 123–124
Fort Washington State Park, 204
Fowler's Hollow State Park, 152
Frances Slocum State Park, 144–145
French Creek State Park, 213
Friendship Hill National Historic
    Site, 108–109

Gallitzin, Prince, State Park, 59–60
Gallitzin State Forest, 54–57
Gettysburg, 178–180
Gifford Pinchot State Park, 181–182
Glaciated Northwest, 21–44
Goddard, Maurice K., State Park,
    30–31
"God's Country," 75–81
Gouldsboro State Park, 93–94
Grand Canyon of Pennsylvania, 81–83
Great Shamokin Path-
    Cowanshannock Branch, 112–113
Greenwood Furnace State Park, 132
Gwynedd Wildlife Preserve,
    203–204

Hammond Lakes (Tioga) National
    Recreation Area, 82–83
Hanover Impounding Reservoir, 178
Harrisburg, 171–173
Harrison, Leonard, State Park, 81

Hawk Mountain Sanctuary, 147–150
Heinz, John, National Wildlife
    Refuge at Tinicum, 223–225
Hickory Run State Park, 94
Hillman State Park, 104
Hills Creek State Park, 83
Holtwood & Lake Aldred, 180
Huntingdon, 127–130

Indiana, 113–116

Jacobsburg Environmental
    Education Center, 195–196
Jennings Nature Preserve, 39–41
John P. Saylor Memorial Trail, 55–56
Johnstown, 53–58

Kahle Lake, 61–62
Kettle Creek State Park, 80–81
Kettle Creek Wildlife Sanctuary,
    163–164
Keystone Dam, 116
Keystone State Park, 106
King's Gap Environmental Education
    and Training Center, 168
Kittanning, 110–113

Lake Aldred (Holtwood), 180
Lake Erie Coastal Plain, 11–20
Lackawanna State Forest, 89
Lancaster, 183–190
Laurel Highlands, 47–52
Laurel Ridge State Park, 51–52
Lehigh Gorge State Park, 90–91
Leonard Harrison State Park, 81
Lewis, Charles F., State Forest
    Natural Area, 57
Lewis, Samuel S., State Park, 182
Lewisburg "Cellblock C," 140–141
Little Buffalo State Park, 153–155
Little Pine State Park, 83
Locust Lake State Park, 149–150
Long Arm Creek Reservoir, 178
Lyman Run State Park, 79

Marsh Creek State Park, 212
Martin Hill Wild Area, 159
Mariton Wildlife Preserve, 194–195
Maurice K. Goddard State
    Park, 30–31
McCall Dam State Park, 144
McConnell's Mill State Park, 36–37
McKeever Environmental Learning
    Center, 31
Meadville, 25–26
Meesing Site, 164–165
Michaux State Forest, 165
Middle Creek Waterfowl
    Management Area, 187–188
Mill Grove (Audubon Wildlife
    Sanctuary), 207–208
Milton State Park, 142
Minsi Lake and Bear Swamp, 194
Mont Alto State Park, 165–166
Montour Preserve, 139–140
Moraine State Park, 37–39
Morris Arboretum, 208
Moshannon State Forest, 73–75
Mount Pisgah State Park, 85–86
Muddy Run, 184–185

Nescopeck State Park, 145–146
Neshaminy State Park, 226–227
New Castle, 36–41
Nockamixon State Park, 196–198
Nolde Forest Environmental
    Education Center, 190–192
Norristown, 203–208
Northeast Northern Tier, 84–86
North Park, Pittsburgh, 100–101

Octoraro Lake, 188–190
Ohiopyle State Park, 48–51
Oil City, 42–44
Ole Bull State Park, 77–78
Oil Creek State Park, 43–44
Old Fort Mifflin (Philadelphia
    Sewage Ponds), 225

Powdermill Nature Reserve, 57–58

Parker Dam State Park, 73
Patterson State Park, 79
Peace Valley Park, 198–199
Penn Roosevelt State Park, 133–134
Pennypack Park, 222
Pennypack Wilderness, 205–206
Philadelphia, 219–223
Piedmont, 169–214
Pinchot, Gifford, State Park, 181–182
Pine Grove Furnace State
    Park, 167–168
Pine Ridge Natural Area, 159
Pittsburgh, 98–108
Pittsburgh Aviary, 100
Pittsburgh Plateau, 96–116
Pittsburgh Zoo, 99
Pocono, Big, State Park, 94
Pocono Environmental Education
    Center, 161–162
Poconos, The (Eastern Glaciated
    Plateau), 86–95
Poe Paddy State Park, 137
Poe Valley State Park, 136
Point State Park, Pittsburgh, 101–102
Pool Wildlife Sanctuary, 192–194
Presque Isle State Park, 16–18
Prince Gallitzin State Park, 59–60
Promised Land State Park, 87–88
Prouty Place State Park, 79
Pulpit, The, (Tuscarora Summit),
    157–158
Pymatuning Area, 26–30
Pymatuning State Park, 29–30
Pymatuning Wildlife Management
    Area & SGL 213, 26–29

Raccoon Creek State Park, 106–108
Raystown Lake, 127
R.B. Winter State Park, 142–143
Reading, 190–192
Redbud Valley Nature Center, 159
Reed's Gap State Park, 137–138
Renovo, 76
Reynoldsdale State Fish Hatchery, 122
Rickett's Glen State Park, 85

Ridge and Valley Province, 117–168
Ridley Creek State Park, 209–210
Roaring Run Trail, 112
Rocky Ridge Park, 182–183
Roderick, David M., Wildlife
    Reserve (SGL 314), 19–20
Ryerson Station State Park, 104–105

Samuel S. Lewis State Park, 182
Sand Bridge State Park, 143
Saylor, John P., Memorial
    Trail, 55–56
Scott Park, 15
Scranton (Wilkes-Barre), 144–146
Second Mountain Hawk
    Watch, 154–155
Shamokin, Great, Path-
    Cowanshannock Branch, 112–113
Sharon, 31–32
Shawnee State Park, 120–121
Shenango River Reservoir, 31–32
Shikellamy State Park, 142
Shippensburg, 175
Siegel Marsh (SGL 218), 23–24
Silver Lake Nature Center, 226–227
Sinnemahoning State Park, 76
Sizerville State Park, 75–76
Slippery Rock, 41
South Mountain, 165–168
South Park, Pittsburgh, 102
Sproul State Forest, 80
State College, 132–138
Stone Valley Recreation Area, 128–129
Strip Mines
    Curllsville Strips, 60
    Dunlo Strip Mine Reclamation
        Area, 54–55
    Mount Zion Strips, 61
Susquehannock State Forest, 84
Susquehannock State Park, 186–187
Susquehanna River, 173–175
Susquehanna State Park, 139
Swatara State Park, 154

Sweet Root Natural Area, 155

Tannersville Bog, 164
Taylor Arboretum, 222–223
Tinicum (John Heinz National
    Wildlife Refuge), 223–225
Tioga/Hammond Lakes National
    Recreation Area, 82–83
Tobyhanna State Park, 93
Trough Creek State Park, 127–128
Tuscarora State Forest, 150–153
Tuscarora State Park, 149
Tuscarora Summit (The Pulpit),
    157–158
Tyler Arboretum, 210–212
Tyler State Park, 199–200

Union City Dam, 24
Uniontown, 108–110

Valley Forge National Historical
    Park, 206–207
Valley View Park, 124

Warren, 65–71
Warrior's Path State Park, 122
West Chester, 208–214
Whipple Dam State Park, 135
White Clay Creek Preserve, 213–214
Wildwood Lake Nature
    Center, 172–173
Wilkes-Barre/Scranton, 144–146
Williamsport, 139–144
Winter, R.B., State Park, 142–143
Wolf Creek Narrows, 41
Woodbourne Sanctuary, 91–92
Woodcock Creek Lake, 25–26
World's End State Park, 84–85

Yellow Creek State Park, 113–115
York, 176–183
Youghiogheny River Lake, 47–48